WORKING GIRLS AND THEIR MEN

Working Girls

AND THEIR

Men

Male sexual desires and fantasies
revealed by the women paid to satisfy them

Sheron Boyle

SMITH GRYPHON
PUBLISHERS

First published in Great Britain in 1994 by
SMITH GRYPHON LIMITED
Swallow House, 11-21 Northdown Street
London N1 9BN

A CIP catalogue record for this book is available from the British Library

ISBN 1 85685 063 3

Typeset by Computerset, Harmondsworth, Middlesex
Printed in Great Britain by Butler & Tanner Ltd, Frome

FOR MY SISTER,
MARIA

CONTENTS

ACKNOWLEDGEMENTS

I wish to thank all those who agreed to be interviewed for this book: first, the working girls – thank you to every one of you. As the cliché goes, without you all it would never have been possible. Thanks also to the clients and others involved in the sex trade who gave their time to offer rarely voiced insights into the business. Some participants agreed to use their real names, others requested to use false or working names.

Other thanks are due to friends and family whose ears I talked off in the six months I researched and wrote the book. Special thanks to Maggie Heaton, Jane Bower, Claire Casey, Mark Dransfield, Jacinta Devenish, Margaret Emsley, Sarah Gibbons, Lynn Heenan, Deborah Holmes, Adrian Levy, Daniel J. Lockwood, Mark Bickerdike, Gaye Paisley, Ian Stuttard, Adrian Troughton, Ruth Unwin and Damian Whitworth.

I would like to pay thanks and a special tribute to a friend and respected journalist, Amanda Marsh, who, despite being in the final weeks of a spirited but unsuccessful fight against cancer, kindly agreed to read the text.

Thanks to Alice Mahon MP, Kath Grogan of Genesis Leeds Project, Nikki Adams of the English Collective of Prostitutes, Jill Coles of Cardiff, Hilary Kinnell, Julie and Kim of Birmingham Safe, Woody Carey of the Bristol Drugs Project, Andrea Denovan and her team in Glasgow, Cheryl Overs of Soliciting for Change, Jane Mezzone, Noreen and Cait, the Josephine Butler Society, Meg Strong of ACE, Bradford, Sir Frederick Lawton, John Bland, Michael Mansfield QC, Anthony Scrivener QC, Mark Turner of Home Office Research and Statistics Dept, Colin Neason of Birmingham City Council and Professor Norman Tutt. Among the police officers, I would like to acknowledge particularly Chief Constable Richard Wells of South Yorkshire Police, DCI Ian Cowden of Lothian and Borders Police, PC Dick Brittan of Avon and Somerset Police, Inspector Roger Smalley, Inspector Andy French, Inspector Richard Powell and the Eight Area Vice Unit, Metropolitan Police. (Positions of officials and MPs are those held when they were interviewed.)

Thanks to Helen Armitage and Elisabeth Ingles for editing the book and to Mark Bickerdike and Ian Stuttard for taking the photographs.

Finally, thank you to Robert Smith, of Smith Gryphon, for giving an unknown, aspiring writer her first break.

Photographic acknowledgements: Mark Bickerdike, pp. 1, 2 (bottom), 3 (top), 4, 5 (bottom), 7 (bottom left), 8; Sheron Boyle, pp. 2 (top left), 3 (bottom right), 5 (top right); Ian Stuttard, pp. 6 (top centre and bottom), 7 (top).

PREFACE

A group of working girls I met through my work as a journalist on the *Yorkshire Evening Post* first sparked off my serious interest in the subject of prostitution.

At an initial church hall meeting an assortment of prostitutes – two sisters, a young mum and a single woman – sat round a table drinking tea and chatting. They were a lively lot, full of both humorous and alarming tales of their lives and work, which immediately caught my interest. One showed me bruises that her 'boyfriend' (pimp) had given her. She then lifted up her long hair for me to see the bald patches on her scalp where clumps had been pulled out.

Like most people, most of what I knew about prostitution and prostitutes was gleaned from magazine articles or the occasional tabloid newspaper's titillating exposé.

During the time I was researching and writing the book, I understood why people constantly enquired about the women, though the repeated questions were a sign to me of how little was known about the trade. The whole culture is shrouded in a hidden twilight world, despite it being so universal. Prostitution, and therefore prostitutes, are seen as alien to what the Establishment has branded as the norms of behaviour in society. This attitude has been moulded and perpetuated by centuries of legislation, most of which was and is created and enforced by men.

After that meeting I wanted to know more about why these women did such work, the laws that governed their working conditions and anything about the culture that would broaden my obviously narrow knowledge of it.

At bookshops and libraries, I was amazed by the dearth of contemporary works available on the subject. While a couple gave me an insight, none offered a comprehensive picture about the trade in the United Kingdom. Interestingly, there seemed to be far more books on male prostitution.

My research took me the length and breadth of the country. I visited massage parlours, saunas and private brothels. I stood on street corners of numerous red-light areas to interview the women in the slack times between their 'doing business'. Many of the women kindly invited me in to their homes, and some have since become friends.

I interviewed women who charge £1,000 a night for sex and women who ask for £10. Though their personal circumstances and fortunes varied, their attitudes about the work of a prostitute did not, as you will find out.

The men who participated in this book must also be acknowledged. The clients bravely withstood questioning on what is a very personal matter. It was easy to find men who visited prostitutes, but getting them to talk about it was another matter. I suggest people consider this an illustration of how common it is for men to pay for sex.

I cannot ignore those people who control prostitutes. While I abhor what they do, they gave their time and spoke honestly of their work, providing me with an insight into their world.

One of the women I met in the church hall, Liz (about whom you will read later in the book), explained to me how the prostitution laws worked, or rather how they did not. I was disturbed by what I heard. I set about finding out more, and gradually my work developed into this book.

Each chapter looks at a different aspect of the prostitution trade in the United Kingdom. I could have explained how it works, but it is much more worthwhile to hear about it from those really in the know – the prostitutes, clients and controllers. I have allowed them to speak for themselves – in their own unedited words.

Unspoken and unique rules governing the oldest profession are revealed by its participants. One of the most common is 'never kiss a punter', but, just like any other trade or profession, some workers break their own rules.

I attempt to explain the parliamentary rules that apply to prostitution and hope to highlight a few of their not inconsiderable weaknesses. The prostitution laws have three main aims, as set down in 1957 by the Wolfenden Committee: to preserve public order and decency; to protect the citizen from what is offensive or injurious; and to provide safeguards against exploitation and corruption.

There are growing calls for changes to these laws. For the first time in history, an All-Party Committee of MPs has been formed to examine legislation. The final chapter looks at options open to the law-makers.

I hope that, by the time you finish the book, you will agree that the present laws are unworkable. What you would like to see in their place is down to you.

When I began the project I was fascinated by this hidden, twilight sub-culture. The extensive travels and numerous meetings completed during my research broke down the stereotypical views I had about this much maligned section of society – the prostitute. I hope the book offers you, too, an insight and understanding into the practitioners and patrons of the oldest profession.

A postscript – I understand that a prostitute in the south of England has adopted my Christian name as her professional name!

CHAPTER ONE

The Top of the Range

ALEX

'W hat I most like about this job is that I just suit my bloody self. I work hard to keep my customers happy and plan to do so while ever men are willing to pay to see me. The thought of working nine-to-five fills me with horror.'

Alex sells sex. She is one of an unknown army of women who rent out their bodies for sexual services for money – and she proudly claims she is worth every penny of the £100 an hour she demands.

'I consider myself a high-class call girl. The term prostitute conjures up an image so alien to me and the skills – a mixture of sex therapist, social worker and actress – I offer to my patrons. They tell me I'm worth it because I take time, make them feel important and give them the best – within my rule book.'

Alex works from home, an elegant two-bedroom apartment. Her work routine is put into action immediately her pale pink telephone rings.

As pleasant but perfunctory greetings are swapped, she lifts a small pink plastic box on to her lap. When the voice at the other end of the line greets her with, 'Hi, it's Peter/John/Andrew/here,' she skims through the several dozen cards packed in the box until she finds the client's.

The alphabetically ordered white cards are a valuable time-saver and allow her to add a personal touch to her service. 'I wouldn't

1

remember who was who without my box. When I ask if the pet dog is better or something like that when they call, I've got them eating out of my hand. You see, they think I remember their visit as if it was important to me.'

Time-wasters are her most annoying problem. 'It's taken me months to develop my phone skills to suss if a caller is genuine, but you still get a lot of down-market rubbish. A client has to be at least executive level or he doesn't walk through the door.'

While small chat is made she quickly scans details noted on the card from conversations during the client's last visit:

Peter. Lovely, from Wales. Stressful job, therefore has problems with sex. Only ever had sex with wife and she isn't interested any more. We attempted intercourse but failed. Ended with oral. Has huge complex about size of his body and 'c' [cock]. Biggest fear is premature ejaculation. Left on cloud nine. Said if he had known how beautiful I was he would never have had the confidence to visit.

Once Alex has booked her caller in for an appointment she hangs up the phone and switches on the answering machine. Rule number one in her book has been followed – see no more than one client a day.

Alex's professional approach to being a call girl has led to a 'streamlining of her operation' over past months to ensure she makes maximum money for minimum time.

Clients who read her advertisement – 'Cardiff: attractive, sophisticated lady for executive gentlemen only' – in one of the more up-market top shelf men-only magazines have to pass Alex's rigorous phone quizzing before being directed to her apartment in one of the city's most expensive suburbs. 'Of course, I am very careful how I word things over the phone and just say I offer a full professional service. Sex is never mentioned as I don't want to be done for soliciting.'

She works between 11 am and 2 pm only and the tastefully decorated flat is always in pristine condition for the business of the day.

Auburn-haired Alex always ensures she is at her door to greet a client. 'Most are up-market people who come to me because I am very discreet and there is no chance of them being recognized.

'I aim for a smart but sexy look. If he is a regular, I wear skimpy panties and a bra, but for a new one I'll put on a teddy and a nice jacket. I always wear suspenders and stockings – Marks and Spencer usually as they're quite thick and last a while – and I have a pair of extremely high black patent stiletto-heeled shoes which have never seen the light of day outside my flat.

'The client is guided to the settee and we chat about the weather, his holiday or how nice it is to see him again, or if it's a new one, I will outline my procedure. I don't take anything off at this stage. It's all a nice controlled situation. I very politely get the money off him and place it on a nearby side table.'

She rarely works at weekends, except for a regular, there being little call as most of her clientèle are married with families. Skimming through her vital box, she pulls out the card of a Bristol accountant who is 'quick and easy', according to her notes.

One of her best clients, a magistrate, has tried on several occasions to persuade her to visit his home. Alex notes:

> Peter: lively chap, late middle age, important post in education. Married, comes a long way specifically to see me every 2/3 weeks.

Clients include company directors and top-notch professionals, mainly from neighbouring English and Welsh counties. Details of their sexual performances are also in her vital box.

> Andrew: his biggest fear is premature ejaculation. We managed it with me on top (not for long). He was pleased how long it lasted (not long)! Wife not interested in sex. Has two sons.

Once the fee is handed over, Alex launches into what she calls her patter. With her slender figure clad in a black top and leggings and her glossy hair perfectly bobbed, a fixed smile suddenly appears on her handsome face as she begins to purr in a soothing voice. ' "Let's take off your lovely suit and go to the bathroom where I will give you a nice wash to relax you. I know this is rather a strange situation and you must be nervous, but I want you to have a good time." That's how I tend to start.'

In her three years as a call girl, she has found most clients are initially uptight and some so nervous that they shake. Should a client turn nasty, Alex's only means of defence are a can of hairspray and a personal alarm hidden at the side of the settee. 'I am at my greatest risk while ever a client has his clothes on.'

Once he is undressed, Alex will lead him to her spacious bathroom, where towels and soap are neatly laid out, and the patter continues. 'I get the shower attachment and explain, "I'll just check the water is OK, after all we don't want you going home with blisters on your willy."'

'God, I've said that so many times,' she laughs. 'I only wash their willy and around it to relax them, check they're clean and give myself a chance to check out their size. I don't like well-endowed men and if it is I silently groan and mutter to myself, "Oh God, a big one". All men are self-conscious about the size of their pricks and think women only want big ones – but they can be so painful!'

She takes them into the spare bedroom – never her own – and encourages them to lie down. Two pillows are strategically placed one on top of the other in the middle of the bed and over a continental quilt. 'My message is, I am not lying down next to you like your girlfriend or wife. Off comes my jacket and jewellery at this stage and I again ask if they're comfy. I never remove my stockings because I feel more in control and it's easier to perform if I'm in costume,' she adds.

'I kneel in the middle of the bed and if they're having full sex, I start off with a little massage and a bit of oral. Several clients have told me I am the world's expert on oral. It is an art. The secret is to give it very, very slowly and really think about what you are doing. I always start off by the balls and lick all round there. Most start to moan at this point and I think, "Good". I don't like it if there's no reaction. Then, very slowly, I trail my tongue all the way up to the tip. A couple of clients have ejaculated before I've even got there. I used to feel guilty but now I think, "Don't be stupid, if I wasn't so good at it, they wouldn't have come." I don't let them have two orgasms. If it's quick – tough shit!

'Most women don't like giving oral and I didn't before I started doing it for a living. I don't always make them wear a condom for oral but I never let them come in my mouth. Another rule I have is not to allow a client to put his hand on the back of my head when I'm doing oral as I like to control how much goes in.'

Alex is rarely excited by a client but admits to having an orgasm once with one. 'He didn't realize and I was disgusted with myself. I was never much of a shouter or screamer in sex before I started this job, but I do now as they love it and it can bring them to climax. And I make sure it sounds real.

'A lot of my clients don't come here for sex but because I let them kiss and cuddle me, although I don't want to. It amazes me how many men haven't the slightest clue how to kiss. One chap's idea is to purse his lips like they did in the 1950s movies and I sit there while he presses them on mine.

'The main rule I have is that I refuse to let them give me oral – that's for my personal life – or interfere with me down below. I don't care if they kiss or fondle my tits. Clients always wear condoms for sex and I usually offer a choice of position for intercourse but more often than not I go below.'

She allows customers to relax in bed for a short while after sex, though she does not stay with them. Her aim is to get them into the bathroom as quickly, but tactfully, as possible. To achieve this she turns on her patter – 'Gosh, that did spurt a long way! We'd better get you tidied up' being a favourite ploy.

'My job is finished at this point and he goes to the bathroom alone – that is the only time I leave him – while I dash into the lounge and hide the fee. I then wash my hands, rinse out my mouth with an antiseptic wash and check my make-up.

'I want to look nice when they leave as, having put all that effort in, I don't want them to go away with final images of me looking tatty. I run through a check list, making sure they've got their keys, watch and such things and tell them it's been lovely to meet them. I don't put on any clothes until they've gone and I've had a shower. I think there must be a psychological reason for that.'

Her whole service generally takes an hour. If some of the older or more anxious clients are taking a little longer to perform, Alex does not rush them but keeps things moving in a professional manner. 'I'm always very pleasant to them. I have to be as they're my wages and I want them to come back as that makes my life easier. Because I am so expensive, I class regulars as anyone who makes a second visit within three months.'

Alex describes her job as the biggest secret in her world. How many colleagues she has nationwide it is impossible to know, so secretive are most prostitutes about their work. A pressure group campaigning to abolish prostitution laws believes two million women are or have, at some time in their lives, been on the game. The English Collective of Prostitutes admits the figures are seven years old and 'a guess based on our experience'.

Alex's method of working is about the closest a prostitute can get in the United Kingdom to selling sexual services legally under the present laws. 'My brothers, all extremely successful businessmen, don't have a clue about my work. My parents, who live in Cardiff, think I am a genuinely straight escort. But they are embarrassed about that and tell their friends I do telephone sales. I get away with it because I'm a "nice" Hampshire-born girl, a consultant engineer's daughter, and people would never think someone like me – from a good home and comfortable background – would do this for a living. A handful of friends know the truth but it can be very lonely not being able to talk about it.'

It was while doing a spot of sunbathing in a local park that the idea of becoming an escort came to her. 'I was in telephone sales and got sick to death of the pressure, the long hours and being a slave to work. It was a gloriously sunny afternoon and I thought, I'm 37 and should be able to do this whenever I want. I made a list of what I wanted out of life – to work part-time, for myself, earn good money and have plenty of free time.

'I studied the list and thought, no such job exists, but then hit on working as an escort. In my naive way, I genuinely believed that was all there was to it and I put an ad in the local paper. I had a massive response, my answer machine never stopped. But when I explained sex was not on the agenda, they'd laugh and say, "You are joking, love."

'I was terribly prim and proper and got no work so I decided to try and do sex. If I couldn't have coped with it, I would have gone back to sales. I never drink but I got half-pissed to see my first client, a man in his late 60s. He was very nice, but to be honest all my clients are.

'I did a few dinner and lunch escorts, charging £20 an hour plus extra for sex. I love eating out but, having streamlined my operation, I decided I didn't want to spend four hours with a person I wouldn't be seen dead with in normal circumstances. Some of my regulars ask me to go out or even on holiday with them but I tell them that a rule of mine is not to get too involved with clients.'

Streamlining her work has seen the axing of certain services such as £50 blow jobs (oral sex). 'Details of those clients were kept in a blue box. But I was putting as much effort and time into that as for sex and I believed I was worth more than £50.'

On a working day, she rises at 8 am and enjoys a leisurely morning. 'I spend about 30 minutes putting on my make-up. I do it very carefully as I want it to stay on in times of stress, so to speak. I don't put on my working gear until I know a client is on his way. I won't see anyone before 11 am and if I have no appointments by 2 pm, I call it a day. I set a deadline otherwise I'd be waiting about all day.'

She spends about £1,000 a year on advertising. Her best week saw her earn £700; on average she sees three men a week and there are occasional weeks when she has no business. Having registered with the Inland Revenue as a professional escort, Alex bought her flat in the suburbs with the job in mind. Though it is extremely well furnished, she has deliberately not put a single family photo on display. 'That's partly because I do not want the clients to know anything about me.

'I want to draw as little attention to myself as possible so I only see one client a day. And because I aim to attract the right sort of people, I had to be in a good area. My neighbours think I do telephone sales from home.'

Free time tends to find Alex relaxing with friends or alone at home. 'My working life is brilliant now – but I've been through hell to get to this level of confidence. All I am is an actress for an hour. Because I do what I do, I feel pretty drained by evening. Showing so much interest in a person you're not the slightest bit bothered about is hard work. Men who come to me are lacking in some ways, otherwise they would have a mistress. When I first see a client and he looks like Godzilla or is extremely shy, I think, "I know why you are here!" The worse they look the more relaxed I feel. It's when I get young good-looking guys that I'm a bit apprehensive.'

She leads a lonely life, by choice to some extent, but forced on her to a greater degree by the nature of her work. But she says she is happy with her lot. 'The last thing I feel like doing at the end of the day is dating some guy. I like to unwind and watch TV or maybe do some yoga. I do have one boyfriend whom I see now and again and he's fantastic in bed – that's the main reason I see him. It's heaven to have sex with someone I fancy.

'I have always been a perfectionist and worked hard at whatever I do. I treat this job no differently. I love the lifestyle it has given me. Clients bring me flowers, bottles of champagne and gifts.'

Being so good at her job means that clients occasionally lose track of the true nature of the relationship. Alex says when they phone and casually suggest calling round for a coffee or chat she has diplomatically to remind them that her time is money. 'I can't say I don't give a fuck what they're up to so I worm my way out of it.'

A minority of prostitutes, like Alex, hire out their bodies purely by choice. The high-class call girls are not treated with the degree of contempt reserved for their poorer street sisters. Indeed, once any of the select band who provide sexual services to the wealthy, privileged and famous become publicly known, they can become minor celebrities. One only has to look back over recent decades – Christine Keeler, Mandy Rice-Davies and the Profumo affair; the Lord Lambton scandal; the case of Major Ronald Ferguson, father of the Duchess of York – to see how money and power add a veneer of glamour to something that is considered dirty and distasteful among the poorer echelons.

Indeed, royalty and the upper classes have been no exception to sampling the charms of illicit sex. One historian of the prostitution trade claims a rough survey of the English nobility showed that a significant proportion of nineteenth-century aristocracy either had an ancestor (often female) who had moved the family a step up society's ladder by performing sexual services for royalty, or else the family itself descended from the wrong side of the royal blanket. Often a woman's family pulled strings for her to become the mistress of a powerful man.

The acting profession was a launch pad for many a good prostitute in past times, Nell Gwyn being perhaps the most famous. The daughter of a woman believed to have run a brothel, she survived her poor upbringing by treading the boards. This brought her to the notice of many noble men, to some of whom she granted sexual favours. Her most prestigious role, however, was to be the favourite courtesan of and mother of two sons to King Charles II.

In ancient Greek society, the high-class courtesan – or *hetaira* as she was known – enjoyed a position unrivalled by other women, who were kept very much under control. Almost every important public figure visited *hetairae* and they had considerable unofficial, though no recognized, status. Would-be *hetairae* attended a special school to be educated in their future career. A broad curriculum, including the art of love-making, was studied alongside the arts and sciences, making them the best educated females in Greek society. They often raised their daughters to join them and passed their skills on to the younger generation.

Such status is achieved by very few in our society, and prostitution is considered shameful. Yet, as the law stands, within the United Kingdom being a prostitute is a legally recognized profession. Any woman who wants to contract out her body and skills is as much entitled to do so as a construction worker on a building site or a freelance computer programmer. But it is the manner in which they ply their trade that sees hundreds hauled before magistrates' courts across the country for prostitution-related offences. The present laws are so designed that most methods used to practise their work are illegal.

Alex, working indoors as a lone prostitute, is not a law-breaker. Her advertising is discreet and, since she sees only one client daily, no public nuisance is created by a stream of callers at her flat at all times of the day. But if she stepped outside her front door and on to the public highway to tout for business from a nearby corner, she would face the possibility of being prosecuted, as a 'common prostitute', for loitering or soliciting for sex.

Thus, selling sex as a lone woman is legally, if not personally, safe. It is impossible to estimate how many 'respectable' women are 'honest hookers' as, like Alex, they tend to cloak their work in secrecy for fear of being found out. Few women who work in the up-market end of the trade are prosecuted, partly because of the extensive precautions they take and the often clandestine circumstances in which they work.

This band of working girls tends to cater for wealthier clients who have neither the time nor the desire to be caught touring the usually seedy red light areas for sex.

SUSAN

Charging top rates does have its drawbacks, says Susan, a freelance masseuse. 'Rich punters expect more for their money, they make you work harder. The working-class fellows are easier to please,' she moans.

Commanding £100 an hour, she visits private homes across London, giving individual massages and extra services to clients.

It is difficult to imagine Susan working in the sex industry. Painfully shy when discussing herself, she speaks of her job with excruciating embarrassment, despite having done it for two years. She later reveals this is because she is so unused to talking freely about what she does.

Indeed, so scared is she of losing her two young children if the social services discover how she earns a living, that she goes to amazing lengths to keep it secret and dares discuss her work with only a handful of close friends.

'When I started I went to the English Collective [of Prostitutes] for advice on how to keep safe. I advertise as a visiting masseuse offering a full personal service and never ever have people at my home. I had a separate phone with a different number installed at home purely to take clients' calls.

'As I don't want to arouse my neighbours' suspicions, I wear flat shoes, no lipstick and a long coat which hides my short dress (it's very easy to take off), stockings and suspenders, when I set off for work. I'm sure some of them must wonder what I do.

'I try to sift out cranks by explaining that I will be chauffeured to a client's house. Some men never call back after I've said that. I pay a friend £15 or £20 to drive me to my appointment and then he walks me to the door and when the punter answers, he says quite clearly that he will wait for me in the car.'

Susan visits at least two clients a week, in the afternoons or evenings. 'My starting fee is £100 an hour and for that they get a massage and sex but if they are prepared to pay, I consider doing extras. When I first started it was a bit of a shock and I had to psyche myself up to do it. No one had ever paid me so much for my time in my life before. My ex-husband used to force me to have sex with him.'

She has six regulars, two of whom she sees weekly. 'One is 28 and the other is 50 years old. He is just lonely and likes to have someone to talk to.

'Clients try and persuade me to let them not to use a condom, saying sex is better without one. Another told me the whole set-up excited him, even just making the phone call.

'I start with a bit of a massage – it's a way of keeping their hands off me – then we have sex. I always keep my stockings and suspenders on and, if I can, my bra. Some want me to leave straight after while others prefer me to stay for a drink.

'It is quite shocking how many men go with prostitutes and very difficult to get a sense of how common it is.'

Born and raised in Sheffield, she moved to London at 17, married a year later and had two children. After the marriage failed and she and her husband had separated, Susan worked as a barmaid at weekends and had an evening job in sales for several years to make ends meet. 'I never seemed to get any time with my kids. Doing this was the easiest way to get money, see them and be able to afford to do things with them. I spoke with a friend and I decided it was crazy to work as I was to make ends meet when this was so much easier. The money convinced me more than anything.

'Life is much easier when you have it. I can afford to buy my kids shoes whenever they want them now. They have a better life but the fear they could be taken from me is never out of my mind.'

The laws that control the sex trade are saturated with double standards. The prostitution trade is akin to an iceberg – nine tenths of it are hidden – with street girls being the visible tip. An unguessable number like Alex and Susan submerge large parts of their lives through fear of exposure and its consequences.

They are among a minority of prostitutes who manage to work without breaking the laws in the United Kingdom. Alex sought legal advice on how to devise a means of operating without gaining a criminal record, and employed an accountant to deal with the financial aspect of her work. Though she and Susan are legally as safe as can be, they are personally vulnerable and isolated.

Much of the present legislation governing those who sell and – in far, far greater numbers – those who buy sex is anomalous, discriminatory, difficult and expensive to operate in terms of time and money, and ineffective in the eyes of the prostitutes, pimps, punters, courts and many police officers.

Stereotypes of prostitutes range from the glamorous hooker who loves her job so much that she would do it even if she were not getting paid, to the dirty slag whose drug- and disease-ridden body is held responsible for the spread of AIDS and other sexual ills. A popular myth surrounding the prostitution trade is the amount of money a woman can make from selling sexual services. In reality, many work long hours and after paying their overheads – babysitters, taxis, pimps – they can be left with nothing or even out of pocket.

Undoubtedly, the money-making prostitutes are the ones who work for themselves – and there are many. While they do not all enjoy lives of luxury, a better quality of life is provided for them and their families through the best means of making money that the women know of.

But there is a body of prostitutes who make highly lucrative livings from sex. They are not great in numbers and rarely have to advertise their specialist services, as clients always know where to find them. No tacky signs, no hand-written posters on the back of cardboard boxes proclaiming 'exotic model', no red lights ever grace the private, up-market houses or flats they tend to work in.

These are the women who specialize in fantasy work, who help create or enact the client's wild and weird desires. Some of the requests defy belief, say the women. At the simpler end of the scale are common fantasies such as the patient/nurse or teacher/pupil scenario, where the woman will dress up in a uniform and the client has to obey her orders.

But the women who act out these requests do not rank among the highest paid for being amateur dramatists. They earn their money by being prepared to inflict, or to have inflicted on them, flagellation and mutilation, sometimes to the extreme, and in so doing to fulfil clients' instructions and wishes which many people would consider abnormal or sick.

DIANA

A stylish mews cottage in one of the select side roads dotted around London's Regent's Park houses Diana's thriving business.

Beige-carpeted stairs to the first floor lead to an open-plan lounge where Diana's maid, Sue, greets clients – including TV stars and several MPs – and safeguards their anonymity.

For Diana is one of a handful of high-earning women in the capital who specialize in fantasy work. As a dominatrix, her work revolves around fantasy and S&M (sado-masochism) or, as the Americans know it, B&D (bondage and discipline).

And because most of her clients' tastes are bizarre, there could be several red faces if they came face to face with others, especially if in drag, says Sue. 'I've had one waiting in the toilet, one behind a screen, another with a curtain around him and someone else in the spare bedroom. I've had them waiting a couple of hours for her but they know she's worth it. You see, she's one of the best in London at what she does.'

Yorkshire-born Diana is 30, petite with beautiful waist-length brown hair and a slender but curvaceous figure. She has specialized in fantasies for the past two years. After changing from leggings and flat lace-up black boots into a white chiffon negligee and high-heeled strapless sandals, she carefully makes up her pretty face for the start of business and, as she does so, lists with typical native bluntness 'what she does'.

'I don't do much of the normal stuff – 95 per cent of my work is specialized. I have about 60 regulars who visit weekly or fortnightly.

'There's a basic temptress where the punter is tied to the bed and teased. I usually touch him with something like a silk glove, never my body, until he comes. There's the schoolgirl and French maid acts where I give a light spanking.

'A popular one is the nursing fantasy. I examine them and tell them they must have treatment. They like that because I am so dominant. A new service, which has turned out to be extremely popular, is to give enemas. The client then either wants a big nappy put on them or they 'go' in the toilet or bucket. Some ask for a catheter to be stuck up their backsides. Many a man has crumbled at that,' she laughs.

The costumes are just one part of her work. To submerge herself and the client into his desired fetish, she will have to role-play, maybe speak in baby or obscene language, and stretch her vivid imagination and broad mind. Diana has spent several hundred pounds on numerous outfits for work. Unless a specific uniform is requested, she wears a PVC or rubber cat suit, leather gloves, mask, boots and gold chains to carry out domination fantasies.

'I'll wear all that if I'm a mistress and a client is my slave. Or we'll do some body worship where they kiss my boots and follow me around on a dog lead and obey my orders. Usually I get them to massage me or clean the toilet. It varies according to the client, one will want affection and the other wants to be dominated.

'I love doing the Nazi interrogator one. I tie them up and dress them in a full body harness, mask, gag and spiked collar. Clamps are attached to their nipples and balls which are then connected to cord wired to the ceiling hook. I pull it all up and begin the torture which usually involves gently dropping hot wax on their privates. If they want they can have electrodes attached to their body and I give them mild shocks.'

Diana says before carrying out any new fantasies on clients she likes to try them out on herself, usually with the help of a regular. That way she gets a better idea of what a client wants and what he gets out of it. Some of the fantasies, such as the cling-film suffocation one, can be dangerous.

'A very good regular told me about it. A client is laid on a rubber sheet and his body totally wrapped in the film. The last thing you do is place a wet towel or piece of film across his face. There's a certain way of doing it and they pass out within 90 seconds. All the time I am holding his hand and as soon as he utters the panic word I have three seconds to get him to come round and then he ejaculates. You have to be experienced to do this. If they don't want the suffocation, a popular request is to be massaged while wrapped in cling-film. I've tried that and it's a lovely sensation.'

For those who do not know what they want, she offers 'a taste of everything', where for £500 a client can sample a range of fantasies during a 90-minute session.

Despite massive overheads, she makes up to £1,500 profit a week. The softly-lit bedroom is testimony to her work, with a wall cupboard holding a range of gold chains, leather whips and canes. A pink feather duster sits on a child's blackboard leaning against a wall. Next to it is a stethoscope, handcuffs, black patent thigh-length boots and a variety of manacles.

Taking a central place in the main wardrobe is a beautiful polished black leather saddle and beside it is a riding uniform, a schoolgirl's outfit, a vibrator and a variety of sexy underwear. A red towel is laid across the centre of the covered mattress on a brass bed frame and directly above it a large metal hook hangs ominously from the ceiling.

In the bathroom, a pink hot-water bottle with a long pink tube connected to it dangles from the shower rail. This home-made piece of equipment is part of Diana's private 'health service' administered to those 'needing' enemas.

Three phones, each with different numbers, sit next to each other on a coffee table in the lounge. Labels are stuck to each, outlining details corresponding to one of the three different cards she has had put in city centre phone booths. Diana and Sue then know which card a prospective client has read when he phones, be it the 'beautiful brunette damsel', 'young model' or the strict nurse/teacher/riding instructor.

Films and TV series often stimulate weird fantasies in many of the punters, says Diana. 'After that series about a nun, *Body and Soul*, men came to me asking for a nun's rig-out so I had to go out and buy one. One punter wanted me to stand over him in my nun's dress while he tossed himself off. Then there's the riding mistress. I think that's from one of those best-seller TV programmes. I'll put the saddle over a stark-naked client's back and a bit in his mouth while I ride him around the flat and he gets a stiffy on. I lead him to the bath and make him drink from it or the sink or an ashtray as if it were a trough. Sometimes, I put down little obstacles like pillows and he has to jump over them. Then I tell him he needs grooming and give him hand relief. It's very funny but I don't laugh out loud.'

Sue, the maid, agrees. She has never been a prostitute and works for Diana three days a week to help pay off debts, during which times she has seen some incredible sights: 'Oh yes, but I daren't titter otherwise it spoils the fantasy for them. Diana will be trotting around the lounge with him and I have to carry on as if it's normal!'

When Diana asks clients why they want a particular fantasy, their answers usually relate back to something in their childhood. 'Why else would a strapping six-foot tall guy want to be a baby and shit in a diaper, or want to be fed out of a bottle? Some stories are very sad. I've even had women on the phone asking if I'd do a service for them! Most of my clients have their own companies. Some are very young, in their early 20s, and the majority of them are ex-public school boys. The only thing I won't do is degradation, where you shit on someone. I can't do it.' But pointing to a well-stacked fruit bowl, she adds: 'I simulate it with bananas and cream instead!'

Among her clientèle are several cross-dressers (heterosexual men who get a thrill out of wearing women's clothes) and transvestites (TVs): 'A lot of the cross-dressers usually look frumpy. But one is very smart and just wants to come and dance with me. He's told me he doesn't find me attractive. For the TVs, I wear a man's hat, shirt and tie, strap on a dildo, go up their bum and say, "You naughty boy". I tend to do a couple of them a day and get quite a lot of their business. That's all down to word of mouth.

'I've only been doing this fantasy stuff for a year and I reckon I'm one of the top three in London. I used to run a restaurant in Sheffield and envied people walking round in nice clothes. I had two children and was desperate for money and a friend suggested working in a sauna for extra cash. Then a girl told me how good the money was down here. I came down for the day and have stayed ever since. I've always had a good imagination and this has earned me a fair packet. My kids go to good schools and have a private tutor at home to help them.'

Diana tells people she is self-employed and runs a promotions agency. 'Sometimes it gets me down but I have a very good friend I can talk to. It's a very lonely job and not even my boyfriend knows what I do. You can never just start up a conversation with someone about work. You can't even talk about it to other working girls as jealousy creeps in.

'The clients are very good to me and at Christmas the place was covered in flowers. I got a Chanel watch, CD player, perfume and chocolates. But I'd never go out to dinner with one because as soon as you do that you lose them. They'd have you on their territory and would think they don't have to pay.'

The other mews houses in the cul-de-sac are all tastefully cared for and her neighbours include one of Britain's best-known actresses. Diana would live at the two-bedroom house but she does not want her children to find out what she does. Instead, she arrives by taxi at 11 am every weekday and allows an hour to prepare for work.

Once fully dressed and made up for work, she covers up with a towelling robe until a client arrives. Apart from the practical reasons of keeping warm, the robe provides a further opportunity to make money. 'If a client wants me to dress up I tell him it's extra to my basic £100 fee for me to put on another outfit. By the time they've requested fantasy and costume the bill soon mounts up.'

Diana employs three 'card boys' – actually in their late 20s and early 30s. Each is paid £50 a day to cycle three times daily around the city depositing in phone kiosks up to 2,000 cards advertising her services.

Such cards, which are mainly used in London and Brighton, range from the tasteful to the tacky. Some card boys say the prostitutes they work for pay them in kind. Diana does not: 'I used to pay them £70 but reduced it by £20 until we weather the recession. The lads are among the best in the city, very loyal and trustworthy, and came with the flat when I took it on. They treat it as a job, not as a cash on the side thing, as they have families to look after.

'I expect them to work 8 am to 7 pm because as soon as the cards are up, they get ripped down by British Telecom people, the police or public. I take a lot of time over my cards and try and put something different on. Some of the ones in boxes look really trashy but mine are good quality. So they should as I spend £100 on printing 10,000 – and they might only last me four days.'

Diana's other major expense is the rent on the flat – £180 a day for a property which normally commands £900 a month. It is collected for the flat's unknown owner by a man who manages several other places used by prostitutes. Extortionately high rents are common in London and this is a factor in the exploitation of prostitutes. Many of the estimated 200 women who work in Soho flats – often nothing more than a small dingy room partitioned off from the maid with a curtain – are paying between £150 and £180 a day, but their business is not as exclusive as Diana's and some offer sex for as little as £15.

Another regular outgoing is her maid, who gets a flat rate of £30 a day and ten per cent of everything she makes. If Diana works overtime, Sue gets a further £10 a customer. The maid has several functions. Her most important one is to answer the phone so that the prostitute does not lose business while with a client.

She offers the client a drink on arrival and if Diana is running late, gives him a choice of sex films to watch. Once Diana is given her fee, she hands it over to the maid, who usually hides it in case a client attempts to rob her, as does happen.

Just as important, a maid offers a degree of protection for the woman and, as in Diana's case, she is often a friend, someone to talk to and laugh with during her regular 12-hour working day.

Like every other trade, prostitution has been quieter over the past year. 'I'm hoping things are going to pick up with the start of the tourist season. I'll be busy until August and then it will go slack for a short while and start to pick up again in the run up to Christmas. It also usually dips the week before the household bills or mortgage is due. If the restaurants are busy, then I am. I don't know why but it does seem to follow.

'On a bad day, I'll see about five men, and on a good day I'll do 15. The most I've ever done in one day is 25 and I fainted from exhaustion at the end of it!'

English men have long had a fondness for flagellation: indeed it was known as the 'English vice' in the 1700s. Nickie Roberts in *Whores in History* remarks: 'Both the upper-class taste for defloration of virgins and the penchant for flagellation among the rulers of British society spread [across Europe] like wildfire.'

'Flogging brothels' mushroomed throughout the city's most fashionable streets. One of the most famous was based in Covent Garden and patronized by King George IV himself. By the mid-1800s, she notes, London was revered by rich masochists the world over as the capital of the flagellation scene.

LISA

Diana was the highest-earning prostitute interviewed for this book. The only other near her earnings bracket was Lisa, one of the few women working in the north of England who offers a similar service to Diana. Apart from that and the fact that both are handsome, articulate women, there end the similarities.

Campaigning organizations such as the London-based English Collective of Prostitutes dislike sex workers being portrayed as victims of abuse. Yet other people who offer professional support to prostitutes all speak of the high percentage of women on the game who have backgrounds of mistreatment or being in care.

Lisa says she owes her career as a £200-an-hour specialist in sado-masochistic sex services to her wealthy stepfather, who 'sold' her at the age of 15 to a woman who ran a torture chamber.

Her brutal life – albeit cloaked in silk, luxury travel and money – is far removed from any saccharine-coated Hollywood whore, as personified by the actress Julia Roberts in *Pretty Woman.*

Trendily-dressed and attractive, 28-year-old Lisa has spent all but the first ten years of her life indulging the perverted sexual peccadilloes of a select group of hospital consultants and top businessmen.

Her speciality is to have extreme violence and pain inflicted on her or to dispense it on her select clientèle. She does not offer as wide a range of fantasies and role-plays as Diana. Lisa's skills are truly and purely sado-masochistic. Humiliation and bondage are all part of the service. Straight sex is never offered and rarely wanted – except once when she was raped by a client two days after the birth of her second child.

Lisa considers it miraculous that she was able to give birth, considering the number of times she has been cut up, burnt and had a variety of everyday objects stuffed inside her 'down below'. A high pain threshold and a body with an ability to heal quickly has helped her cope, she says.

In return for massive fees, clients want to be beaten, whipped, burnt, branded or treated as babies. In between servicing them, she has gained five A Levels, a university degree and borne two daughters.

Like a substantial number of her colleagues, Lisa became a teenage prostitute after years of abuse at home, in her case an up-market detached house in a picturesque Kent village.

She believes her stepfather sold her to Jane, a woman who ran a torture chamber at her home in a nearby town. Lisa became one of three girls who worked for her. 'I came into my own there. I could do anything because I healed so quickly and so I was very valuable. The clients were all doctors from the south-east or London. Some were OK, especially those who had foot fetishes. They just wanted to ponder over your feet and kiss them.

'Some wanted violence. Jane had all the equipment. Two popular requests were nipple-piercing and branding, usually pictures on their arses. Sometimes it was something specific. One always wanted a bead on a piece of string pushed up his penis and then having it pulled out.'

But the sinister side of this ugly world soon showed itself to the teenage Lisa when Jane would video the doctor clients as they violently tortured and cut up the girls. Lisa believes she owes being alive today simply to her amazing ability to endure pain. 'I have no fear of it and I suppose that's why I'm relatively uninjured today. Unlike the other two girls, I never cried, screamed for help or begged for mercy so I wasn't much of a turn-on for the men. Remember, these were doctors, so they knew how to cut up. I'd watch but would never have a reaction. I don't know how much these men were paying but I never saw any money. I suppose my stepfather got some share.'

Lisa left Kent for Yorkshire when she was 19 but carried on working. During the 1980s she saw eight regular clients from a detached house in a quiet Leeds suburb which she bought specifically for the job. The room where most of the violence is inflicted is decorated purple, a colour Lisa says she hates. Clients are 'city people' – wealthy, married, aged late 30s to 60s. One was sent to her by her stepfather and the others learned of Lisa by word of mouth. 'They're not all public school types. The only thing they have in common is, without exception, they were all only children, including my stepfather.'

Her services vary and include the 'usual' – being tied up, handcuffed, beatings. Trigger words have a vital role in S&M and domination. 'The two of you work out a word which as soon as it is uttered by the clients, it has to jog you out of whatever you are doing. It can be a daft word, like potato, but if they don't say it you totally ignore their pleas for mercy, begging, cries of no and orders for it to stop. Most of them aren't sleeping with their wives or even in the same bedroom so I suppose it's quite easy for them to hide any scars or marks.

'In S&M there's a top and a bottom, with men usually in the latter role. But with domination, the client is helpless. One of mine, in his 60s, pretends to be a baby and likes to be covered in a body suit with small breathing holes and eye slits and left alone to watch videos of *Watch with Mother* or *Andy Pandy*. He wants me to be his mother and he gets an erection when I have to tell him off or hit him. I've had an adult-size high chair built for him and bought a potty too which I decorated with nursery transfers.'

Michael, a rich, handsome insurance executive in his 40s, saw Lisa for nearly ten years on her stepfather's recommendation until he wed last year. 'He took me on trips to Europe and bought me expensive clothes but he repulsed me. He got really turned on by reports of a child rape and would want to re-enact it in some way with me. I was so appalled by this that I beat the shit out of him once and even though he said the trigger word I just kept hitting him. Afterwards he was really humble. He never normally wanted sex but he raped me two days after my daughter was born – because he knew it would hurt.'

The image of S&M women dressed in plastic mini-skirts and thigh-length boots is just that – an image, says Lisa. 'These men want class. I usually wear a well-cut long black dress and have to be immaculately groomed. Good underwear, preferably silk, is essential. It doesn't matter if it's going to be ruined and only worn once, it has to be good quality.'

The abuse of Lisa, the elder of two girls, began at the age of ten when her mother remarried, to a senior executive in the building industry, and they went to live with him. 'It started within days of moving in. He bought me a doll and touched that up before quickly moving on to me. We were having full sex before I was 11. He was very keen on photography and would get me to pose in my school uniform and take pictures of me in our front room.

His other hobbies were also tuned into satisfying his lascivious cravings. 'He was very clever with his hands,' she said bitterly. 'He was a DIY enthusiast and carved a wooden penis which he'd stick in me and then take photos. He made a wooden pulley and after hauling me up, he would cut or shave me. One time he burnt me with a blow torch. This would go on every night or during the day if mum was away. It's funny, but I never felt any pain as a child. I still don't, I can't tell you why.'

Though he never touched Lisa's young sister, her mother was often a victim of his violence and was put in hospital on several occasions as a result. Lisa never dared tell anyone of the horrific goings-on for fear he would kill her mother. 'He never said he would, but he didn't need to. I don't think my mother knew what he was doing to me.'

'We stopped having sex when I was 12. I knew he didn't want me as I was too old by then. But I realised I was a prostitute and thought I might as well make money out of it.'

When desperate attempts to get teachers' attention failed, she turned rebellious and was suspended twice for lengthy periods – once for drug-dealing in the school toilet. Her stepfather passed the photos of her posing around his circle of friends, who would then come to the house to take pictures of her with objects stuck inside her: 'It could be anything – from vegetables to telephones. A favourite was the hair-dryer. It really hurt when it was switched on, but I got paid a lot of money.'

In the past couple of years, Lisa has attempted to wean herself off the game, her initial efforts being inspired by a male counsellor saying he cared for her. 'That changed how I felt. It began to hurt and I wanted to get out.' But today, she is back working after at least three failed attempts and she seems resigned to it being her life. 'It's what I was born to do. I keep going back because I think how else can I deal with the mental pain. I've tried to give it up but have no real desire to do so. It's like smoking. You can only stop it when you really want to. It's much easier to work and not face what brought me to do it in the first place. I was created for this, that's how it is. You know, when I first came up north, it was at the time the Yorkshire Ripper Peter Sutcliffe was stalking the area and killing prostitutes. I saw some police poster saying the next woman could be innocent and I remember thinking I was an innocent victim.'

Because Diana and Lisa are the only prostitutes working at their premises, they could not be charged with running brothels, as under British law there have to be at least two prostitutes working at the same place to constitute a brothel. However, both are law-breakers because of the services they offer and could face prosecution under a 'catch-all' offence, set down in statute more than 200 years ago, of running a disorderly house.

Under the 1751 Disorderly Houses Act, a disorderly house is a building visited by people who conduct themselves in a way that violates law and good order. The disorderly conduct need not be visible from the outside of the building, nor do visitors have to take part, they can just be spectators. The indecent acts must either outrage public decency, tend to corrupt or deprave, or otherwise injure the public interest.

The police still use the 1751 act where there are complaints from the public, live sex shows, premises specializing in sado-masochistic services or even, as with the infamous Operation Spanner group of men, on private property with consenting individuals taking part in such acts.

In the notorious 'Spanner' case, a group of sado-masochistic males was found guilty of assaulting each other, despite the willing participation of all of them. The Court of Appeal said that whether the participants consented to the assaults or not was irrelevant, since it was not in the public interest for them to behave in the manner they did. One of the men was jailed for four years for keeping a disorderly house.

Like the Spanner defendants, prostitutes such as Diana and Lisa and their clients can be prosecuted for assault – despite the fact that both parties consent to give and receive treatment which could result in injuries. Under the 1861 Offences Against the Person Act, an assault is classed as anything from bruising and scratching (actual bodily harm) to inflicting more serious damage (malicious wounding or grievous bodily harm). Diana and her maid face the risk of brothel charges and they both might have to prove that Sue did not offer sexual services.

Those who cater for the exclusive end of the market may operate for years without ever coming to police notice, and probably stand more chance of being exposed by a Sunday newspaper than a vice unit. Generally these women have their professional and personal lives under control. They rarely claim state benefits; most are registered as self-employed and can afford to work discreetly, thus attracting little attention.

Nevertheless, late last summer, Diana received several phone calls from a police officer who has gained a notorious reputation among high-class call girls for demanding 'favours' from prostitutes working in the capital. The first call was to let her know he would be paying her a visit. The second call soon after was to say he might want 'favours'. She fled to Spain for a week to avoid him.

On her return, further calls followed and she sought advice from a solicitor. He told her she was the fourth big-earning prostitute to see him for advice about this specific officer. One woman so feared him that she packed up work and fled to Italy. It is thought another handed over several thousand pounds to him.

Diana decided to play along with the officer. 'He was always very careful what he said on the phone. I couldn't win either way. If I attempted to trap him, I'd have my face blasted across every paper and never be able to work again. If I went along with him, I'd have to give him sex and/or money,' she said.

Another phone call revealed his thoughts. She was OK, he had decided. Diana lay low for a few weeks and changed her phone numbers before resuming business.

CHAPTER TWO

Calling for Company

T he safest way to avoid arrest, if not attack, is to work as a call girl for an escort agency. These women are considered, particularly those that operate in London, as the *crème de la crème* of the trade, catering for wealthy clients in top hotels. International business visitors or tourists are often charged higher rates than local clients. Some agencies organize women to work in the hotels of a particular city where a business conference is held. It has been known for companies to arrange 'entertainment' for guests and colleagues attending a major event.

ANNABELLE

'I always say there are two kinds of agency – mine and the "fuck it and chuck its",' Annabelle breezily asserts.

'I run an extremely professional up-market service and have 80 girls aged 19 to 46 on my books. They can be as ugly as hell but what matters is their personality. All women are prostitutes in one way or another, the difference being that genuine prostitutes are honest about it.'

Annabelle takes great pride in the escort agency she set up four years ago in one of the south of England's livelier cities. She runs a call-out agency: the escorts stay at home and are called out by Annabelle when a client rings the office. The other type of agency is the sit-in, which involves the women waiting at the office until a client calls in person or phones and she is selected by him or the agency boss.

Annabelle's office is the dining room of her home, where on a broad desk sit three constantly ringing phones and an answer machine. Beside these are several index card boxes crammed with details of the women who command and the clients who are willing to pay £100 an hour.

Filling one wall of her cluttered office is a large map of southern England dotted with more than 50 coloured pins, each representing one of Annabelle's employees. A red one denotes an escort with a car who is prepared to travel to meet a client or to entertain him at her own home. Green is for those who will travel but have no transport and blue for those who have cars but won't entertain at home. The map is highly useful, as it allows her to see at a glance who lives closest to a client.

When a man rings requesting company, she immediately asks his name and number and quickly dials it to check it is engaged. She then scours her boxes to see if he has done business with her before. If he has, Annabelle will have recorded whom he last saw and any comments the escort thought were important about him or his behaviour. More importantly, she checks to see if he is on her black list. Men are placed on it if they have been violent to their escorts, paid by cheques which have subsequently bounced, whipped off condoms at the last minute, or are known time-wasters. 'One client, a doctor, took off his condom while having sex. I just don't want and will not tolerate that sort of business. The only time I would expose a client was if he did anything to one of the girls.'

Regular customers include solicitors, doctors, businessmen, tradesmen and disabled men from across southern England. 'I have a vicar who comes just for fun. MPs always prefer to visit the girls so they don't find out who they are. Some pop stars who've been performing in the city have used my service.'

Annabelle takes a £30 booking fee per client from the women for arranging the meetings. Any 'extra services' are paid as tips by the customer directly to the woman in the privacy of the hotel or bedroom.

Agency fees can vary from £25 to £70 and many escort company owners declare their profits to the tax man. As most of the women are self-employed, it is left to them to declare their earnings.

Without this arrangement, Annabelle could face being charged under section 22 of the 1956 Sexual Offences Act which states that it is an offence to procure a woman to become a prostitute or to leave her home in the United Kingdom to become an inmate of, or frequent, a brothel for prostitution.

Few females, however, are convicted of this, as Government statistics show: 45 in 1989, as opposed to 557 men (rising from 300 men and 15 women in 1986).

The other offence she could be accused of is exercising control over a prostitute for the purpose of gain. This is used most often against 'madams' and is a crime that can only be committed by females. This is the male equivalent of living off immoral earnings, 'pimping', as it is unofficially known.

The legal situation quickly stokes up Annabelle's temper. 'I am trying my best to run a reputable agency where the girls are protected. Yet if I say I know what is going on then that means I am acting illegally, but if I didn't know then I wouldn't be able to do the business. The law is an ass! Prostitution is the only crime where there is no victim.'

Many requests fall through the letterbox of Annabelle's terraced home from women eager to get on her books, but before they do she puts them through a rigorous vetting procedure. 'Nine out of ten haven't a bloody clue what escort work involves. I have to tell them there are "extras" to it rather than just going out for meals. I am always dubious if they give financial reasons for wanting to be an escort as they might try to skip paying my booking fee. Or if they are saving up for something like a holiday because once they have the money, they'll bugger off and I am left high and dry.'

Annabelle places emphasis on a girl's character and anyone found not to be up to standard is sacked: 'It's personality, not looks, which makes the first impression when an escort calls a client. If a potential employee speaks to me on the phone asking for a job application and her personality doesn't come across I tell her not to bother. I've got one big, big girl, 18 stone, and she's a great character. She goes down great with the men and sees a couple of local handicapped fellas. I tell the girls if they are enjoying the man's company, don't rush as he will always come back.'

Once a woman is accepted on her books, Annabelle sends her a starting pack containing a letter of welcome and a job contract. It is this slip of paper, along with the payment arrangements, which safeguards her in the eyes of the law and she will not employ a woman unless she signs the contract. It lists the following points:

1. The agency introduces clients to escorts for the purposes of dining, dancing and theatre only.

2. The £30 agency fee must be collected by the escort and given to the agency as soon as possible.

3. The escort works on a self-employed basis and is responsible for making her own income tax returns and national insurance payments.

4. The agency does its utmost to vet all clients before introduction to escorts but cannot accept responsibility for damage or theft while an escort is with a client.

5. Escorts are requested always to look their best and be polite and well-mannered when with a client.

6. Any escort divulging her phone number to a client or offering immoral services will be dismissed immediately.

Also in the pack is a typed sheet of A4 detailing safer sex guidelines and written by Annabelle. It advises: 'Never do anything you don't want to. Remember we are always being blamed for spreading disease. Let's make sure this is not true.' She gives practical advice about the use of condoms: 'If they want French [blow job or oral] use an allergy or flavoured condom. Don't use baby oil or oil-based lipsticks as they break a condom. If he wants oral without a condom you can always say you have a problem with your wisdom teeth and can't open your mouth wide enough.'

To tackle the problem punter who wants condom-free sex, she advises: 'You will always come across this sort. Tell him the smell of rubber turns you on.'

And she adds: 'Don't forget to offer them a shower or bath afterwards as questions could be asked when they get home.'

Her women live in Kent, Berkshire, Hampshire, Dorset and London. Most are equipped with mobile phones or bleepers, and some have fax machines installed at their home so as not to miss out on vital business. Some who are available 24 hours a day for work have pagers.

'Many of my escorts are career-women with the escort work giving them a bit of extra cash. Some have public school education and are from comfortably-off families. A lot are married. They are the best ones, as they are reliable and hard-working. In fact, two of my girls have wed clients and I lived with a punter for five years. The women trust me because I've worked myself.

'I don't care for brothels as girls have to submit to any Tom, Dick or Harry. In many ways, escort agencies have replaced brothels. At least I give girls a choice to work or not.'

Most employees of escort agencies offer sexual services. These semi-legitimate organizations have become the acceptable face of prostitution and are rarely raided by police, since the people who own and run them are controlled by legislation. Men who use escort agencies can freely avail themselves of their services in the knowledge that they are not breaking any vice laws in the United Kingdom, unless of course a prostitute is under-age.

Advertising escort agencies or their services is not illegal, either. Women who work as such and their clients do not break any laws. Because Annabelle does not publicly acknowledge or have anything to do with what happens between the escort and the client, nor does she receive payment for any sexual services performed, her business is above board.

Despite this, Yellow Pages refused to accept orders from Annabelle for £7,000 worth of display advertisements in ten different editions covering her business area. The adverts would have shown a woman in a sexy evening dress and described the service as an escort agency. Other services are never mentioned in any publicity and are always left for the escort and client to arrange. Nevertheless, all Annabelle was granted was a one-line advert, stating her business's name and number.

'The girls employ me and I suppose if anyone was soliciting or procuring it's me,' says Annabelle. 'I spend £900 a week on advertising in newspapers and contact magazines, £3,000 a year on phone bills and have just been landed with a £16,600 VAT bill. On average I do 80 bookings a week. The most I've done was 115 and the least 65. I am not doing anything illegal – the contract protects me.'

But she angrily denounces the hypocrisy of the laws: 'I am open about what I do and have gone to great lengths to ensure everything is as legitimate as possible within the existing laws. The tax man is only too willing to cream off his fair share of money earned from the agency, yet I could be done if they considered I was openly employing prostitutes. I often look at that poster' – nailed to her office wall, it states, 'The only pimp I know is the tax man' – 'and swear profusely. What do we get in return for paying taxes? Nothing. Ideally, every town and city where prostitutes operate should have a drop-in centre for them, which offers help and advice. But there's nothing for us.'

The friendly 49-year-old has the healthy looks and manners of a Home Counties farmer's wife, but was born in Corby and her father was a church army captain. On leaving school she went into secretarial work before moving to France with her husband where they ran a restaurant for 13 years. After he left her, she returned to England and took on various jobs, including housekeeping and school cleaning, in return for a roof over her head.

She drifted into prostitution at the age of 40 after the marriage break-up left her in dire financial straits. 'I worked for an agency for about 20 months and believe it or not I was pretty popular, probably because I was versatile. I didn't mind travelling and I would entertain at home.

'I went to work for one agent but she was a real scrubber and that put me off the idea. But a while later a friend called to say one of his girls had not turned up and would I do him a favour and take his agency's phone calls. A chap rang for a girl and no one was available. I refused straight away to do it but after a chat with the client, an ex-journalist, he suggested I see him for a few drinks. I went, we had a good evening and his cheque paid my bills. It seemed to me to be money for old rope.

'I worked for the agency for a while but then decided to set up on my own in 1989. I started off with a handful of girls and gradually built up the business. I want to make as much money as possible and retire in a few years.'

Advertising is vital for businesses such as escort agencies and massage parlours, and for those women who work indoors or as independent escorts. Somehow they always manage to find ways of working around the increasingly stringent laws which hinder their efforts to attract work discreetly.

Both Yellow Pages and Thomson Directories refuse to publish display adverts from escort agencies or massage parlours. Thomson issues its sales representatives with two pages of strict instructions explaining what is and is not acceptable. Having checked with the

Institute of Complementary Medicine, which said there were two types of massage, therapeutic or remedial, Thomson insists that the word 'massage' can only be printed if it is prefixed by either of these words. There are also limitations on the size of print used and the size of advert. A spokeswoman said any genuine parlours would be listed under alternative medicines.

The Yellow Pages company follows the same policy but insists it is not being moralistic. 'For some time we were unhappy with the style and content of many of the parlour and sauna ads that were coming in to be published,' said a spokesman. 'We are a public source of information and we were becoming increasingly concerned over the matter. We were spending a lot of time censoring the ads, stopping stuff getting in, and we didn't like that.

'We are not taking a moral stance over the issue. We have a responsibility to the 25 million people who have Yellow Pages in their homes and did not want to offend people. Sadly, genuine businesses do lose out but we still allow free one-line entries.'

Though advertising prostitutes' services does not constitute soliciting, it may be an offence for two reasons. First, an advert might be considered to be 'obscene' if it encourages men to use prostitutes. An obscene article is defined as one having a tendency to deprave or corrupt people likely to see, hear or read it. So any kind of advertisement could be classified as obscene, whether in a magazine, a shop window, or broadcast on radio or TV.

Secondly, any male involved with a magazine, newspaper, shop, radio or TV station which earns advertising revenue from prostitution could be prosecuted under section 30 of the 1956 Sexual Offences Act – the same offence used against pimps – for living off immoral earnings. The prosecution would have to prove that the payments were received in the knowledge that they were earned by prostitution. Evidence of this might be exorbitantly high advertising rates charged to prostitutes as opposed to other customers. This rule also applies to taxi drivers who put up their fares to escort punters to prostitutes and vice-versa.

British Telecom tried two years ago to block prostitutes' phone lines advertised on cards in phone booths. But the telephone watchdog organization OFTEL ruled that BT could not do that as it contravened its obligation to provide a universal service free from discrimination against particular customers. BT responded by saying it would introduce a clause into its Customer Service Contract enabling it to block incoming calls on lines advertised in its phone boxes. This has not yet been done.

Annabelle has designed a tight set of safety precautions for her women and not one of them has been attacked while she has been in business. This must be partly due to the strict working regulations she drums into the women – checking on punters' names, informing the agency when and where the meeting is, and letting the punter know people are aware of who she is with.

Unfortunately, not all agencies are so vigilant or caring, as Stella discovered.

STELLA

The fresh-faced 28-year-old has worked her way from street girl to pub stripper to high-class escort in the four years she has been in the sex trade. She found her present London escort agency in Yellow Pages. After calling them she was invited for an interview, where they explained how to deal with credit cards and other work practices.

The image of a high-class call girl's job is that she is wined and dined by a rich client before she succumbs to his charms in the privacy of a luxury hotel bedroom. In reality, most men are happy to skip the food and get down to what they are paying for. Stella is occasionally taken to dinner but usually she goes straight to the client's hotel room or private home. She used to work every night, but has cut down to four. 'They're usually one- or two-hour appointments and when I go in I have a chat or a glass of wine with them before getting down to work.

'I fake an orgasm every time. Most of my clients are international businessmen who spend nine months of the year jetting around the globe and only one has ever said to me, "Look, you don't have to pretend, it doesn't bother me."

'It's all very clinical. I give guys the impression there's a hell of a lot of physical contact between us, but there isn't. I have my own limits – I don't kiss, I couldn't do that. And there's no going down on me, but I don't tell them that. If I think a guy is about to, I'll say, "Ooh, come and kiss my breasts." I give oral and sex with a condom and maybe some fantasy stuff if I trust the punter.'

She usually signs off with the agency at about 10.30 pm but if she needs the work she might wait up until midnight before ringing in.

Of her £200 fee she has to give £50 to the agency as a booking fee. 'When I first started it seemed so much money. But you get used to it and then the work gets very wearing. It can be very stressful. Even if a punter seems a nice guy and is staying at a top hotel, there's always a niggling worry that he is going to hurt you. Whatever way you work, you are on your own.'

She discovered the truth of this after being raped at knife-point by a client who held her hostage at his flat for nine hours. 'My agency never realized anything was wrong or wondered why I hadn't phoned in.

'I'd not been in London for long and hadn't sussed out which were good and which were dodgy areas. I turned up at this guy's flat in Hammersmith and I thought it looked a bit rough. He said he was a doctor and it soon became perfectly clear that he wasn't but I couldn't think of a way to get away. I suppose I panicked.

'When he told me he didn't have a cheque card I said I would come back tomorrow. That's when he produced the knife. I tried to call the police but he ripped the cord out of the wall and he raped me several times. It went to court but such a big deal was made out of what I did for a living. They found him guilty of kidnap but not of rape and he was jailed for two years.

'The police were sympathetic but one of the most humiliating things of the whole business was in court when the prosecution said it cannot have been as bad for me as for a "normal woman"! I did try to stop working but gradually fell back into it.'

A prostitute's job and previous convictions can be publicly disclosed in court, whether they relate to her present occupation or not, if she is a witness in a case. A lawyer can cross-examine her about these and other situations if questions designed to attack the witness's character are allowed. This is known as cross-examination as to credit and aims to show that the witness made an earlier inconsistent statement, or is biased.

Stella started on the game in her West Midlands home town after being sacked from her job in a shop. Estranged from her highly religious, working-class parents because of losing her job (she refused to say why), and faced with a long-drawn-out battle for benefits, she 'crashed down' on the floor of a friend's flat, which happened to be situated in a red light area.

'I waited nearly seven hours to make a social security claim and when I went into the booth, they told me I was in the wrong office and I had to go to another the next day. I was totally skint and as I walked home a kerb-crawler pulled up. I had been solicited before but just ignored them. I was so distraught that I got in his car. We did full sex but I can't remember how much he paid me. I went home to recover from the shock of what I had just done but from that day I started on the streets.

'I couldn't survive on my £42 a week dole money and whenever I was short I'd do a bit of work. Once you have done it, you have done it.'

She moved to London to escape the unhappy memories of her home town and to look for work. But again, with little money or job hopes, it was not long before Stella was using her feminine wiles – not for money, but food. During the day she would visit a nearby hotel for coffee and pocket the free bread rolls to keep her nourished.

The hotel was a popular haunt for businessmen on an evening out. 'I'd go in dressed reasonably provocative and order an orange juice. When a man sat near me I'd look at him, really look at him, to give him the impression that I was a working girl. Usually he would come over and be embarrassed about what to say. One way or another I would get them to buy me dinner and after he'd paid I would make it clear that I wasn't a prostitute and play the innocent so he wouldn't have the courage to ask for business. I did that until I got thrown out of the hotel.'

She became a stripper. Seedy pubs and clubs around the East End of London were her venues for a year after she had read an advertisement boasting of £500 a week earnings. In reality, pub landlords paid £10 for her to strip naked. 'My agent was a complete sleaze-bag. I didn't have a clue what it was all about when I first started, never realized I had to buy my own equipment and records. I'd make up the money by passing a jug around the customers after my act.'

Today, registered for tax purposes as a self-employed cabaret worker, she is working full-time as an escort. Although the money is good, she has to juggle her finances carefully. 'I own a house out of London which I rent out because I have to live in the centre. When a client wants to see you, they mean in 20 minutes not two hours, so I rent a flat and that costs quite a bit. Taxis are a must as you can't be getting buses to and from an appointment and agency fees are so high because of their advertising.'

In her free time she has gained A Levels and is studying for more qualifications. She is well-spoken, with a neat blonde bob; her pert face is free of make-up when she is not working and she dresses her boyish figure in a trendy rather than glamorous fashion.

Most of her friends are working girls. 'I need them as there is so much of yourself you can't disclose to people and that's because there's such a lack of understanding about the whole business. I don't find it hard to accept that I am a prostitute but I would like to stop before I get too old and have to charge less money.'

Not all escorts work for agencies. Ann is one of an unknown number who freelance at night while having a 'respectable' job during the day.

ANN

'I call it dessert. We'll have our meal and then I usually ask if they want to go to my flat for a nice dessert.' Ann laughs with a hint of bitterness as she explains: 'I don't speak like that in normal circumstances. It's all part of the role I play when I'm working. I say what a client wants to hear.'

Ann is an expensive sweet. She will not step out of her Kensington flat for a 'dinner date' for less than £350, do an overnight stay in a hotel for under £1,000 or visit less than up-market hotels and restaurants in London. Similarly, clients will not see the other side of her apartment door without handing over a minimum of £150.

As with most prostitutes, money was her main motive for turning to the job but, ironically, her disillusionment with men had some influence in her decision to sell sexual services: 'I felt that men expected sex at the end of the night if they took me out for a meal.

'In my experience, a lot of men don't tell you they're married and I thought why should I be used? I wanted to get something back at the end of the day – and I was struggling to make ends meet. I did have a full-time job but by the time I'd paid my mortgage and bills I was left with nothing.'

A friend told Ann about her job as an escort and after consideration she decided it was a way to earn extra cash, meet people and socialize. 'The dining companion side appealed to me. I was awfully scared at first and still am with new clients. Now I have about 20 regulars but it is difficult for them to always get to see me as I don't work so often. One guy, whom I've seen for seven years, is like an old friend. He's even guaranteed loans for me. I see him once a week if he is in the country or once a month otherwise.'

Like many women who secretly work in the sex business, Ann most fears being arrested by the police or exposed by tabloid journalists searching for titillating stories. These anxieties, coupled with the fact that she works independently of an agency, mean she is cautious about how she operates. She believes she jeopardizes her safety by not employing a maid, because this might increase the risk of being found out.

The softly-spoken Ann outlines her predicament: 'The most frightening thing is working on my own. I have worked as a maid for a friend for £50 a day but have never worked as a prostitute with another girl in the same flat. I don't employ a maid. I'm too scared to for legal reasons. I've never been prosecuted but I do feel vulnerable.'

Although, as we have seen, escort work is legal, she takes care with the wording of her advertisements and telephone conversations with clients. If she entertains at her flat a client who has read her advertisement – 'attractive, discreet escort for all occasions. Dinner dates a speciality. Hotel visits' – she will phone his given number up to four times to establish he is genuine before giving out her address.

As she works independently, Ann does not have to pay any agency fees. But the lack of official back-up support has led her to setting up her own security system for dealing with potentially troublesome clients. 'Screening is really important. I check them out as thoroughly as I can before even describing myself. If they think I'm suitable I insist on a number from them or I won't see them. I try and get a girlfriend to call ten minutes after a client arrives to check everything is OK.

'If it is, I pour the client a drink and have a chat before I give them a massage and whatever service they require. I'll wear a nice dress with the right sort of lingerie underneath. Most of my clients are married businessmen, aged 40 to 60s, and treat me like a lady for the time I am with them. They usually say they don't get on with their wives in the bedroom but they share a house to keep up the family image. Half want straight sex, the rest hand relief. I have a few in their mid-30s, guys in good Government jobs. One is extremely shy and has only ever had sex with working girls.

'Occasionally I'll get young men who've saved a month's wages and seeing me is their treat, but they can be very demanding. Flat visits are mostly English businessmen while the hotels tend to be lonely and bored American or continental travellers.

'The recession has changed things a lot in the capital. Three years ago I could have had a dinner date every night and maybe a couple of clients at home during the day. Now I'm doing a lot of business at my flat.'

She refuses to visit hotels in the seedier areas of the capital. Most of her appointments are at five-star ones and fees for a four-hour dinner date are between £350 and £500. 'I usually wear a little cocktail dress for a dinner date or a suit for a hotel visit. I spend a lot on clothes, usually classic designer stuff, as I have to look good. I aim to be discreet and, for hotels, as inconspicuous as possible. I don't want to look like a floozie on some guy's arm and hate the busty blonde stereotyped image.

'Dinner dates can be good fun, though I do get some where I am counting the minutes. Everything is up-front. I get the money sorted out straight away. I normally tell them over the phone to have the money in an envelope and pass it to me 10 to 15 minutes after my arrival to save embarrassment on both sides. I've been to most of the best eating places in the city – Le Gavroche, Bibendum, Mr Wing's. I certainly wouldn't be going to some of them if I was paying.

'You know, men love their ego boosted. Even though they are paying for my time and company and we have only just met, many kid themselves they are taking you out and want you to like them. I do some. A few are so nervous that you have to be on the ball conversation-wise.

'I kiss my regular clients or those I like. I won't do anything kinky as I don't like it and find it draining. As for the sex, I don't even think about it. I'm playing a role and most men can't tell the difference between acting and for real. I can have a giggle about it afterwards with a girlfriend. At home, the sex usually only lasts seven to ten minutes and they never get into bed. I take my time with the build-up and talk to them as I do the massage. I always use condoms but it's the married punters who don't want to.

'I know my clients see other women, partly because I am not always available and also because they like the variety. I had a relationship with a married client but it was a horrible experience. After he stopped paying me, I was at his beck and call. I had lost control and felt I was being emotionally and physically used. I know quite a few working girls who have developed relationships with clients.'

Born into a middle-class New Zealand family, she arrived in England on her travels around the world ten years ago and stayed. She started on the game a year later at the age of 20 and works full-time, or part-time when she has a 'straight' job. Currently she has a part-time job as a doctors' surgery receptionist, and while it is enjoyable it fails miserably to meet the £200 a week rent on her Kensington flat.

She also cuts down her escort work and, in the past, has stopped doing it altogether if she is in a relationship: 'It is difficult for a partner to accept that you can switch off while having sex with a client. I told one boyfriend what I did and it went down like a lead balloon.'

While she makes a good living from being an escort, she pays out £150 a week on advertising and clothes are a further expense: 'I spend a lot on underwear and go through so many pairs of stockings.'

Ann, with the appearance of a rich businessman's wife, does cause people to cast a second glance at her as she walks along the street. Her svelte figure was clad in black patent pumps, tailored black trousers and jacket topped with a hat trimmed with fake fur covering her bobbed hair. A few discreet items of jewellery – delicate gold chains and pearl earrings – were added. Throughout our meeting she never removed her hat or her large tinted glasses.

She is presently involved in a serious relationship with a woman. Money earned from escorting is paying off Ann's debts, then she and her partner hope to set up house together and have a family. 'We get on very well. She is not in the business and it was difficult at first but we discussed it and it's OK now. I've always been bisexual to some degree and had a relationship with another woman when I was 19. I think everyone has some bisexuality in them.'

It is perhaps understandable if a prostitute turns to a lesbian relationship for comfort. Cardiff, for no obvious reason, has a number of working girls who are involved either with other prostitutes or 'straight' (non-prostitute) women, as working girls call them. As one of the city's outreach workers explains: 'Some of them hate men, probably because they've given them a hard time in the past.

'But there is also the adage that if you eat sweet stuff all day you want something savoury when you go home. Some of the straight prostitutes don't like "the dykes" as they call them.'

One thing Ann has learnt from the job is never to be surprised at the numbers and types of men who pay for sex. 'Their excuses to their partners are usually the same – working late at the office, having a drink with mates, going shopping is a great one. At Christmas, a lot of men will visit me while their wives are at Harrods.

'At the end of the day most working girls are here for one reason – there is a market for us.'

CHAPTER THREE

Anyone Can Be a Punter

KEVIN

'Life certainly began at 40 for me. Well, my sex life did,' recalled Kevin with a nervous chuckle. It was on that memorable birthday that the self-employed builder decided to buy himself a present – sex with a prostitute.

It was to be several visits later before he embarked on a sexual journey that 'nearly sent him through the roof' and has led to him paying for sex ever since.

Kevin, now 58 and a grandfather of two, appeared ill at ease as he explained why he paid for sex. 'I'd heard and read about prostitutes and just thought, well I'm 40 now, I'm going to try it.

'A friend told me of a woman, Yvonne, who worked from her own home. I decided a visit there was to be my treat and I paid £5 for sex with her. I was terrified as hell and you know something, that fear has never left me. Even when I go now I'm still nervous and tremble. I don't think I'll ever get over that. I did feel ashamed after my first visit and vowed never to go again – but thought better of it!'

For ten years he attended the same parlour four miles from his northern home until a police raid closed it down a few months ago. On average, every third Friday night he saw one of the same two women for sex or oral sex. If he was flush with money visits were more frequent, but they would slacken off in the winter, when work and cash were thin on the ground.

Kevin always followed the same routine. 'I'd come home from work, have my tea, get changed, go out about 8 pm, park a few streets away from the parlour, have a drink, chat and sex with them, then about 9 pm go to my local for a couple of pints before going home. It's a very relaxing evening.

'I have built up relationships with the two girls. They were in their early 20s when I first started seeing them. One time we all went to a wedding together. One asked me once if I minded having the other as she was going out with her husband in an hour! During the first three years, I didn't have to wear a condom but do now.

'A lot of the women don't kiss but these girls do. We have a laugh and chat before getting down to it. The massage turns me to jelly even though it only lasts a few minutes before the girls strip off.

'I always go on my own, even though a couple of other pals use the same place. When I go on weekends away with local rugby club members, I slope off on my own for a couple of hours. I've always gone to parlour girls as I think they are more attractive than street ones.'

His sexual ventures nearly met an abrupt end in the early days. 'I was gobsmacked one day when I walked into the massage parlour I'd been using for a while and saw a good mate's wife behind the counter, in charge of the place. I thought, "Oh Christ, this is it. I've had it now." But she said, "Don't be a prat, I'm not going to tell anyone." And she hasn't, ever.'

Kevin describes his wife of 37 years as beautiful and smart – but very religious. They have not had sex since she had a hysterectomy eight years ago. Now they have separate bedrooms because of Kevin's loud snoring – well, that is the excuse they tell their children. 'I adore my wife and we had good, if predictable, sex for years. But she is very Roman Catholic, a prude and has not been that interested in sex for years. There were certain things she wouldn't do such as oral sex, which she told me was disgusting and unnatural. I'd never had it until I went with one of these birds and now I like it better than ordinary sex. It was Yvonne who introduced me to oral sex. I nearly went through the roof the first time I had it.

'I've had two affairs and even then we didn't do oral. I got myself into so much trouble with the affairs. It's much less hassle paying for it. The wife knew about the relationships but she doesn't know about my parlour visits and since I've been going I've not had any affairs. I sometimes think she must know I'm doing something but she never mentions it.

'We took our grandchildren to Blackpool for the weekend and while she showed them the Tower I sneaked off for a visit to a parlour. I looked a few up in the local newspaper, made a call and got a taxi to one. I love my grandkids and know it must sound awful but I just got an urge and fancied a bit of sex.

'I am scared of being caught. One of my worst fears is what my family would think if I was found out. My wife would probably walk out on me if she knew. I still have feelings of guilt. I was brought up a strict Methodist.

'I think even if everything was OK between me and her, it wouldn't make any difference now. We both get embarrassed if either of us try to talk about sex. She says she is celibate and happy to stay like that. We're still together though I don't know why we didn't split up years ago. It's too late now. I'm not unhappy – but we never hit the heights. Maybe we married too young, I was only 21 and knew nothing about life. We were both virgins and courted for two years before I got near her. When we did it for the first time a month before the wedding, she caught on [became pregnant].'

Kevin has not used a prostitute for five months. He says the desire is not there at the moment but he expects to resume visits soon. 'A scout-master pal recommended another parlour to me but I stuck with the same one until it closed. My wife read of the parlour's police raid in the local paper and asked me if I'd seen it. I said yes and just thought thank God I wasn't in at the time. I enjoy seeing the girls and get a thrill out of it but I'm not a kinky guy. It's an erotic experience. I suppose I'm a good customer as it only takes me three or four minutes to come.'

There is no such being as a typical punter. That is one of the few issues prostitutes and police agree on. Another fairly safe but maybe distressing bet is that a male member of your family, circle of friends or work colleagues has paid a prostitute for sex. Statistics from surveys carried out over the past few years suggest that up to one in five men have paid for some kind of sexual service at some time in their lives.

The image of the 'dirty old man' getting his sexual kicks from slavering over a hooker for a few pounds is one which many people might prefer to retain, perhaps feeling detached enough from it to smirk at it. While a few customers may fit this mould, the majority do not. White-collar workers appear to make up a large proportion of the clientèle of the women interviewed for this book. One maybe should assume that some punters lie about their personal life to conceal their identity. But of the numerous interviews with clients, on and off the record discussions and sightings of punters I had, none of the men could be described as either dirty or old.

A Glasgow study of 100 men who visited prostitutes revealed that more than half were married, and most were in serious relationships. Only two had told their partners they used prostitutes.

Some, like Kevin, visit the same women or place for years, others enjoy the thrill of having a different woman each time. A few men said it was easier to pay for sex than have an affair, while many said they would ask prostitutes to perform something, such as oral sex, which they felt unable to ask their partner to do.

Those who want 'specialist' services such as S&M or fantasy work may reveal their tastes only to the prostitute. The excitement and dangers of illicit sexual encounters with a type of woman with whom they may never come into contact through their normal social habits can be as pleasurable as the sex act for others.

Why, when men can use an escort agency or visit a luxurious parlour with little fear of arrest or exposure, do they persist in touring the streets looking for sex? The danger of it all, coupled with the seediness, must be part of the attraction for many punters.

Surely Sir Allan Green could have afforded to visit a discreet call girl if he had wanted? The then top solicitor in the country was spotted just before 11 pm on an October night in 1991 in a seedy King's Cross back-street by Metropolitan Police officers patrolling the area in an unmarked vice unit van. He was confronted by a uniformed officer after he left his car and crossed the road to talk to one prostitute. A second was close by. He was asked to identify himself, which he immediately did, told he would be reported to senior officers, and then allowed to drive home. After a report was presented on the incident, a chief superintendent decided Sir Allan should receive a written warning about his future conduct. He resigned days later from his £77,000-a-year job as Director of Public Prosecutions.

Many prostitutes say clients deliberately go for women who are total opposites from their partners at home. Compare the scrawny, lank-haired, badly-dressed prostitute Sir Allan was seen with, to his elegant blonde Swedish wife, Eva, who tragically killed herself several months after the incident was revealed. Is this a man's way of keeping separate in his mind sex with a prostitute and sex with a partner?

Some of the most extensive research undertaken on clients, the services they purchase and where business is done, has been carried out by the Birmingham Safe team in the seven years it has existed. Comprising social and health workers, former and working prostitutes, the health authority-funded organization provides an excellent service for sex workers in the city.

Studies by the project manager Hilary Kinnell and her team have shed new light on the prostitution trade. Via their prostitute contacts, Safe managed to get 130 punters to fill in questionnaires. A further eight prostitutes who worked in various ways kept records of 300 client contacts, giving brief demographic details of them and details of services given.

Two-thirds of the 130 said they had partners with whom they did not use condoms. Half were in blue-collar jobs or unemployed, and tended to go to street or window girls. Professional and managerial types made up about ten per cent.

'We estimate there are 50 to 100 punters for every prostitute. We asked when they last did business with a working girl and the average answer was five weeks. They looked for business roughly every fortnight and that means an average 10 to 26 visits a year,' said Ms Kinnell.

'Birmingham has 400,000 men aged 17 to 79. Based on interviews with 1,200 prostitutes, we reckon about 30,000 of the city's male population would visit a working girl. It could be up to 80,000 – one in five. We say between one in five and one in 12 men visit working girls and average it out at one in ten.'

Ms Kinnell's respondents were asked to record the sexual services given to each client on the last day they worked and information was gathered on a total of 1,157 prostitute/client contacts. Straight sex was the most common service with 649 incidents (56 per cent), 237 (20 per cent) had oral sex and 141 (12 per cent) were masturbated.

As she states: 'The predominance of vaginal sex calls into question the myth about commercial sex catering mainly to minority sexual interests.'

The average age of the 130 men was 40 and of the working girls 25, though nine women were over 40. Only a handful of the men said it was their first visit to a prostitute. The rest had all used a prostitute within the previous six months, with the average career of a client being ten years. 'One man was in his 70s and had been seeing prostitutes for 50 years!' recalled Kinnell. 'Yet so few admit to doing it – I am sure that is because a view prevails that it is not macho to have to pay for sex.

'It is the shame and embarrassment attached to it. No one should be blamed for needing to express their sexuality with another consenting adult. We have totally unrealistic images about sex – "good" sex is within marriage and for having babies, naughty sex is much more exciting.'

Ms Kinnell's research put paid to the myth that women who work indoors see more men than do street girls. Wherever they worked, women saw on average 22 punters a week. Surveys carried out in 1988 and 1991 showed the average was exactly the same.

Of 258 prostitutes interviewed over nine months, 109 (42 per cent) met clients exclusively on the street; 104 used several means, including the streets; 45 met clients in places other than the street. Off-street prostitutes used several methods to meet clients. Hotels topped the list, followed by contact magazines and visits for massage. Escort agencies were third choice with sauna/massage parlours not far behind.

It is only since 1985 that men have been criminalized for picking up prostitutes from the streets of England and Wales. Prior to this – and as still happens in Scotland and Northern Ireland – they were dealt with under the 1361 Justices of the Peace Act: the charge was breaching the peace by conducting himself in a manner likely to cause alarm, annoyance or disturbance to the public. It is punishable by fine only and is still used on occasions in England and Wales when the offence is more serious than one needing a letter but there is insufficient evidence to secure a conviction under the 1985 act.

Kerb-crawling laws are set to be introduced in Ireland this year for the first time ever, under a new sexual offences bill. Meanwhile Scotland

and Northern Ireland remain very much kerb-crawlers' paradises, as no such offence exists. Extremely regular visitors to the red light areas of Leith, four miles from Edinburgh city centre, or around Belfast's city hall area, are dealt with for breaching the peace. This remains a rarely used legal tool, while prostitutes in these areas are prosecuted in a similar vein to those in England and Wales.

Detective Chief Inspector Ian Cowden, head of Criminal Intelligence for Lothian and Borders Police which covers Edinburgh, admits the Scottish laws almost condone kerb-crawling.

He explained: 'There is little we can do to deter clients, as it is not an offence for a man to pick up a prostitute. If the police catch a punter and woman together, they probably go for her and take his details in case she pleads not guilty and they have to call him as a witness. In reality, prostitutes rarely deny a charge.'

The offence of kerb-crawling in England and Wales was created by the 1985 Sexual Offences Act (SOA), which resulted from recommendations made by the 1984 Criminal Law Revision Committee's (CLRC) 16th report, 'Prostitution in the Street'. The act was introduced to the Commons by Miss, now Dame, Janet Fookes and supported by the majority of MPs. Their argument that it brought equality into the prostitution laws, as the client was also to be punished, was condemned by the English Collective of Prostitutes, who said it was a further infringement on prostitutes' right to work. 'That's like lowering men's wages to make them equal to women's,' said its spokeswoman Nina Lopez-Jones at the time.

Section 1 of the 1985 act states that it is 'an offence for a man persistently to solicit a woman, or different women, for the purposes of prostitution, from a motor vehicle while that vehicle is in a street or public place; or for a man persistently to solicit a woman or different women for the purposes of prostitution, in a street or public place while in the immediate vicinity of a motor vehicle he has just got out of or off'.

Soliciting does not have to be in the form of words or acts, but the client must indicate to the woman that he requires her services as a prostitute. Unlike the woman awaiting his business – who can be arrested immediately she makes a move towards her eager client – the man kerb-crawling is not committing an *arrestable* offence. If a man is collared by the law, his details will be noted and a file sent to the Crown Prosecution

Service, which will decide whether there is sufficient evidence to prosecute or not.

Officers constantly blame the wording of the act and the level of evidence needed to bring charges for there being far fewer clients prosecuted compared with prostitutes. Quite simply, a kerb-crawler soliciting one prostitute on one occasion does not commit a crime. Even if he is caught with his trousers around his ankles sitting in his car with a KCP (police jargon for 'known common prostitute') he is not guilty of a kerb-crawling offence unless it can be substantiated by police officers – but the woman could be arrested for soliciting.

The key word in the 1985 act is 'persistently', which was a House of Lords amendment hastily added to prevent innocent drivers from being mistakenly arrested for kerb-crawling. Home Office guidelines state that a would-be punter has to be seen soliciting a minimum of two women or a single prostitute on two separate occasions over at least a half-hour period.

In practice, a man drives around a beat, maybe flashes his car lights at the chosen prostitute, or parks and approaches her on foot. Punters looking for business tend to achieve success on the initial approach to a woman requesting business – and it is all usually done within a few minutes. So police stand little chance of successful prosecutions with a man – yet under existing laws there is plenty of evidence to charge the woman. Further inequality applies to the prostitute and the punter, as the latter can only be charged on the evidence of uniformed officers. This adds to difficulties in gathering evidence, as many vice squads patrol in plain clothes.

Many police say they would prefer to target the punters rather than the women but are frustrated in their efforts because of the wording of the act. Yet there are means available within it to clamp down on those whom many consider the real nuisance – the punters. Metropolitan Police from Charing Cross's Eight Area Vice Unit's street squad say they get around having to prove that a man 'persistently' solicited by charging him under a clause of Section 1 which covers kerb-crawling 'in such a manner or in such circumstances as to be likely to cause annoyance to any woman solicited, or nuisance to other persons in the neighbourhood'.

This section is an alternative to those requiring evidence of 'persistent' soliciting. Officers do not need to show that anyone was harassed or to have a specific complaint against the client. Instead, they use residents' past letters of complaint about the nuisance caused by punters to support their case.

Though the Met's vice unit admits this policy has yielded only a few successful convictions, it does pose the question that if officers were serious about pursuing kerb-crawlers, why do more forces not use the mechanisms which are ready and waiting idly in place?

'Cruisers' who drive around 'beats' (red light areas) in slow-moving vehicles and 'eye up' or shout abusive comments to prostitutes are greater problems than the genuine punters in some areas. Such voyeurs can also be prosecuted under the nuisance section of the 1985 act.

In its report, *Prostitution in the Street*, the Criminal Law Revision Committee questioned whether prostitutes' pedestrian clients should be penalized by the law. 'We . . . had to ask ourselves whether the man who merely accepts the prostitute's offer should be guilty of an offence. [Interesting to note that the committee assumed it was the prostitute and not the client who made the advances.] We think not. His presence on the street until that moment [the approach is made] provides no greater risk of public nuisance than that of any other male pedestrian.'

They admitted it was inconsistent to draw a line between a man soliciting from a vehicle and one who does it on foot. 'On the other hand there are arguments the other way. Men often make sexual advances to women in the street and public places, as well as elsewhere, which may or may not be welcomed. It would, in our view, be most unwise that such conduct should of itself give rise to the possibility of a criminal offence.'

They concluded that the pedestrian punter's actions should only be treated as a criminal offence if there was a degree of persistence but admitted: 'We appreciate that this creates a discrepancy between the case of the prostitute on the one hand, and that of the client on the other.'

It seems that it is not the male himself who causes the nuisance – but his means of transport. However, pedestrian clients are not totally let off. Section 2 of the 1985 act states that it is an offence for a man persistently to solicit a woman or different women in the street or public place for the purposes of prostitution. The use of a motor vehicle is not an essential ingredient in this offence.

Home Office statistics reveal the increase in kerb-crawling prosecutions in England and Wales since the act was introduced: from 163 Section

1 offences in 1986 to 1,132 in 1991. Section 2 offences were 26 in 1986 and 51 in 1991, with a peak of 70 in 1990. Fines during the above period for kerb-crawlers have increased on average from around £66 to £117, falling far short of the maximum £1,000.

Comparing the figures with the number of women prosecuted for soliciting, one client is found guilty on average for every ten prostitutes.

Sir Frederick Lawton, the now retired Appeal Court judge, sat on the CLRC from 1959 and chaired it from 1977 to 1986. He was instrumental in the act's conception and admits now it is weak. 'Our proposals were watered down by over-enthusiastic lawyers, therefore it is not very effective. The law is unrealistic and fails to meet the actualities of the problem. It is almost impossible to get evidence of a kerb-crawler soliciting twice.

'We wanted to make it easier to punish them but the act is a non-starter. I don't expect it will be changed for at least 20 to 25 years. It should be made more severe. I don't think kerb-crawlers should be jailed but fines should be stiffened and they should have their car confiscated.

'It should be an arrestable offence. But you have got to be careful, some of the police are a pretty nasty lot and if you had them paid by performance, they could be stopping everyone.'

The ex-Conservative MP Sir William Shelton, whose former Streatham constituency embraces a red light area, sponsored a Government-backed bill in 1990 which would have strengthened the kerb-crawling law if it had not been talked out of the Commons at its third reading by the Labour MP Ken Livingstone. Shelton proposed to have the word 'persistently' removed from the law, make soliciting by men an arrestable offence and double the fines. A well-orchestrated campaign highlighting the dangers of this move, primarily that any man could be arrested for approaching a woman on a single occasion, helped block the bill's progress.

Shelton's efforts to get the Home Office to consider electronically tagging persistent kerb-crawlers and prostitutes also failed. However, the Government has since pledged to re-introduce the proposal 'as soon as a suitable legislative vehicle can be found' (see Chapter Ten, question 7).

STEVE

Undoubtedly, some men feel threatened because women are slowly but increasingly gaining more independence generally and shedding their subordination in all areas – including the bedroom and the sexual arena. Some men who feel worried by this take comfort in buying sex. Prostitutes are non-demanding, non-committal, non-threatening, and there for your pleasure, said one punter. 'You know what you are getting for your money. If you don't like the service, you try another.'

One suspects the reasons why Steve regularly picks up prostitutes are not as straightforward as Kevin's. The 28-year-old sales representative is from a family whose name is known throughout the country. He describes himself as a 'spoilt little rich son of an incredibly boring middle-class family from the north-west'.

His flamboyant 'live life for now' attitude, coupled with an attractive personality and looks, endears him to women. But he seems to lurch from one emotional muddle to another. Already he has one failed marriage behind him and is currently engaged in a rocky relationship with a former work colleague.

Steve is from a moneyed background and his job leaves him with plenty of free time and cash – much of which goes on casino tables around the country and generally having a good time. The evening we met he was £900 richer from an afternoon's gambling and he insisted on getting drunk before discussing why he regularly paid for sex.

He has used prostitutes from streets and massage parlours for sex and oral sex since the age of 20, usually when he is between relationships. He estimates he has used the services of up to 60 girls on his travels around the country through work. 'A lot will ask what I want them to do, and then they often say, "Oh, that's my favourite position!" I think, "Don't mess me about." I know they just want to get you to come as quickly as possible and so they can get on to the next punter.'

If his first experience with a prostitute had been unpleasant, he probably would never have gone to one again, he believes. 'But she was very tender and gentle, almost like having sex with a girlfriend. I anticipated feeling dirty but I felt really relaxed and during sex I thought how good it felt. Afterwards she gave me a kiss and said, "Look after yourself, you don't need to do this."'

There was a lull of a month before he saw another prostitute; the gap narrowed to two weeks, then a week. 'After that, I started seeing them a couple of times a week, around the same time I was introduced to casinos. I'd win massive amounts of money. There's a risk to picking girls up. It's like a lottery, wondering if you're going to enjoy it or if they're going to rip you off.'

Steve estimates at least half of his 20 close male friends have been with prostitutes. 'Men seem to find it easier to reconcile going with a girl in a parlour than off the street. In many ways, it's safer to have sex with a hooker as practically all insist on using condoms. But if I met a girl in a club I might take a risk.

'When you have picked a prostitute up once, you'll do it a second time, then a third. It's like lying or stealing, the more you do it the easier it gets. I've never been so desperate for a shag that I'll pick any girl up. I go if I find them attractive, feel horny or lonely. Some men like women who look and seem to be rough because they don't have to be concerned about their emotions or feel inhibited in saying what they want, whereas with an attractive girl a bloke might feel shy about explaining what he wants her to do.

'I get a mixture of fear and adrenalin picking a girl off the street. I've done it in their flats, industrial estates and car parks. To begin with I always wanted straight sex, simply because I was too nervous and shy to ask for anything else. But I was like that in general then.'

He did not lose his virginity until he was 18, which was quite old compared to his friends, he says. 'The first time I had sex it was a complete and utter disaster. The next day I cried, felt really dirty and spent ages in the shower. Then I went out with loads of girls but I didn't have sex with many of them, sometimes I couldn't.

'I like girls who take the initiative. Most don't. When I've had sex with girlfriends, I have always had to make the moves. I've always had a thing about not wanting to be a chauvinist – unlike my father – so much so now that I don't get really turned on even if I am pleasing a partner.'

Steve met his wife when he was 22 and, until they had sex 12 months into the relationship, continued to use prostitutes occasionally. They were married less than a year when he started buying sex off the streets again. 'Our relationship quickly went downhill. Before we married we were rutting [having sex] every night and everywhere. When I restarted seeing prostitutes I was still having some sex with my wife but I always wore condoms with the girls. I have been offered sex without a rubber but I wouldn't entertain that.

'I don't have a big conscience about using prostitutes. The fear of being caught never enters my head. At the time I didn't want my wife to find out because I thought she might blame herself. I have a high sex drive but I didn't feel as if I was being unfaithful to her as there's no real emotional link with the prostitutes.

'It would be a major disaster for me if I came first during sex with my wife or girlfriend. I'd feel so ashamed. But it's not something I worry about with a prostitute. I knew my wife would have sex with me when she didn't want to and probably fake orgasms and that would upset me. But I never feel obliged to try and please a prostitute, not because I don't want to but because she doesn't have to be, though there have been times when I have thought they seemed to enjoy it.

'I suppose it's my way of getting my own back and saying "Fuck you, I am going to be a male chauvinist bastard". I can imagine why punters think they're in love with prostitutes because even though you're paying for sex, it can still be a very intimate experience. Kissing is all it would take sometimes.'

Vice officers at Belgrave Police Station, who police Birmingham's infamous Balsall Heath red light area, collated information last year for the city council on 883 'men who had come to their attention for prostitute-related matters'. The confidential document, which until now has remained unseen by the public, explained that while the men questioned were not necessarily prosecuted, the very least that happened was that a 'letter of advice' was sent to them regarding their involvement in the Balsall Heath area. The document goes on: 'Obviously it has not been possible to gain full information on the male person, but the information gleaned is I think very interesting as it does provide, for the first time, the basis of a profile of the type of male person that frequents an area where prostitution is operating.' The table on page 52 shows a breakdown of what the survey revealed.

The figures back up previous research, which shows that the majority of punters do not travel miles to buy sex. Of the 833 men questioned by Birmingham's vice squad, 629 were from the city or surrounding regions.

Avon and Somerset police say the same pattern occurs in Bristol. Most punters live along the M5 corridor, between Cheltenham and Exeter – within one hour of Bristol's red light area. They tell their wives

Ages	No.	%
18–30	393	44.5
31–40	177	20.0
41–50	144	15.9
51–60	38	4.3
60+	8	0.9
Unknown	127	14.4

*Employment

Blue-collar	385	43.6
White-collar	292	33.1
Not stated	206	23.3

Areas of residence

Birmingham	399	45.2
Midlands	230	26.1
UK	251	28.4
Other	3	0.3

*Police classification

they are going for a drink but can be in Bristol, do the business and get back home without attracting suspicion. And they are all 'Mr Average "collar and tie", not the creepy crawlies people expect,' said one local officer.

Roughly half the kerb-crawlers caught in London are from the city, with mid-week being their peak time for touring a beat. 'It's difficult to say why this is so. Maybe it is because a lot of the women don't work weekends or they are so busy with punters, others are left cruising about,' said a London street vice officer.

He admitted that though kerb-crawlers were often a greater nuisance than the prostitutes, the police still pursued a policy of targeting the women. 'Residents complain to us more about being harassed by kerb-crawlers than by the women. But kerb-crawlers are infinite and prostitutes are not. We can remove the street girls but not the punters. Generally our aim when on patrol is not to get the punter, even though they are more of a problem than the women.'

The prominent barrister Michael Mansfield QC offers a reason for such unfair policing: 'Most police units are populated by men and I suspect they see a punter and think, "There but for the grace of God go I", and so do not home in on them.'

Kerb-crawlers in the capital benefited from the knock-on effects of the Allan Green incident, as one Met vice officer explained: 'After that saga, we went through a phase of not charging clients. As Sir Allan wasn't prosecuted, it raised the problem of why prosecute Joe Public when the ex-DPP was not.'

Their statistics support this. In 1992, they made 2,905 arrests on prostitutes and 661 cautions, compared to 62 kerb-crawlers being prosecuted and 234 'ticking off' letters sent to men's homes saying they were seen in a red light area. Many others simply received verbal warnings.

Nottingham Police Force's anti-vice boss Inspector Dave Dawson says that, unlike many other squads, they target punters more than the women. 'Our figures for bringing the men to court rank as one of the highest in the country and I don't think we are touching the tip of the iceberg. But we decided that because the laws were useless in deterring the women, we would try to get rid of the purchaser rather than the seller – and that is a policy we have pursued for the past five years.

'We split them into two groups – fully-fledged offenders and voyeurs

– and act against both. Those who have picked up a woman and paid for sex are treated just like any other person caught breaking the law. I know some forces give cautions the first time, but we don't. Though the voyeurs do not buy sex, they affect local people's quality of life. We make sure they appear in the same court as kerb-crawlers and are usually bound over to keep the peace. If we don't prosecute we send letters to their homes unless they give a very good reason why we shouldn't, such as a critically ill relative. It is deliberately worded in a guarded fashion, never once mentions prostitution and we see it as a deterrent.'

This is a copy of a letter sent to alleged kerb-crawlers by one particular police force. Most other forces have similar ones. They are sent to the man's home either in a plain envelope or in one emblazoned with the relevant force's crest.

Dear Sir

On   you were interviewed by a Police Officer in connection with an incident that occurred in   on that day.

Whilst no further action will be taken on this occasion in respect of the matter, I would like to advise you that any repetition may well result in your appearance before the Magistrates Court.

Legislation under the Sexual Offences Act 1985 which relates to kerb crawling, together with the application for Bind Over under Section 115 of the Magistrates Courts Act 1980 are being enforced in an effort to eliminate street prostitution.

Should you have any query concerning this matter, please do not hesitate to contact me.

Yours faithfully,

Since the 1985 act came into being, the number of kerb-crawlers dealt with by the Nottingham force has soared from six in 1986 to nearly 300 (158 prosecuted, 132 cautioned or warned) in 1992.

Inspector Dawson admits that pursuing prosecutions depends on the climate of opinion at the time. A crack-down will take place if residents' complaints have increased but if not he concentrates on policing other problems.

CHARLIE

Young, good-looking, single with a muscular body well toned from playing amateur rugby, Charlie has few problems attracting women.

The 23-year-old dark-haired printer has been seeing his present girlfriend for about a year – around the same time he first visited a prostitute. Since then, while his personal relationship has gone from strength to strength, his visits to prostitutes have increased in regularity and moved from the streets to massage parlours.

'I always go with my mates, usually after we've had a few beers or if we're away on a weekend rugby trip and one of the lads mentions it. It's a laugh. I suppose I feel a mixture of guilt and a buzz from the excitement of it all. If my girlfriend found out, she'd probably pack me in. It's no reflection on her or our sex life that I go. I've no complaints in that field though I bet that's not how she'd see it.

'The first time was after four of us finished work on a Friday evening last summer and one had to go to Leeds to pick up some money. We piled in a car and someone suggested going for a drive up Chapeltown. It was about 8 pm and we ended up chatting to a couple of prostitutes stood at a corner on Spencer Place and they seemed nice enough. We drove around the area a couple of times laughing and joking about it all before three of us picked different girls. They seemed OK but I looked at a few and thought "no way!". To be honest I never gave a thought about being caught by the police even though we were dead blatant about it all.

'The lad whose car it was didn't bother. Me and my mate went to a house nearby and the other lad went to another house. Mine was about my age, slim with long black hair. I was attracted by her stocking tops I could see below her tight black dress. I paid her £15 for straight sex. She took her pants off, kept her stockings on and lifted her dress up.

'I tried to touch her breasts and body and she said that would cost extra. She took out two condoms and I thought one must be for her next punter – but she put both on me. I was nervous by now and didn't say anything. It was a bit off-putting at first as she played with me for a short while and that got me slightly aroused. But the sex wasn't very good, she just laid there until I came and never once had any reaction.

'She dressed straight away and waited until I got my clothes on. She got rid of the condoms and that was that. I went back to the car and we gave one of the lads a bit of stick for finishing first. We had a laugh and joke about how we should have had more beer first.'

A weekend rugby club trip to Dublin and a few pints of Guinness set the scene for his second venture into buying sex. Several of the older men on the trip had told him how the previous night they had visited prostitutes in the city centre's canalside area, the main place for street walkers. Flushed with alcoholic bravado, Charlie and a friend decided to do the same. 'We got a taxi to Leeson Street and the driver told us where we could find a prostitute. We saw one aged about 40 leaning against a wall and asked if she was doing business. She told us it was £20 for a hand job and £30 for sex.

'I went first and she took me round the back of some flats, lifted her skirt, put a condom on me and we had sex against the wall. She then did the same with my mate. All the time, there was a man, I think it was her pimp, sat in a van nearby. She was dressed really tarty and throughout sex talked dirty to me.'

Nearer home, his next vice trip was to the decidedly down-market setting of Bradford's red light area, Lumb Lane, known locally as 'The Lane'. A Friday tea-time saw his first visit to a massage parlour with a friend who was a regular. 'We paid £5 to a woman at a front counter for a massage and shower. We were taken to a room where there were about eight girls sat watching saucy videos.

'I was really nervous when one, taller than me and wearing a short skirt but no stockings, came and sat on my knee and asked if I wanted to go for a massage. We went into this dimly lit room and I stripped down to my underpants and laid on the table. It was all nice and clean. She asked if I wanted to be massaged with oil or talc. I laid on my front and we chatted as she did my back and legs. She asked if I wanted my front doing and after she took my pants off she asked if I wanted anything else. I asked how much it was and she said £15 for a hand job, £20 for sex or oral and £40 for sex and oral. I decided on sex.

'She carried on massaging and then started rubbing me and asked me what position I wanted sex in. She stripped off, fixed the condom on me and got on top.'

Charlie's tastes do not run to bondage after he and a friend whiled away a Sunday afternoon calling women advertising in the *Sunday Sport*. 'We followed up one advertised as Dominique and when we got to her house, there was this fat black girl with a scar on her face rigged up in suspenders and the lot. We went into a room painted in black and there were two TVs on with dirty videos playing. At the side of a double bed was a cabinet full of sex toys, various uniforms, a rubber diving suit, and some blow-up dolls. Whips and chains hung from a wall. I was broke and told my mate I wasn't staying there even if he was paying for me. I didn't like the set-up, made my excuses and left. She was OK about it.'

His most enjoyable experience with a prostitute was when he and a gang of friends paid an afternoon visit after a few Christmas drinks to a massage parlour in his home town, near Leeds. 'We'd finished work for the holidays and the women were also having a few drinks. We paid £6 for the massage and all sat round in this room, waiting to see which one of us would be brave enough to be the first to pick a girl.

'Mine was aged about 19 and pretty. I didn't feel as nervous, probably because I felt as if I was taking the upper hand. I said I only had £30 on me and she gave me oral, full sex and a hand job. She kept asking me what I wanted and I was with her about 30 minutes. When I rejoined my mates, two of us decided to go with one of the other women. She started off quoting us £30 each with a further £4 to the front woman and we bargained her down to £20 each with her paying for the massage.

'The three of us stripped off and we began going with her at the same time. One of us would be having sex with her while she was giving the other oral and then we swapped around. We both came but I don't know if she did. We got her to lie on the bed and we watched as she played with herself. I was quite surprised when she agreed to that but it did arouse me. I much prefer it in a massage parlour, you feel more relaxed and you're not being rushed.'

Charlie and a pal took part in another threesome while staying at a Heathrow hotel during a weekend rugby trip to Wembley. While having a drink at the hotel bar, they made inquiries with the barman about the availability of girls. He gave them a calling card and ended up ringing the prostitute for them. When the girl arrived, she went with Charlie and John, one of his pals, to their room. 'We all stripped off and she laid between us. She then went from me to John and gave us both oral sex. John had sex with her and I watched. That turned me on a bit.

'I couldn't do anything as I'd had too much to drink to get an erection so I started acting about. Just for a laugh I put her underwear on and after she gave me oral I started dancing around the room while they were having sex. Next day I found out we were in a ground-floor room and about eight of my mates had been watching through the window and laughing at us! She charged us £180 but while she was giving me oral John took some of it back from her pocket.'

Charlie has been with seven different prostitutes in the past year and says the thrill of illicit sex adds to the excitement. 'It's because you know you're not supposed to be doing it and you know there's no pretence. I don't think I'd ever visit a prostitute on my own. When it's happened it's always been a spur-of-the-moment suggestion. There's nothing serious in it like trying to find something missing in my life – it's more being one of the lads.

'I suppose that's a bit chauvinistic. I have a good relationship and a healthy sex life with my girlfriend and would feel more guilty if I picked up a girl in a nightclub and slept with her. Going with a prostitute doesn't mean anything. You know you're not going to see them again, there's no commitment.'

None of the punters interviewed for this book ever admitted doing violence to the women whose services they purchased. Nevertheless, prostitutes believe the 1985 act has considerably increased risks to their working practices as the punters, nervous at the possibility of being arrested, will not dawdle and so the women have less time to check them out.

Violence perpetrated by clients against prostitutes largely goes unreported and, therefore, cannot be measured precisely. But it is clearly tied to street prostitution. One only has to recall where Peter Sutcliffe approached most of his prostitute victims.

Practically every prostitute has suffered some degree of physical attack but many shrug off all but the most serious as occupational hazards. The English Collective of Prostitutes estimates that more than half of prostitutes are raped by punters but only one woman in 12 reports the attacks. A commonly voiced reason for this is distrust, caused by previous treatment received from officers. 'Women don't get police protection from violence as others do. They pour time and money into arresting prostitutes and punters yet refuse to do anything for King's Cross prostitutes when there has been a series of rapes and attacks on them,' claims the ECP spokeswoman Nikki Adams.

Of 115 Birmingham prostitutes surveyed, more than half had been raped, three-quarters of these attacks committed by punters. Workers at a prostitutes' drop-in centre in Glasgow were told of 69 attacks on women by punters and had reports of 66 in 1992.

Despite this, few women report them, mainly because they believe sympathetic legal ears towards prostitute attacks are few and far between because of the work they do.

Hilary Kinnell, of Birmingham Safe, says prostitutes are the only section of society to be ostracized and vilified, yet their clients suffer no such stigma. 'Society views sex workers worse than murderers,' she said. 'Whatever happens to them, people seem to adopt the attitude "they deserve it", "they were probably asking for it" or "it doesn't matter, it's only a prostitute". Yet all she is doing is making it possible for some man to have an orgasm.'

The renowned barrister Helena Kennedy says the law is more sympathetic towards buyers than providers of sex. 'Selling sex as a commodity is seen as depraved, but it is the seller, not the buyer, who bears the responsibility. The purchaser is seen as the victim of his own sexual needs . . . the law promotes the myth that men are ruled by their libido.'

She tells a colourful if disturbing tale which occurred in a pornography trial and bears out her view. The judge called the barristers involved, except the one female counsel, to his private room. According to one of those present, the judge said words to the effect, 'Come on, chaps, we're all men. The acid test for this stuff is our own reaction – did any of you get a rise out of it?'

A judge gave a rapist a jail sentence two years less than the recommended five-year minimum because his victim was a 'common prostitute'. The court was told how many convictions the woman had as the judge said 'someone who for years has flaunted their body and sold it cannot complain as loudly as someone who has not behaved in such a way'.

The women often try to police themselves. Word of mouth about dangerous punters is one piecemeal way. 'Ugly mugs' lists are another increasingly effective way and operate in many red light areas in the country which have outreach workers. Women tell the support workers of a violent client and a poster will be drawn up giving his description, vehicle details and a brief outline of the incident. These lists have led to the capture of several punters.

Safer working practices are also encouraged by outreach workers. The murder of two Glasgow prostitutes within two years shocked the scores of women who work 'the drag' in the city's Anderston district. As in the days when the Yorkshire Ripper, Peter Sutcliffe, stalked the north, the Glasgow women stand in pairs and when one gets a client, the other will take a note of his car registration number and the girl in the car makes sure the client knows this.

Attitudes to assaults on prostitutes are improving, say police. However, while individual officers were singled out to me for praise, most prostitutes and social workers feel there is considerable scope for improvement in police forces' handling of working women.

Most prostitutes – and punters – like to keep their encounters on a strictly business level. Many more men speak fondly of prostitutes than vice versa. Maybe having temporary delusions of love or false impressions of friendship is their way of coping with having to buy sexual satisfaction.

At the other end of the scale, a very few prostitutes become fond of and good friends with a small number of regular clients. Several women have dated and had genuine relationships with punters, but invariably it has gone wrong because they lost control of the relationship.

Helen went a step further than most of her colleagues – she married a punter.

HELEN

Her life story sounds like a script for a film: young, curvaceous, blonde and attractive – she becomes a hustler to get money for her babies' nappies. Makes a good living, marries a wealthy punter who helps her escape a violent pimp; he has his own factory, a boat docked in the South of France and a private plane.

There can be little doubt that in her prime Helen was a big attraction to punters. Her five-foot frame remains trim and neatly-clad to this day and though the ravages of years of alcoholism have taken their toll, it is not difficult to picture how attractive she was even ten years ago with her petite features, framed by high cheek-bones, and good skin.

Her friends say she has gone from nothing to everything and back to nothing again. The large luxury bungalow in Lancashire is replaced by a run-down bedsit; mink coats and gold jewellery were pawned years ago, cars swapped for buses; her annual eight weeks of holidays abroad have long since disappeared over the horizon.

A £30 booze bill was the motive behind her desperate phone call to me demanding an immediate interview. Her prime reason for hustling these days is to pay for the bottle of vodka she continues to drink daily after a recent three-week drying-out spell in hospital failed.

Her speech becomes increasingly slurred as the interview and generous swigs of vodka and lemonade progress. By the end of the meeting, she cannot remember when she married her former punter George, what year they split up or if they are divorced. She announced George's mother had died two days earlier – but then spent several minutes pondering whether she had dreamt that.

George encouraged her to leave her pimp Selwyn after Helen caught him with other women while she was pregnant with his child. Fourteen years Helen's senior, George had been a regular client for eight years. She recalls him affectionately: 'I feel rotten saying I wasn't in love with him. He'd take me flying for the day and I'd stay with him for weekends. He came one day and said, "You are getting out of this." He loved me and I thought I loved him but I didn't, not as a husband anyway.

'I was young and had been brought up with nothing. I did love Selwyn but I loved George for what he had, not for what he was. He was a suave guy with kind eyes. Aye, his eyes were nice.'

She can count on one hand the times they had full sex while married. 'We never did it when he was a client. He'd always bring nice underwear – fishnets and stuff like that – and I'd have to wear it and stand by a wee wardrobe while he wanked himself. We had sex a few times and it was fucking awful. He was all right size-wise and had kids from his first marriage so there was no reason why he couldn't do it.

'But he was kinky and not long after we married, he took me to a council house in a small town. This grotesque woman, massive she was, lived there and had it done out like a bondage place. She had to touch me up and he'd watch. Then he got someone else, a man, to go with me while he watched. I went there five times in all before I put a stop to it. He wanted to get in touch with those magazines to meet other couples.

'One holiday we were on his boat on the Riviera and he tried to make me go with a group of guys from another boat. He was telling them behind my back to go with me. That was his fantasy – to watch while I had sex with other men.'

After they wed, Helen stopped working as a prostitute and joined George at his dress factory, where she worked for eight years in the office. But she gave it all up one morning, packed a bag and drove away from it all. 'I got up and told him I'd be in to work later but I couldn't take any more. He just did my brain in, trying to make me as he wanted me to be. He never tried to understand. He'd do anything for me but nothing for my family and was mean to them. We weren't on the same level.'

Yet she admits leaving him was her downfall. 'I don't regret it. I miss the lifestyle but not him. We'd have a drink, usually a bottle of Mateus Rosé or Asti Spumante, with our evening meal. But the heavy stuff started when I came back to Leeds. Now I know I've got a drink problem. I put myself in Jimmy's [hospital]. I'd be OK but all the people I mix with drink so I was soon back on it – and back working.'

Helen looks much older than her 42 years and her life appears to be set on a tragic downward spiral. She laughs bitterly and becomes tearful when she admits she now works for a fraction of what she used to command. 'I only have two regular punters who come to my place on a Sunday afternoon. One's 70 and he can't get a stiffy so he just rubs it against me. He bangs away on my couch like he's really at it but there's nothing there. Do you know what I do – fucking lie there and watch TV.

'I fucking hate shagging punters. I don't do anything weird or gam [oral] as it makes me sick, just pure sex or a strip and sex. I only hustle when I'm desperate for money for drink. I'm an alcoholic and a prostitute – just that. It doesn't matter what a punter looks like so long as they have money to pay me. I always insist on using condoms. A lot of punters ask for it up the arse these days and a few girls give it to them. They must be crazy. That sort of thing was never even talked about in my day.'

She fled her native Scottish village and a gambling, drinking butcher husband when she was 20 for Leeds, where her sister, who had also escaped an alcoholic husband, lived. 'We rented a Paki room in Chapeltown, me and her. It was awful – mice, holes in the floors. My kids were aged two and three and she had two young ones as well. I'd seen these women walking up and down the street. We had no money for food or nappies, the wee ones were bleating and my sister sent me out. She'd never do it and never has to this day.

'I'd no idea what to do, ask for or about Durex. I came from a wee village near Glasgow and didn't know about condoms. In my early days I did it without one until one punter showed me how to use rubbers. It was easy money and meant we could get the washing done at the launderette and buy the weans [children] things.'

A friend introduced her to Selwyn, who was to father one of her three children. They set up home together in Manchester, where she stayed and worked for ten years. 'I suppose he was a pimp because even though he was a labourer and would give me his wage packet, he got me punters and took my money. I worked through my pregnancies and one time I got home to find Selwyn had five men sat waiting in a line on the settee for me.

'He hit me a few times but wasn't violent on a regular basis. I didn't work the streets then. We lived near the beat and I was clever and would walk to some nearby shops with a shopping bag, buy a few things and pick up a punter on the way back. If the police stopped me, I'd kid on I was doing a bit of shopping.'

One of her regulars – a Chinese restaurant owner – fell in love with Helen and wanted to leave his wife for her. But Yip's twice-weekly £25 visits were abruptly curtailed when his wife discovered him enjoying sex in Helen's back room after spotting his car parked outside her house.

'She broke into it and kept her hand on the horn and then started banging on my front room windows. My brother was visiting me at the time. He hates prostitution and panicked like mad. I didn't care, it wasn't my problem. But I thought I'd better get him out and as he tried to get over the back wall my Alsatian bit his leg. The last I saw of Yip was him running away from my dog and his wife.'

Like most other prostitutes, Helen has had a fair mix of straight and kinky punters. 'Some were terrific and the money was great. A big Irish fellow always wanted me to dress him up, paint his lips with ruby red lipstick and kiss him so that it smudged all over his face. I'd give him a coffee and he'd give me £80. Another, Adrian, was a top executive with an insurance firm. He'd bring me roses and took me, my mother and my fellow to his house. He could never get an erection so I'd just have to kiss him, offer him a bit of comfort. He was divorced and took me to his work's dance in Chorley where his boss tried to proposition me.'

She always gives her clients nicknames. One solicitor, who would wait hours outside her house for her, she knew as 'briefcase'. She was later to come in contact with him in more genteel surroundings. After she had married George, it transpired that among her mother-in-law's circle of bridge party friends in Cheadle was 'briefcase'. 'He liked to be pissed on. He'd lie on the floor, I'd stand over him and piss and he'd drink it.' Discreet to the end, Helen took his secret with her when she packed her bags and left her comfortable middle-class life.

Now, passing trade is done on her way to the shops. 'Write it down,' she insists, 'I have never been a street walker. I haven't got one conviction so I'm not a prostitute at all. I never go with punters in cars as I'm too frightened. I don't care how much they offer, I always take them back to my place. Once you've got hustling in your blood, you can't stop. It's too easy money. I've never taken drugs but I suppose prostitution is like an addiction and once these pimp cunts get in on the act. . . . They reckon black guys never pay to go with white women but I've two aged 20 and 25 who regularly see me. Them and my Sunday ones are my only regulars. I hate the sight of punters and when I see one approaching, I think "Jesus Christ here we go again". I'll kiss a punter. I'd kiss anyone for money.'

The average prostitute, research has revealed, sees between five and seven clients a night. In Birmingham, as we have seen, the weekly average for each of its estimated 1,200 working girls is about 22 men: that equals 26,400 acts of sexual service a week and a staggering total of nearly 1.4 million a year. Most clients are aged between 20 and 50, though men continue to buy sex well into their 80s. Prostitutes reported nearly half their clients were married, a quarter were separated or divorced and the rest were single or widowed. The reader can be forgiven for wondering whose fathers, husbands or sons they all are.

CHAPTER FOUR

Modern-day Madams

SAM

She could be considered a classic victim of the 90s recession. Made redundant three times from high-powered accountancy and civil service posts, based in London and answering to government ministers, she did what the arch-Conservative Lord (Norman) Tebbit advised and got on her bike to look for work. Leaving the capital behind, she returned to her home city of Bristol, where she directed her energies and obvious business acumen to owning and running a massage parlour.

Sam became a madam.

Although the title sounds rather grand, in sex trade terms it simply means that she keeps or manages prostitutes in some form of organized premises which under present laws would be deemed a brothel.

As with all aspects of the prostitution trade, brothels can be traced back to the early civilizations. They were an established and honoured part of ancient Greek society. The Romans had two types. One was staffed by slave girls who were bought and sold at auctions by brothel-keepers. The other was run on very similar lines to the majority operating today, whereby independent prostitutes pay rent or set fees to an owner or manager.

Women who manage massage parlours and saunas are the modern-day madams. Some are ex-prostitutes who have decided they are too old to work. Some have never worked as prostitutes and would never offer sex; they see their job purely as managerial. Many, such as Sam, have not and never would work on the streets. Big-time madams can be found operating escort agencies, massage parlours, health clubs, hostess bars and saunas in every major town and city across the United Kingdom.

The term 'brothel' traditionally conjures up images of bawdy, voluptuous women led by a well-endowed, sharp-witted madam-type figure, lounging on brocade *chaises-longues* in their frilly satin dresses having a grand ol' time until their handsome clients saunter through saloon-type doors and grace their beds with their presence.

Massage parlours and saunas are today's equivalent of nineteenth-century brothels. Vast numbers have opened over the past 30 years, with most of the public not only tolerating but accepting, albeit with a nudge and a wink, what goes on behind closed doors.

After eight months in the sex trade, Sam, 32 years old, the cheery and self-assured blonde daughter of an RAF officer, is seeking to expand her operation and open a second parlour back in London.

In business terms, she is a 'hands-on' boss, working alongside the eight women she employs when they are all busy. 'After I was made redundant a third time, I decided to work for myself and that's how I see this – purely as a business. I am not causing any harm and treat the girls well. I don't employ anyone under 21 or drug-takers and I make sure they have fortnightly medical check-ups. On average, each girl does two or three men a day and I might see that many in a week. I look at the money and think this job has got nothing to do with sex.'

When Sam returned to Bristol she worked as an accountant for a company running 0898 telephone sex lines before moving to a travel agency, which soon after went into receivership. 'I'd heard of a job going in a parlour and went for it.' Every prostitute remembers her first client, and Sam was left feeling distinctly down in the mouth about hers. 'After doing the business, I promptly threw up in the bath next to him!

'The girls would tell me I wasn't the type to do the job. I work now, but not that often and only if I have to. I don't think I would have lasted that long, to be honest. You can only switch off to a certain extent.'

She quickly moved on to managing the Bristol parlour, situated near the local police station, and within several months the opportunity arose to own and run it.

Having gained O and A Levels at school, she moved to London ten years ago and got her first glimpse of the sex trade. 'I had a job with the Civil Service and worked for a brief spell as an escort after I was made redundant the first time, but gave it up as soon as I got another post. I had my picture in the agency portfolio and they would call me with details of the escort. I had to go to dinner at the St James's Club with some old guy. I also visited men's homes but I didn't like that.'

Dressed in her working gear – a blouse open to her waist, revealing a lacy bra, a mini-skirt complete with the ever-favourite stockings and suspenders – she proudly offered a guided tour of the premises.

Fully carpeted, freshly decorated and centrally heated, it was immaculately clean throughout. There are two lounges, one where the girls can relax and enjoy a drink while waiting – sometimes hours – for a client to walk through the door, the other for the customers. A small but comfortable sofa faces a TV and video where they can watch a selection of erotic films.

Off from the lounges is one of the smallest massage rooms. Downstairs, in a converted basement, are two more; one, with a jacuzzi, is considered the VIP suite. Centre stage in each room is a black massage bed with, at the sides, pine cabinets filled with tissues, neatly folded peach and maroon towels, and condoms of all varieties.

Tight security is in place on the premises. Ironically, considering the illegal nature of the work, the burglar alarm system automatically alerts the police station via an alarm company should it be activated. Cameras monitor the entrance and the customer lounge, giving Sam the opportunity to scrutinize the clients. Each room has a panic button.

Sam employs three of her women a day to work 10 am to 11 pm, but will extend that to 1 am if business is good. Customers pay a £10 entry fee which includes a video and 'splash about' in the jacuzzi. Other services range from £25 for hand relief, £35 for a full strip, £50 for sex to £90 if the client wants a two-women simulated lesbian act.

She has made rapid progress in a short time but works hard to present an acceptable and professional face of the trade. 'There's many parlours which are seedy, rough or don't treat the girls right. That's not for me. I aim to run a good business. I have never been raided and get on well with the local police. But if this fails I won't be out of work, I'll find another job.'

Brothels exist in practically every reasonable-sized town and city across the country, whether in the guise of a private flat or house, or run on more commercial and professional lines, such as massage parlours, private health clubs or saunas.

A brothel has no statutory definition but the courts have held that any premises where two or more women practise prostitution, or where a number of prostitutes occupy separately-let accommodation in a building with some common management, constitutes a brothel. This can even apply to blocks of flats (see page 80).

There have to be at least two women working in the same premises, though not necessarily at the same time of day or even the same day. Thus, two prostitutes who rent a flat, share running costs but work alternate days could be prosecuted for running a brothel. The wording of present English law means it is not even necessary to prove that women who offer sex are paid for their services or are prostitutes (but, as one police handbook notes, 'they invariably are').

Brothel-related offences are set down in the 1956 Sexual Offences Act. It states that brothels are premises used by persons of the opposite sex for 'illicit' intercourse or other 'indecent behaviour' such as masturbation. Illicit intercourse is defined in Section 24 of the act: 'Unlawful [intercourse] means illicit: outside the bounds of marriage'.

Some cities have a thriving indoor prostitution trade. One outreach worker in Edinburgh estimates that all but 40 to 60 of the 700 prostitutes in the city work indoors. Those who do ply their trade on the streets do not work in the elegant centre, but four miles away in Leith. Scotland's other major city, Glasgow, has a massive street prostitution trade.

Similarly in Wales, Cardiff has very little indoor work and those men who prefer to use parlours and saunas have to go to Swansea. Those in the trade say there is no obvious reason why this should be so – maybe history and tradition have shaped its structure. Other cities, such as Birmingham and Leeds, have equal amounts of street and indoor trade.

Within Bristol, police estimate there are more than 40 massage parlours operating, and reckon on an average of five staff per business, giving a total of around 200 'parlour girls' in the city.

Some places operate with just three or four women, but others have up to 20 on their books. Parlours relaunch themselves fairly often, with new names and 'fabulous new girls', so they boast in newspaper advertisements – usually not true and all done in an effort to attract more business. Multiple ownership occurs nationwide. For example, a handful of people are believed to own up to 30 parlours in Swansea and Bristol.

Anyone involved in a brothel's running, from the owner to the cleaner, can be prosecuted. Madams, like maids and female escort agency owners or managers, can also be charged with exercising control over a prostitute for gain.

As with street prostitutes, women who work in English and Welsh brothels can be arrested on the sole word of a police officer, with no other evidence needed. The degree of proof needed for prosecutions under Scottish law means that evidence is needed to support a police officer's allegations. Partly because of the difficulties entailed in this, brothel prosecutions are few and far between north of the border. In Northern Ireland, the 1885 Criminal Law Amendment Act, covering brothel offences, is similar to the 1956 SOA.

I have classed commercial brothels as those which operate under the guise of massage parlours, saunas and private health clubs.

PAT

Her 11 years' banking experience was the prime qualification which clinched for Pat the job of manageress at a busy sauna. Ensuring its smooth day-to-day running and keeping the books comes easily to her, since she had previously worked her way up to supervisor of a Midlands branch of one of the big four banks.

Pat was a late-comer to Birmingham's sex trade, taking it up as a full-time occupation only four years ago at the age of 35. While the sauna closed for refurbishment, Pat took a temporary banking job but declined their offer of a permanent job, preferring to return to the sex business.

Pretty and articulate, Pat laughs as she recalls a former bank colleague visiting the sauna. 'I don't know who was the more embarrassed. Both of us changed colour! I still see some of my old work mates but they think I'm doing promotion work.'

Pat started at the bank after leaving convent school at 16 with six O Levels and four CSEs. She married at 18 and separated at 29. 'He was going out with other women. He worked hard and we had a beautiful home but I couldn't take it so I took our two children and moved into a private rented house.'

The road to her becoming involved in prostitution is lengthy and stretches back six years. 'I didn't want the bank to know what was happening at home but I had to take a couple of months off to sort it out. My husband never took me out and once we split up I started going out while off work.'

After resigning from the bank, Pat and her children got by on her savings and help from her family. A chance meeting with a woman, Sue, in a nightclub toilet led to a friendship developing over several years. 'One evening she asked if I was struggling and said I could earn good money, being a pretty coloured girl with a nice figure. I asked her what she meant and she said she was an escort and went out with men for meals and money and worked in a sauna.

'I never really clicked and she never mentioned it for another year, during which I was temping in offices. One day I was moaning about some bills I had to pay – my ex-husband used to pay them all before – when Sue asked me if I had thought any more about what she had said about sauna work. I honestly and truly did not know what she meant as the only saunas I knew were in health clubs.

'That's when she dropped the bombshell – "I have sex with men for money" – and I was shocked. Someone who did that was terrible, that's the way I was brought up. I remember looking the word prostitute up in a dictionary after hearing my parents talk about it when I was a child. I thought if my mother found out about Sue she'd die so I asked her to leave and avoided her for ages.'

The friendship was revived months later after a chance meeting. 'She said, "Look, I'm still the same person. I haven't changed." And she was right. She told me about a friend who needed someone to manage his sauna and do the banking on a Friday. I didn't know what to expect and my heart pounded as I walked in the place. It was high-class, with a lovely bar area and girls sat around.'

Pat ran the place for two years and earned £300 a week. Dressed in a suit and blouse, she offered clients a friendly face when they walked in, a drink and chat while they relaxed – but never sex. 'We were getting accountants, men with chauffeurs and I was a bit in awe of them. I knew what was going on and men asked about me but I was scared. It was the first place I saw a blue movie.'

She made the leap to working girl after Sue rang her and said she had a client who wanted to 'do a double' with a coloured girl. 'He wanted to watch while Sue played about with me. He never touched me and I got £50. On the next escort I did hand relief and thought I maybe wouldn't mind working.

'I'd only do hand relief at first until another girl told me I'd have to do other things to make any money.'

Today she is in charge of four women at a sauna in a Birmingham suburb. It opens from 10.30 am to 1 am Monday to Saturday, noon to midnight on Sundays, with 15 to 20 customers a day walking through its doors. For every punter the girls see, they have to give the owner (a woman) £5. The girls work one day on and one day off.

Apart from the lounge area there are three centrally heated rooms. The largest room has beige-painted walls and fitted carpet, a large olive-green corner bath, a settee and a massage table. Next to that are the oils, a neat pile of peach-coloured towels, numerous condoms and a box of tissues.

Clients have to hand over £7 to Pat for a shower and massage or £15 for a sauna. 'The girls negotiate their own deals in the room,' Pat explained.

Her second husband, a mechanic, thinks Pat, now 39, works purely as the manager but she sees between 10 and 15 clients a week for hand relief, occasional sex and a sprinkling of strange clients. 'There's one I call the wrestler as all he wants me to do is wrestle with him just like on TV. I have Joanna, who's a man. He comes here to dress up and be ordered about by us.

'But it all goes to helping my daughter buy her flat and I have a lovely house and nice sports car.'

Much of the present anti-vice legislation was created in the 1950s, an era which placed a great deal of emphasis on traditional family life. Memories of how the Second World War had obviously torn families apart was at the forefront of the Conservative Government's thinking, according to Carol Smart, in *Controlling Women: The Normal and the Deviant*.

The Wolfenden Committee, the originator of much of the current sex legislation, was established in 1954 amid an atmosphere created from a successfully orchestrated moral panic over prostitution, she says. 'This arose from the number of tourists in London due to the Coronation, and the shameful reputation the capital was acquiring as the vice centre of the western world at the time of a new Royal era. It was also felt that big-time organized crooks would be attracted to Britain because of prostitution.

'The second panic wave was caused by immigration and the "problems of prostitution" became linked with the "problems of immigration". Public opinion was enraged by tales of black and foreign men "living off the bodies of white women".' In reality, there was some doubt whether prostitution was on the increase in the 1950s or whether the police just made more arrests to increase pressure on the government for further legislation.

The guiding principle of Wolfenden was the distinction between law and morality, and the individual's right to make choices without legal interference unless harm or nuisance was inflicted on another. The committee stressed that it was not concerned with private morals, ethical sanctions, clients' personal lives, or to enforce any particular pattern of behaviour beyond what was necessary to carry out their stated purposes.

But that is exactly what they did. Double legal standards apply in the extreme to brothel-related laws, most of which are based on nineteenth-century legislation. A client commits no offence by visiting a brothel and paying a woman or women for sexual services, but the men and women who run brothels and provide sex break the law.

There can only be one brothel-keeper in the set-up and the accused does not have to be on the premises, only appear to be in charge – even if she or he is not.

Other related offences are set out in the 1956 Sexual Offences Act. Sections 34, 35 and 36 state that it is an offence for a landlord, tenant or occupier to let premises or permit them to be used as a brothel. In these circumstances it is necessary only to show that the premises are being used by one prostitute. Such charges are heard at magistrates' courts only and there is no right to a crown court trial. Maximum penalties across the United Kingdom are six months' jail and/or a substantial fine. However, landlords and owners of such property are rarely prosecuted. They are often able to afford to remain faceless, employing people to collect rents and front the businesses. It is not uncommon for brothel workers never to know who the true owners of the property are.

Charges are more frequently brought before courts under Section 33, which states that it is an offence for a person to keep, manage or assist in the management of a brothel.

Managing means that the person concerned has exercised an active part in the running of the premises as a business. To prove that, evidence must show that the accused exercised control and did not carry out purely menial or routine duties such as sweeping out the cubicles, washing up and changing towels. Answering the door is considered a menial job but there is less clarity over whether answering the telephone implies some degree of responsibility.

Far more women than men are found guilty of brothel-keeping offences, as Home Office figures show: over the ten years 1981-91 a total of 698 women (with a peak of 105 in 1990), as against a total of 194 men (rarely more than 20 a year).

Many police from forces across the country admit to paying little attention to saunas and parlours even though they know sexual services are sold, unless they have complaints, for example, of too much traffic around the area, or they believe drugs or under-age girls are on the premises.

An Avon and Somerset Police Force officer says it is policy to 'leave massage parlours and the like alone', and in the last ten years they have brought prosecutions against no more than half a dozen people for keeping a brothel or disorderly house.

Inspector Roger Smalley, who heads King's Cross Police vice unit, says that, while there is a reasonable number of brothels operating in the area, policing them is low on his list of priorities. 'We deal with drugs first and prostitution second. We do not pay a great deal of attention to saunas and such-like. Our key objective is to take it off the streets. My personal view is that if it is off street it is not a problem. We don't actively seek out brothels as it can be a very time-consuming and expensive process.'

John Blandford, a Croydon solicitor who has represented defendants in more than 50 brothel cases in England and Wales over the past six years, says police have on occasions tried to get 'freebies' from the women, threatening to arrest them unless they are given sex. He believes brothel prosecutions are a waste of massive amounts of public money and police time.

'Police costs can easily run into six figures as they attempt to get evidence. Officers can observe the premises from static posts – neighbours' houses – or mobile positions, such as unmarked vehicles, and in court they do not have to disclose which they used in order to get photographs of people entering and leaving the place, or logging car registration numbers.

'I have known observations last from three days to five months – and when the case has gone to trial some of the women, under the unit fine system, were only fined £40.'

MANDY

Mandy manages 14 girls at one of the established massage parlours in Leeds. In the four years it has been open there has been no trouble with the police.

She earns a few hundred pounds a week for running the place, one of four owned by a woman. Mandy's name is on many of the business papers – a front the real owner paid her to undertake. The police know who the real owner is but Mandy is unsure of the woman's true identity.

Being on the game for 13 years, she knows most of the tricks of the trade, and her girls quickly summon her if a punter is troublesome. 'I've just had to see a Paki. He got into the room and began haggling over the price. I told him for what he wanted to pay he should go to the streets. They never want to pay the full whack.'

Going rates at the establishment start at £20 for hand relief, £25 for sex, £30 for oral and sex. 'The less girls wear the more a punter has to pay. If they want tying up or domination that's between £50 and £150. We open 10 am to 10 pm with five girls to a shift. They pay £30 a cubicle and we insist they use condoms. If we discover they don't they are sent packing. I greet the customers usually in a mini-skirt, basque and stockings. They choose a girl and she offers him a glass of wine or lager. They are taken to a room and usually have a shower. A lot know the score and don't bother with a massage.

'I start hard on their back and legs – usually a Swedish massage – and finish with a gentle Korean where I touch their genitals. By the time they turn over they are erect. Most will touch you and ask what else we do. Half the time I don't even take my pants off, just pull them to one side. They can shower after and have refreshments in the lounge area.'

It is her plain brown spectacles which Mandy, a 34-year-old mother of three, believes have fooled vice squads over the years. 'I mean, people just don't think hookers wear specs. In all my years on the game, I've only ever been brought before the courts four times – that's not bad going,' she laughs. She could be taken for a mature student or a middle-class mum with her shoulder-length wavy brown hair, petite features and slim figure clothed in leggings and T-shirt.

Mandy worked on the streets for years before moving indoors. Raised near the red light area in Leeds, she knew a few working girls who would call into her family's shop and regale her with stories of how easy it was to make money on the game. 'I'd walk along the street and could be approached ten times in 100 yards. One day as I was on my way to my mother's, I decided to say yes to the next guy who propositioned me. I did and he had to put me right about how much to charge and what to do! I took him home, he laid on top of me and showed me how to put a condom on. After that he called every week and I never looked back. I could earn three times what my husband got and I thought I was so clever.'

When Mandy and her husband split up, she carried on working and in 1984 went to London after being told of the money to be earned there. Within a couple of hours of her arrival she was working from a rented room, charging £60 for full sex 'and a play around', £10 of which would be handed to the landlord.

She also got on to the books of an escort agency. 'I'd give the agency £25 a client but could earn £700 in a few hours. I'd see Canadians and Americans here usually on business and we'd have a meal and a few drinks. They always treated you like a lady.

'We always had lots of problems with the Arabs as they were arrogant and thought they had bought you. I'd go up to their suites and there'd be dishes of cocaine and other drugs set out, but I never touched them. Some would want me to go through a marriage ritual before we had sex! I had to be married for the sum of £200 for three hours and when the time was up we were divorced. Some offered hundreds to do anal sex but I'd never risk it and it's too personal to do with clients.'

Hotels such as the Park Lane, Grosvenor and Hilton were Mandy's stomping ground and, thanks to her glasses she says, she was never stopped by staff as she walked to a client's room. 'I raked in loads of money – but spent it as quickly.' The one time in six years she was arrested, she managed to hide her condoms in the police van. 'They apologized and let me go!'

When she returned to Leeds she met the man who was to father her children and went back to work on the streets. She was to become his 'main woman' out of a stable of four or five he ran. 'The trouble began when we lived together and he made threats for me to hand over my money which then developed into daily beatings. Most white girls have pimps at some time. Mine had other women at the same time as he saw me. In Leeds the ponces tend to be black, in Bradford it's mainly Asians but in London they are every nationality.

'He'd tell me what to wear and then patrol the streets getting business for me. I'd work 1 pm to 7 pm and pull about £400. I'd give him that and he'd hand me back £10 for Durex and cigs. When I came off the streets while I was pregnant, he'd bring punters back to the house. He knew how many condoms I had on me at the beginning of the night and would count how many I had left at the end to work out how much I would have earned. I couldn't hide anything from him.

'I was frightened of him but I loved him. He'd say another girl was getting him more money and I'd work harder. Once he battered me with a hammer and I passed out. I pressed charges but he persuaded me to drop them as he said he loved me and would never do it again. But he did and I've been out on the streets with black eyes and horrific injuries.'

She fled to London with her children but he tracked her down, snatched the youngsters and Mandy was forced to go to court to get them back. 'If I was in a refuge, he'd get one of his girls to ring and say she was a relative. He'd always find me.'

A near-fatal attack by him led Mandy to bravely press charges and see through the court action. 'I was in bed one night last year and he came in, kicked me in the face and ordered me into the front room. He told me to stay down and kept thumping and kicking me in the head. I fainted and he threw a bucket of water over me and tied a dog chain around my head.

'My body was covered in chain marks and he kept shouting, "Once a prostitute, always a prostitute. I am going to leave you for dead tonight, finish you off." I felt like throwing myself out of the window. I'm only alive because I managed to keep the children awake and he never did anything in front of them. He'd been on drink and drugs and though I could hardly walk I got the children out and called the police.

'I worked out that in seven years he had 22 cars, about £5,000 worth of jewellery and countless good suits out of me, yet I was dressed in stuff from charity shops. He was charged with living off immoral earnings and assault and all he got was a 17-month suspended sentence.'

Even now, she is not totally free of him. Though she does not work for him and they live apart, he will not allow her to bring men friends back to her house – and she does not. The fear has never gone away. 'He says once the sentence is up, he will come after me. I think he will and I have become philosophical about it – if he's going to kill me, he is going to kill me.'

But Mandy fights on. Having worked independently of her pimp for two years and with her job at the sauna, she feels she has been given a fresh start to some degree, and recently enjoyed her first holiday abroad for years. 'I regret falling in with a ponce – but I have never regretted working as a prostitute. I don't enjoy what I do but I enjoy the excitement of it all, meeting different people. I'd like to open my own parlour one day, I don't want an office job.

'The sex is nothing, I switch off and don't enjoy it with clients and never kiss them. If you have a boyfriend then there's got to be something different otherwise it would be just like seeing a punter. Sex with a punter is a case of bang, bang, on, off, on, off. Most of my customers are white and a lot fall in love with you, especially the older ones who have been widowed. Some will bring bunches of flowers to ease their guilt. I don't go out with white men, they don't do anything for me. Some punters hate women and make you feel degraded, use us and call us names, that hurts. Some have to be sick. They bring needles so we can pierce them. That makes me grimace. The worst thing I had to do was shit in a dish and feed it to him. He told me his girlfriend enjoyed it. Another wanted an aubergine pushed up his bum – now that even shocked me!'

Mandy, a forthright and outgoing woman, is the third generation of her family to go on the game, following in her aunt and grandmother's footsteps. She blames her environment for becoming involved in the trade. She briefly mentioned that she was abused by a man when she was a child but lightly shrugged the matter off. 'I was used to being touched. It didn't matter. I went into prostitution because of the area I lived in.

'But the girls never told me of the dangers involved, only the good things. Once you fall into the vice trap you never get out. Young girls say they'll do it for a few years and get out. I used to think like that. For the time I am in a room with a client I become whatever they have paid for. But when I go home I am just a young mum. My house is clean and my kids are well looked after.

'Just about every sauna or massage parlour advertised in local papers offers sex. Legalizing prostitution might take a lot of girls off the street and do away with pimps controlling girls as they won't bother with all the legal requirements to get a business opened. I think prostitution should be taken off the streets as so many innocent people are approached, even I've been stopped while out with my kids. Here the girls are safe and everything is provided – even condoms. We are normal and have hang-ups, laughs and jokes just like other women.

'I know legally I am branded a common prostitute. I say I am not common – but I am a prostitute. Maybe you do lose your self-respect but I don't give my body away.'

Brothels, along with all classes of prostitutes, were a recognized feature of numerous societies and were subject to various controls. Many Greek states taxed practitioners and regulated fees. To keep track of the women and make sure taxes were paid, a 'whore collector' was appointed with the responsibility of going out and collecting the levy. A special official was employed to supervise brothels. His duties included ensuring that public decency prevailed at the premises, and he would also be called in to mediate in any disputes which arose.

Today, although a very different attitude prevails, some limited form of regulation is in force: in large areas of the country parlours and saunas are licensed.

In Scotland, it is set down in the 1982 Civic Government Act that owners of such premises have to apply annually to their local authorities for a public entertainments licence which costs about £130.

Emergency Services have to be consulted as to whether the premises meet safety standards regarding fire exits, lighting and such matters. The police are also involved and may object, for example, to lengthy opening times on the grounds of the site being close to a residential area.

The police can also call unannounced at the premises to check safety and that licensing restrictions are being adhered to. Failure to do so might lead to the owner having the licence revoked.

Under the 1991 London Local Authorities Act, all the capital's local authorities insist parlours and saunas have a 'licence for special treatment' before they can open. Councils can stipulate that staff are qualified masseurs and occasionally check up on the validity of certificates. They can also say how the business should advertise itself. Those who set up without a licence are prosecuted.

Some believe that licensing is the first step towards legalization of brothels. But, with typical British hypocrisy, licences are granted on the understanding that most saunas and parlours are genuine – there are indeed some, but probably only a small minority, that do not offer sexual services.

Although 'parlour women' are safer from arrest and violence from clients, they are still vulnerable to exploitation, often being pressured to provide services they consider distasteful, deal with punters they would prefer not to, and even offer unprotected sex in order to keep their jobs. One sauna owner said that none of the women he employed could refuse a client if he chose her: 'A nurse cannot pick and choose who she wants to care for according to the colour of a person's skin. The same goes for my girls.'

Unlike the streets, commercial brothel hours are fixed and women often have to work 12-hour shifts. They have to pay the manager a shift fee plus a set amount per punter and any money earned from 'straight' customers (those who just have a sauna or massage).

Shift or cubicle fees can take a large chunk of their earnings – up to £30 a day is quite common. Prostitutes say they can often work a long shift, only see one or two punters and consequently be out of pocket at the end of their day. Some may have to provide their own towels and lotions. Because it is an illicit trade, the women have little authority to act against any exploitation.

Though it is not illegal to work in a brothel, many of the prostitutes who do are often prosecuted for assisting in its running. The courts have held that where a person negotiates fees with clients and discusses the nature of services on offer, she is assisting in the management of a brothel. It is impossible for a prostitute to do her job without discussing prices or which services the client wants. It is interesting to note, again, that the law appears to assume it is the prostitute who broaches the subject of money and sex and not the (legal) customer!

The phrase 'assisting in' is the catch-all clause which can be applied to working girls and maids, and can be extended to others. The porter of an apartment block where prostitutes brought men back to 12 of the 18 flats was held to have committed an offence of assisting in the running of a brothel.

No one is quite sure where 'assisting in' responsibilities begin and end. The police have to show a court that the accused knew either directly or by implication what was going on in the cubicles to secure a conviction of any offence involving a brothel. Officers might rely on conversations overheard with girls or the presence of condoms all over the place.

This is the offence Anna, who works part-time in a luxurious West Country health club, would be charged with.

ANNA

'Prostitution: A Reflection of Female Sexuality in a Male-Dominated World' was the title of her A Level Sociology project, which gave Anna an initial insight into a group much studied by academics – and journalists!

But the 18-year-old took her studies beyond the text book. She became a prostitute and works at the massage parlour she visited while researching her thesis. Indeed, she worked there while writing it. Now that it is completed (she achieved a Grade B) her motive is to save money for a 12-month trip to Canada this year as part of her work for the environmental group Greenpeace.

'Prostitution was always something I was interested in. I'd already interviewed a few girls who work the pier at Weston-super-Mare, and a high-class girl. I came to the parlour pretending I wanted a job as I was skint but I wanted to find out how these places were run. I was quite surprised at how normal the women were as I had all the usual stereo-types about them.

'At the interview, the manageress asked if I had worked before and she explained what they were doing was illegal. I was offered and accepted a job. I'd heard of sauna bosses who like to "personally try out" all the girls, particularly the new ones, but I've not had any trouble.'

Anna is estranged from her mother, a head teacher, and had worked at a Tesco supermarket for extra cash before starting this job a year ago.

'I was 17 but told the manageress I was 18. I look older than I am. I work two evenings, 4.30 pm to 10.30 pm, and 10 am to 4.30 pm one day. I've arranged it like that so it fits in with my course. Doing this job gives me more time for my studies than when I was packing shelves. My family think I'm a waitress.'

While seeing clients, she managed to interview some for her study. 'Their attitudes surprised me. When I asked why they came here rather than use an escort agency, they said it was a pleasant way to relax and forget about their worries. Quite a lot of businessmen put their visit on their expenses or credit cards. They come to be pampered and made to feel special as much as for the sex. A lot go for totally different types of women to their wives at home. One of my regulars showed me a picture of his wife and she was the exact opposite to me,' recalled Anna, a good-looking, statuesque blue-eyed blonde. Needless to say, her college lecturers were surprised at the information she had managed to get!

The sauna's lurid external neon sign gives little indication of the grandeur awaiting clients inside. The building, situated just a mile from Bristol city centre on a busy road, was one of the plushest brothels I visited for my research. Once a client has paid his massage fee at reception, he walks down a winding corridor to the individual dressing-rooms where he swaps his clothes for one of the thick, soft, white towelling robes hanging next to a shower cubicle.

The *pièce-de-resistance* is the white-tiled pool area. Large potted plants, palm trees, plastic tables and chairs, and pale green-painted walls surround a sumptuously deep spa pool. The heating is suitably high, to exude a totally tropical feel, and the whole scenario would comfortably grace any private health club.

She says since starting working as a prostitute, her savings have soared from £300 to £20,000. 'I charge between £30 and £60 for the usual stuff but I specialize in domination and make most of my money from that. These punters hardly ever want sex, they're not interested. It's all the caning, handcuffs, whipping, and tying them to the bed stuff. I am greedy and sussed out there was more money in this. Not all the girls will do it but I charge £100 for a full domination session, that's about 45 minutes.'

Anna's observations on why men want to subject themselves to such treatment sheds some light on a subject which many consider taboo. 'I have found the domination fans always have high-powered jobs and are from upper-middle-class backgrounds. They say they're in such stressful jobs, that they want to be as far removed from them as possible. A couple of judges from London I do tell me because they are sentencing others, they feel they should come here to have some punishment dished back to them.

'I have two regular domination customers a week and see three or four punters a shift. One six-hour shift I did eight. I have to give the parlour boss £15 for every punter but I can clear £400–£500 a week.'

Hotels have always been regular haunts for call girls. As far back as ancient Greece, innkeepers supplied women to interested travellers. Anna recruits business at several of Bristol's top hotels and casinos when work is slack at the sauna. 'I always go with another girl. She is a single parent and when she is feeling the pinch every three months if the bills are popping through the letter box she gives me a ring. We'll wear suits but just to let the men know what we're up to, we'll have a few buttons too many undone or a bit too much make-up on. During the week, there's always some lonely middle-aged businessman wanting company and if you give them a wink or a smile, they'll buy you a drink if they're interested. You can tell by their body language and the way they look at you.

'I tell them I used to work for an escort agency and then they know why I am there. Then I'll say how I used to earn £400 but since we were not really planning anything £150 would be enough. While one of us has sex with him in his room, the other waits downstairs as a precaution.'

With two A Levels under her belt, Anna is currently training to be an outward bound instructor as well as planning her conservation work in Canada. 'I've been a member of Greenpeace since I was 11. I enjoy canoeing and going to the pub with my pals. This job is just financing what I want to do but I do enjoy the money and social aspect. I did worry for a while when I started and reckon it took me a couple of months to adjust. Now when I've finished work, I walk out the door and think about what shopping I have to get.'

Above: 'I see myself more as a pavement hostess than a street walker,' says Pam. 'We don't get turned on doing business. Sex for prostitutes is like waving a pencil about in the Albert Hall.'

Below: This beautiful leather saddle was made specifically for Diana's many wealthy clients who request the 'riding mistress' fetish.

Right: Stocks and the spanking stool stand aside the 15-ft table on which is spread a range of Diana's equipment that she uses in her job as one of the capital's top dominatrix.

Below: Diana, a high-class London call-girl, takes great pride in designing her tasteful 'business cards'.

Bottom: French maid, grand mistress (leather or vinyl) and schoolgirl, all outfits worn by Diana – and occasionally her clients – to enact the fantasy of their choice.

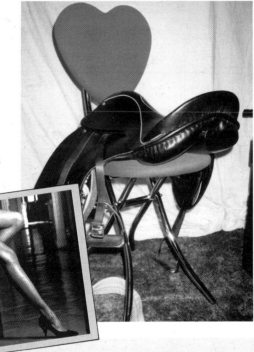

071-224
NAUGHTY BUT NICE
DIANA

Left: Research by
Hilary Kinnel shows
that up to one in five
men could have used a
prostitute at some
time. 'So few admit to
it – I am sure that is
because a view
prevails that it is not
macho to pay for sex.'

Above: Leading
barristers Michael
Mansfield (left) and
Anthony Scrivene
(right) hold opposing
views of the
effectiveness of
prostitution-related
laws.

Above: Marie, proclaimed as queen of Birmingham's notorious red-light district, despite being in her sixties. This grandmother regularly walks these streets to attract clients.

Right: Sally, who at 30 has spent exactly half her life on the game, says: 'Women are simply buying love when they hand their money to their pimp.'

MUGS

UGLY MUGS

25th February 1993

...att Mug Girl"

We have had a report of an attack on a business girl while she was in her own flat in Edgbaston. He is described as an Asian 5ft 11in to 6ft aged 50 he has a turban on but underneath he has long hair that is tied in a bun, he is big built, his eyes are brown and he wears gold rimmed glasses. He wears trendy young clothing. He also has a scar on his chest by his right shoulder.

This client uses the name of Jas, he phoned her last night for an appointment and he never turned up. He turned up this morning without ringing. He wanted domination, he then slapped the girl across the face. He threatened her with rape and said he could rob her. The girl then tried to talk the client out of it.

27th January 1993

The Attack happened on 23rd January 1993, Saturday night at 10.30pm on Balsall Heath Rd.

...atty no reg

The man has a moustache, he is described as white with his eyes are wide apart, he has short brown greying hair and he has a scar on his right cheek.

They were in Sir Harry's car park. The client wouldn't use a condom, the girl refused to do business the client pulled out a flick knife he said that if she didn't do as he asked he would use the knife on her. The girl then managed to get away ...om him.

Above: One of the Birmingham stree from where 'wind girls', like Samant operate, creating night-time scenes more reminiscent times of Amsterd. Left: 'Ugly Mug' l like these, help publicize violent punters to the prostitutes and ha resulted in catchir such clients.

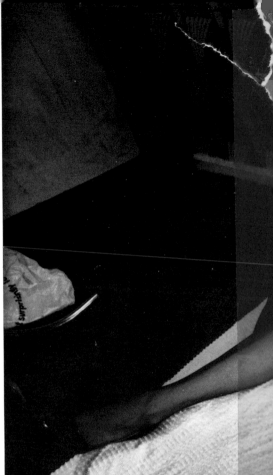

: 'I've another
ears on the game
most, and I want
e the best of it,
e a better
ute,' says 27-
ld Zoe.

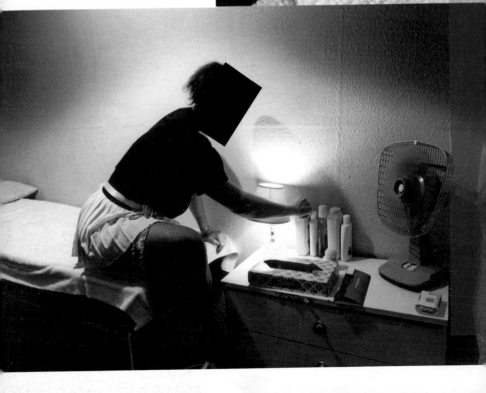

Left: Mandy is madam of 14 women at a busy sauna: 'I enjoy the excitement of my job. The sex is nothing. You never kiss a punter.' She did not wish to be identified.

Above: Liz, 37, prepares for work. Most of her clients are married and in white-collar jobs. 'Though you have a kind of power over them, you feel mucky, abused and degraded,' she says.
Right: A devout Roman Catholic, Crystal's job as a prostitute in a London brothel makes her unable to confess to her priest or take Holy Communion.

e: Pat swapped a
y job in banking
ighly lucrative
r as a madam.
: The author
with Pat.

Right: Preferring the
comfort and safety of
working from home,
another prostitute
called Pat arranges
appointments over the
phone. Business is
done on the lounge
floor.

CHAPTER FIVE

Home Comforts

The celebrity brothel-owner Lindi St Clair, the octogenarian pillar of the legal establishment Sir Frederick Lawton, the Mothers' Union and the radical barrister Michael Mansfield do not immediately spring to mind as companionable bedfellows. Yet they all agree – albeit to differing extents – that there should be changes in the laws relating to brothels.

Ms St Clair, in her role as leader of the Corrective Party which campaigns for sexual freedom, commissioned a Mori poll in September 1991 on the legalization of brothels. Of 1,924 people questioned, 55 per cent – including many women – said they would tolerate them if they were 'small and discreet', 12 per cent were uncommitted, 33 per cent would oppose them; 60 per cent of the men questioned were, not surprisingly, in favour of the move.

Perhaps the British public's stated attitudes to brothels go some way to understanding our views on selling and buying sex – we know it goes on but so long as it is kept under wraps, so to speak, it is OK.

A brief historical outline will help to explain how these attitudes developed. Legislation was increasingly used by medieval authorities for several reasons, one being that brothels were seen as potential centres of public disturbance and were often considered to be fronts for other organized crime. Some cities, such as Leicester and Cambridge, attempted to deal with the problem by banning prostitution within their walls. Sandwich confined brothels to certain areas – was this possibly one of the earliest red light areas or forms of toleration zones?

Bristol classed prostitutes with lepers and both groups were banned inside the city walls. For a time, London attempted to ban prostitutes and established a section where they could live and work just outside the city walls. Brothels found outside this area had their doors and windows removed. If the women refused to leave the illegal brothel, the authorities would attempt to demolish the building.

Another favoured method of dealing with prostitutes in the later Middle Ages was to demand that they dress in a certain way, emulating the ancient Indian custom whereby prostitutes dressed in red clothes. Bristol prostitutes had to wear striped fur on their hoods which was different from that worn by a respectable woman.

Thankfully, a more lenient attitude is taken by the authorities in the city today. One local vice officer says that if complaints are made about private brothels, the police may just visit the occupants and have a discreet word.

I have classed private brothels as those which are run from domestic premises such as private homes and flats, and do not operate as commercial saunas or massage parlours.

CLARE

A crop-haired grandmother of 49, Clare has a penchant for large earrings, slim cigars, gardening, reading and animals. Her aim is to turn her large Victorian terraced house in Bristol into a full-time brothel.

A Thomas Hardy novel was the inspiration for her working name. A fan of the classic Victorian novelist, Clare named herself after Angel Clare, one of her favourite characters in *Tess of the d'Urbervilles*.

At present, she splits her working week between seeing clients and managing her small-scale brothel, employing one other prostitute plus a maid. Clare hopes to expand the brothel and, once she has taken on more women, plans to stop doing business herself in order to become a full-time madam.

She began working from home five years ago after giving up massage parlour work. 'I'd be happy employing three or four girls on a shift system. I don't want to run too big a place as it wouldn't be fair on my neighbours. I like to keep a tight rein on the girls, make sure they eat well, are clean in their habits and look good. I laid one girl off as she'd lost so much weight, it put the punters off. She's just come back and is still skinny but I cook her good meals and keep her in order. I only take £10 per punter off them and that's for everything – their meals, towels, even toilet rolls.

'I keep a low profile and I would not employ anyone too young. The girls have to know the law and what they are doing. This is a dangerous profession and my set-up is as safe as we can get. I don't want any of them putting me at risk of arrest for saying the wrong things over the phone.

'I keep lots of animals and I think if I was arrested or jailed who would feed them. I'm not scared about going to prison – it'd be a bloody holiday! I appeared in court once with two other prostitutes and we later worked out that we'd "had" the bench between us.'

Her career in prostitution coincided with her move to Bristol 14 years ago after one of her two sons was killed in a motor-cycle accident in the city. 'I wanted to be here to be near my dead son. I lived in a squat at the time of his death and my other son was going to be taken into care if I didn't get a job.

'I enrolled on a typing course. Me and another girl were useless and she told me she was going back to her old job – wanking men in a parlour. I went along, the madam interviewed me, gave me a job and taught me how to give proper massages.

'The first trick I did was a double. I took to it like a duck to water and within a week I'd made quite a lot of money. At the time it was the best thing that had ever happened to me. It allowed me to keep a roof over mine and my son's head.

'I'd do about six or seven men a day. The only time I got caught in a police raid was when I was with a magistrate. I was bollock-naked, laid on my stomach and he was massaging me. It never went to court as the poor cunt died not long after from a heart attack. I was sacked as they said I was too hot to keep. We had some great laughs but there was a lot of fiddling going on. We wouldn't hand over half the money we were supposed to. Now some of the parlours have two-way mirrors and record your conversations with the punters to stop fiddling – and let the bosses bring friends in to watch and get a free thrill.'

Clare worked sporadically for ten years in the parlour, never outdoors, before setting up in business herself. 'When I first started on the game in Bristol, there were only a few parlours going. But loads more opened and business got thinner and the girls got bitchier. So I packed it in and went to teach English on a Greek island. I came back skint three years ago, put an ad in a newspaper – "mature, understanding lady offers full body massage" – and started back on the game.'

Today she entertains punters in one of her bedrooms. 'I call it the toss shop and chose that particular one because it's conveniently next to the bathroom.'

She currently employs one other prostitute but is recruiting two more. 'I'm very particular and make sure everything is spot on. I have a separate set of towels for punters. They are not allowed to use mine. We work 11 am to 7 pm and when a punter rings I tell him I live near a local college, not in St Paul's as it puts some of them off.

'Charges are:

£15 for a basic body massage;

£25 strip and relief;

£30 reverse – they can touch me;

£35 breast relief or body to body;

£45 sex or oral;

£50 both.

£60 for anything off the wall [different] – water sports, whipping, handcuffs, or dressing up in women's clothing.

Rules include no kissing and no ripping off clients as I want them to come back.

'Fees also depend on how long they're here. My record in getting a guy to come was three minutes but generally I do it all in 20.

'My maid takes the customer upstairs, shows him where the bed and bathrooms are while I finish my fag, put on a mini-skirt, stockings, suzzies and stilettos. I get the money off them, put it in a clip and throw it downstairs to her. I try to cater for the over-40s but unfortunately I do get younger ones. I don't like it as I have a son who is 28 and I feel embarrassed doing business with someone his age. He knows what I do but we don't talk about it.

'We get everyone from students to pensioners, and there are quite a few workers from the local Rolls Royce factory. I see several disabled men. One can have sex but a lot can't and just like to touch me.'

A Bristol client recently wrote to her explaining why he would no longer be visiting:

Dear Clare,

I owe you some explanation why, after spending several months getting to know you, I will not be visiting again.

As I told you, my wife is not enthusiastic about one aspect of marriage and we decided we might be happier if I let her off and purchased satisfaction elsewhere.

I visited you in the hope that we should get to know each other in the course of two or three visits and after that be regular.

However, my wife has now decided to resume normal relations, and there is no doubt that she attracts and excites me better than any woman. So it is not likely that you and I shall meet again.

I shall remember your patience and sympathy with gratitude.

Yours sincerely,

James

Clare was touched by the letter. 'I did take time with him. He'd come and chat and on his last visit he was beginning to feel really comfortable. We never had sex – that's what he was working up to.'

With business affected over the past months by the recession, Clare has cut her maid's hours until things pick up. She always ensures there is someone available to answer the phone while she or one of her women are working, as they do not want to lose vital custom. Her maid, a lesbian ex-prostitute, is paid £15 a day plus meals for carrying out all the typical duties as well as doing Clare's shopping and banking the money.

Clare first married at 17 to her teenage sweetheart. She left him a year later after he 'tried to stick his mates into me'. She moved to York, ran a shop, met and married a university student and bore him two sons. 'We had our own house and I was quite a career woman for a while but I left him when he turned violent.' She lived in squats and toured with convoys of travellers during summer months for several years before settling in Bristol.

'I don't like the job, but I can't do anything else. I'd like to give it up in the next few years and maybe work as a maid abroad. It's hard to get out of it because you get used to the independence. Most of us in this business have been treated pretty badly by men and this job is one of the few ways of getting money and, therefore, independence.

'In one way, going on the game was the best thing that happened to me because I met other women who had suffered tragedies. I have friends and we can talk about things between ourselves that we can't with other women.

'I think straight women see us as a threat as we take money for something they do for free. Maybe that's why some see us as slags. They're wrong. Slags are women who do it with different guys without using condoms, or those who'll pull a guy in a nightclub on a Friday night.

'Prostitutes do it for money or love – not for fun.'

When the Church of England's Mothers' Union announced in 1992 that, after a three-month debate, one in five of its members would be prepared to accept legalized brothels, the vote revealed a marked move from its previous long-held anti-prostitution stance.

The 200,000-strong organization, traditionally viewed as the upholder of conventional Christian family values, called on the State and Church to do more to prevent further exploitation of prostitutes and requested a fresh examination of the laws.

The 59 members of the union's social concern committee voted 40–13 (with 6 undecided) against legalizing brothels, but suggested that prostitutes be allowed to work in pairs from licensed premises.

The Bishop of Liverpool, the Rt Reverend David Sheppard, supported their efforts and said the debate had shown that 'prostitution raises more complex questions than whether to legalize brothels or not. Some dismiss the question by saying, "Would you like a brothel next door?"'

Both the Mothers' Union and the bishop recognized that many women were forced to sell sex because of economical and psychological pressures.

Calls to legalize brothels are made every few years or when a scandal, such as the Sir Allan Green incident, makes the news.

The last time the government examined the possibility of legalized brothels was in 1985 when the Criminal Law Revision Committee (CLRC) produced its major review of the laws relating to indoor prostitution.

It rejected the argument for brothel legalization as facile, noting that the evils of legislation would be great, and decided: 'Legalizing brothels would remove the incentive to be discreet and they would no doubt increase in number. It would increase demand for the services of prostitutes and attract more girls into prostitution.'

The committee's working party did propose, however, that the law which did not penalize one woman from running a prostitution business from her own premises (unless her activity amounted to keeping a disorderly house) should be expanded to allow two prostitutes to work together without risk of prosecution for keeping or managing a brothel. Sir Frederick Lawton, the CLRC's former chairman, interviewed in 1993 for this book, admitted: 'I suppose this would be a step – though only a small one – towards legalized brothels. My main justification for this is safety and the women would be able to share child care arrangements. But I would restrict it to no more than two women, for fear the stream of men visiting would cause a nuisance.' In other words, the CLRC – rightly – considered the women would benefit from greater security, companionship, mutual help, emotional support and in having daily care for their children.

But objectors to the move eventually proved more powerful than supporters. The former stipulated four main reasons for not relaxing the law: such a change overlooked the fact that a significant number of prostitutes did not live at their work place and so some would also use their homes if the law permitted them to; it was not in the interests of children to be brought up in a house where prostitutes were operating; it would facilitate the exploitation of one prostitute by another; it might encourage the young and homeless to drift into prostitution in return for accommodation. After considering the advice, the CLRC found itself divided over what to do – so it did nothing.

With regard to penalizing brothel clients, the majority of the CLRC was not in favour, claiming that to do so would not help in the process of closing brothels down.

Attempts to shut brothels and to penalize their keepers have sometimes backfired. Perhaps the most famous private brothel madam of recent years is Cynthia Payne, whose detached house in suburban Streatham became notorious for her 'sex for luncheon vouchers' parties. Her local vice unit spent 520 hours investigating the saucy thrashes and went to extraordinary lengths to bring nine charges of controlling prostitutes against her.

An 11-day crown court trial revealed that one officer had cosmetically aged himself eight years by dyeing his hair and acquiring a tan to pose as a country gentleman. False addresses in Egypt were set up by the vice unit who also arranged for mail to be sent from abroad addressed to the bogus chap to strengthen his alibi, gain Ms Payne's trust and thus an invitation to one of her gatherings. Another officer posed as a Welsh bisexual hotelier, dressing in medallions, cravats, silk shirts and wearing heavy make-up. Considering the extraordinary lengths the officers went to in order to secure a conviction, it was ironic that, when the police chief who led the raid on Ms Payne's house gave evidence, he told the court he believed she was obsessed with sex!

The 1987 case, calculated to have cost £100,000, ended with Ms Payne being found not guilty on all charges. Newspaper reports at the time said the police estimated the operation took 42 days to prepare and cost just £500. The woman who began her career at 18 as a Soho prostitute's maid endeared herself to the nation as the acceptable face of vice and has since made a lucrative career out of her notoriety.

LIZ

White lace curtains carefully pulled back and secured to a metal hook in the kitchen give the tell-tale sign for clients that Liz and her women are ready for business.

At 37, Liz has spent 20 years on the game – and it shows.

To many she might appear the archetypal tart – top-heavy, with a blowsy figure, gold-painted toenails, language as harsh as her bleached blonde hair, and a fondness for vodka. Years of walking the streets of Manchester, Leeds and Cardiff have taken their emotional and physical toll on her.

She is 'self-employed' these days as a small-time madam. Her daily morning routine consists of doing the housework in her tidy Victorian terraced home in the Leeds red light district of Chapeltown, shopping and preparing her children's tea.

Weekday afternoons are set aside for work, satisfying the demands of her regular clients. Her 'office' is a spare upstairs bedroom furnished with a double bed and a mirrored ceiling. It is kept locked if the children are at home or when business is being done. Liz earns extra cash by allowing two or three younger street girls to use the room but only during her working hours. She gets £2 for each punter they bring back. The younger women benefit because they can do business only yards from the beat, in greater safety, and do not waste time driving to and from premises. Should any punter cause trouble, they only have to stamp on the floor or call out and Liz is quickly on hand to help.

She says she is too old for street work now. Punters, many of whom she has had for years, either knock at the front door or give a discreet nod if she is standing in the doorway. But they all know to call before the children return home from school at 4 pm.

Liz, a devoted mum, is happy with her routine – but she admits this lifestyle has come with wisdom acquired after years of answering to a pimp who fathered two of her three children. The two eldest know how she earns a living. Liz was forced to tell them after a call girl blurted it out to her eldest son: 'I was heartbroken when my lad said he knew. They always thought lots of friends or repair men were around. But after I told him and my daughter why I did it, they put their arms around me and said they still loved me.'

These days, Liz's rates start at £15 for straight sex and £25 for a full strip and fondle of her bust. Though she appreciates the money, her dislike for what she does and whom she does it with has remained steadfast over the years. 'I don't regret what I've done, but if I had my life again I wouldn't be a prostitute. If I hadn't come to Leeds and got involved with a black man I'd never have gone on the game.

'Though you have a kind of power over the punters, you feel mucky, abused and degraded. There's no feeling in it, never any sexual enjoyment. You look at a punter and think you could spew over their horrible, pink, wrinkled thing. Prostitution puts you off sex in a personal relationship, you don't want it as often.

'I take care of myself and have always used condoms as I'd be frightened of catching something from a punter. I go to the clinic every three months for check-ups and they're aware of what I do. In fact, the only time I got VD was from my kids' father.'

Liz is unsure of how many times she has been convicted, only that it is more than ten. She believes in designated red light areas. 'Let's face it, it's never going to go away. My neighbours are great and know what I do.

But I make sure they never get any hassle.' She is, of course, vulnerable under the 1956 SOA, Section 35, for allowing any part of any premises to be used as brothels or for prostitution (Section 36), though there are only a handful of prosecutions each year for these offences.

Most of her clients are married, in white-collar jobs, and several are into sado-masochistic fantasies they cannot or will not enact with their wives. Men wanting to be prostitutes' slaves are quite common. They do not visit the women for sex, but purely to be ordered about. Sensible prostitutes, such as Liz, make the most of them. 'One head teacher calls every six weeks – but never for sex. He brings women's underwear, stockings, suspenders, a saucy white frilly apron and dusters. He pays me and my sister £100 each to sit and drink tea while he pretends to be a cleaner. We have to order him about while he cleans the house dressed in his finery. In fact, he does as good a job as me!' she joked.

'Another reckoned he was Hitler and wanted me and my sister to walk on his back while wearing high-heeled boots. Then we had to drag him to the bathroom and hurl him into a tub of water. He gave out such a loud scream and shouted, "It's fucking freezing." I told him, "You never said you wanted warm water – and anyway that'll cost you extra!"'

It was Scottish relations' tales of the fantastic nightlife of Leeds which lured the 17-year-old Liz away from her working-class family in Glasgow to a job in a shop in the thriving Yorkshire city.

'There were six of us. My parents worked hard – dad was a labourer and had two jobs, mam was a cook and we had a good upbringing. But it was always a struggle. I went from an environment where there was never any spare cash to one where it ran free and I – who had never eaten out before – was suddenly being taken to restaurants.'

Liz lived it up for three months after she met her future pimp in a club: 'We had a fantastic time. I saw other girls going out with black men and they always seemed to be OK. He was a real charmer, ten years older than me and showed me a lifestyle I never knew existed. He was my first boyfriend and I fell in love with him.'

The northern port of Hull was the scene for Liz's initiation into a career of vice. She thought her boyfriend was taking her for a night out when he parked his car in a pub car park: 'We sat in the car, he turned to me and handed me a packet of three condoms and ordered, "Get in that car over there and have sex with the man inside."

'His only other words were to tell me to get the money before sex. I was that much in love with him I would have done anything and believed if I didn't get the money he wouldn't love me.

'I was terrified and thought, how do I start? I went over to the car, leaned in and said, "Are you looking for business, darling?" I did three that night and got £12. They were all easy punters, caused no problems and had nothing down below so it was done in seconds – and it was good money.

'The next day my man took me shopping and bought me a red suit. I was only ever used to hand-me-downs from my sisters. He took me to a tailor's to have it taken in – all to keep me sweet, the little fucker.'

Liz's man set her up in a rented back-to-back in Hull from where she serviced sailors docking at the busy East Coast port. Come weekends, Liz was left on her own as her man told her he had to return to Leeds to see his mother.

'I worked 7 pm to 11 pm every night. And like an idiot, I'd do it all weekend. My sister joined me and we'd make about £30 each. It would have killed my mother if she knew what we were doing.'

But when the ships came in so did the men and the money. A Swedish deep-sea diver was Liz's first encounter with kinky customers. 'He liked young lassies. We never had sex, would just get dressed up and sit and chat about a right load of rubbish. If he wasn't able to see me he'd send flowers, cheques or telegrams. He'd give me £80 – a lot of money, even then.

'One time I put on one of his rubber suits and he wore my clothes. He always brought his own high heels as mine were too small. I had him for a long time, until I moved back to Leeds when I found out I was pregnant.'

Her man refused to believe he was the father. His claims that it must be a punter's proved fruitless as Liz always used condoms, and still does. She moved into a bedsit in Chapeltown's most infamous street, Spencer Place, and worked from a nearby corner.

Her pregnancy at 18 proved to be lucrative even though she received her first conviction just a month before the baby was born. 'Lots of punters like you being pregnant. It's a common fantasy. They're dying to know what it's like to go with a pregnant woman. It seems many of their wives won't let them do much when they're expecting.'

After her son was born, Liz would work the streets from 1 pm to 5 pm while another girl babysat. Going rates for business in the mid-70s were £5 for a full strip or £3 for straight sex. Liz continued to hand her earnings – up to £80 a day – to her pimp. Whatever the weather she would be out working with 'Fiery Jack' (embrocation) sprayed on her bare legs in an attempt to keep them warm on wintry nights. 'Straight sex would take a few minutes. The most time-consuming part is them taking their clothes off. I was a good hustler, always got a lot of men as they liked my big bust, but I never had any money and would tap my sister for food. Yet I couldn't wait to see my man's face when I gave him my earnings. He told me one day he wanted a full-length fur coat and it took me three days' work to pay for it. He then demanded a car – that took about four weeks. But what really killed me was when he asked for a two-seater sports car and we were a family of three. I smashed it up later when I discovered he had another woman.'

Unaware for ages that her man had served four years for 'poncing' (living off immoral earnings), Liz finally confronted his mother over why she never wanted to see her grandson. She was shattered when the mother said she never knew he existed and that her son went to live with his wife, a white woman, in Bradford on weekends. But when Liz's man discovered he had been found out, he turned violent. 'He broke into my flat and battered me. He hit me so hard on my back with a stick that it snapped and for days my sister had to spoon-feed me. But I took him back. I was that naive. You don't learn with the first one.' It was to be several years before she finally broke free from him – and only then because he had met another woman.

These days, Liz has control of her life and is happier than ever. But like many prostitutes who manage to attain this, it was achieved mainly through her own strength of personality and wisdom gained over the years.

She recently married and speaks almost with surprise of how kind her new husband is to her. 'He irons my clothes and treats me like a lady. The kids like him too. That was important to me because if they hadn't I would have packed him in.

'Most hookers have been brought up hard. They're fighters short of money. Every girl does it for the money – that's what it boils down to. It's hard work but easier than being stuck in a factory. I worked in one for three years and got in a week what I could have earned hustling in two hours – and I never saw the kids.

'Once you've hustled, you'll always hustle. When you've no money you fall back on the game. You're always going to go for the easiest ways of earning money – for me that's selling sex. You have to live this kind of life to realize what goes on. Street work is the hardest form of prostitution and the most dangerous. You've got to be hard to do this job and be able to turn yourself off from what you do.

'I've never lost my self-respect because I've never denied what I do. Prostitutes are judged wrongly. We are just normal people who sell our bodies. If that's what you want to do, you should be allowed to do it. And why should we pay tax on something that belongs to us?

'I am a normal mum who wants better for her children. No one wants it to be their daughter who goes on the game. I'd batter mine if she did. I have a high opinion of myself because at the end of the day I can put my hand up to God and say I kept my kids the only way possible.'

The English Collective of Prostitutes estimates that around 70 per cent of working girls are single mothers. The London-based organization, which has been campaigning for the abolition of prostitution laws since it was founded in 1975, says women see going on the game as their best means of affording better lifestyles for their families. 'They don't do it for the love of it,' said the ECP spokeswoman, Nikki Adams.

'Women have the right to earn a living, however. There's a way of thinking that being poor but respectable is OK but these women have decided the price of respectability is not worth paying. Women want more out of life and money from prostitution does give many a lot more independence. The last ten years have seen more women go on the game.

'Wives have come to us and said what they do is no different to prostitutes and joke about the "Thursday fuck" – husband comes in with his wage packet and the wife does her thing to get her share of it.' Some wives go a stage further.

CRYSTAL

Crystal had just completed her first week's work at a small private brothel in a London council flat. A devout Roman Catholic, her main worry was not how she would face her husband and family but how she would cope with seeing her local priest when she took her four children to church that weekend.

She plans to work three days a week, at a Wandsworth brothel, managed by the madam, Linda, a prostitute who has run several bordellos across London in a lengthy career. Crystal and Linda work alternate days Monday to Saturday with Sheila, the maid, present every day to answer the phone, greet clients, serve drinks and log the services they buy.

'I met Linda at an Ann Summers party [sex toys and saucy underwear],' Crystal explained. 'She told me she worked in a massage parlour and was looking for someone to answer the phones. She said if I wanted to do anything else while I was there I could and I decided to give sex a try. Until then I never ever considered doing it as I thought it would be too dangerous and I am a Catholic.'

Crystal's red lipstick is garish. Thick black eyeliner and clumsily applied mascara do nothing to enhance her pretty blue eyes and clear pale skin. First impressions were that she is docile, a bit stupid; but they crumbled as she explained why she works in a rather grotty multi-storey flat.

A miserable home life with her Turkish-born husband of seven years was the main motivation for going on the game. 'I needed the money. My husband's got his own food takeaway shop, but he only gives me £80 a week housekeeping. He slaps me about a bit, shouts, goes out all hours, gambles a lot and leaves me with nothing. I want a bit of independence, to work for myself.

'I am unhappy at home. He never wants to go on family holidays or days out. We have a good sex life, but that's about all that is OK. He's too boring for me. I wanted to do something exciting. He thinks I'm selling bathroom equipment.'

She wears a skimpy PVC basque, black garter and stockings, which she had to smuggle out of her home for work. 'I was so nervous as I walked through the bedroom door for my first punter. I didn't think I'd be able to do sex but he was a really pleasant older guy. He wanted me to bathe him and said he didn't want sex, but we ended up having it. My second one was a Somalian teenager. He wanted to do anal without a condom but I refused. I don't do that with my husband so I'm not with anyone else.

'They were the only ones I did on my first day. I told them I was new in case they thought I was no good. I didn't think about what I was doing until I got home and then started feeling guilty.'

She notched up another two punters on her second day. 'One said he wanted me to have an orgasm with him and I said I only do that with my partner but, so as not to put him off, I said I took too long. They think you enjoy it so I just play along. None of them have been repulsive but I'd be scared stiff if a cop or reporter caught me.'

Sheila and Linda briefed Crystal on what to do. The bedroom is clean but cannot be considered luxurious. A row of different sized canes is displayed along a wall and hanging down from a hook are several black masks and a pair of black 'nipple and ball' clamps. A large TV and video fill one corner and a bucket, filled with condoms, baby oil and talcum powder, stands on top of a cabinet. Next to it is a box of tissues – man-size, of course.

A punter pays £10 for a massage and saucy film which Crystal plays to relax him before going on to perform 'extras'. Although a newcomer to the business, she reels off the prices like an old-timer: 'It's £20 if he wants to massage me, £30 for hand relief, £40 for oral, breast relief is £50 – that's where he puts his penis between my boobs. Funnily enough, they don't seem to mind that I'm flat-chested. Sex is £60 and any extras or peculiar things are £70.'

Crystal takes the underground from her north London home to work from 11.30 am to 7.30 pm. Out of her wages, she pays the maid £30 per day while Linda pockets £10 per customer and every £10 massage fee. One day Crystal went home with just £10 profit in her pocket.

Nevertheless, she has no plans to give up the job. 'It's something wild and exciting and I'll do it until my husband gets suspicious. If I can do four men a day I'll be OK. I quite enjoy dressing up in the gear.'

The 29-year-old was born and raised in York. She left her factory job there nine years ago to visit relatives in London and never returned. 'I wouldn't tell anyone what I was doing as I'm religious and never miss church on a Sunday, it makes me feel better. I had a fling with my husband's cousin and one of my kids is to him. I kept that to myself and the priest asked if there was anything worrying me. He told me to go to confession and then I could go to Communion.

'I told the priest I couldn't confess what I had done [with my husband's cousin]. I've never been to Communion or confession since. There's no point. I can't confess to doing this because I can't promise I will give it up.'

Working from home presents a different set of problems from those faced by prostitutes who work the streets or in commercial brothels. Any children living at the house could be deemed 'at risk', even if the woman is careful to see clients while the children are away from the premises.

Another legal problem could be presented if the local housing authority discovered a woman operated a small brothel from her home. It could say she had breached planning laws (in the case of a private house) or tenancy agreements (in the case of rented or council accommodation) and order her to stop working. Or the council could serve a 'stop' notice and if she continued working after that it would constitute an offence. Ultimately, the authority could evict the woman from her home.

On the safety front, women do not get a chance to vet clients before these walk through their doors, and so they put themselves at considerable risk of violence, rape or theft. Whether by choice or to limit the risk of being caught by the police, these women lead isolated and lonely lives, and if they want to hide the type of work they do, they may be reluctant to call the police should they need help.

Those who work from home are known to be 'working off the phone'. They get most of their business from advertising in newspapers, men-only and contact magazines and, most commonly in London and Brighton, cards in phone booths. In areas where parlours have to be licensed and masseuses qualified, the women get round this by offering 'relaxation therapy'. Women who rely on the cards for business are up against British Telecom, which employs a team of cleaners at a cost of £50,000 a year to trawl the phone booths three times a day clearing out the cards. But BT admits that as soon as one is cleared it will be restocked within minutes by card boys and girls.

Card boys or 'sticker men' – such as are used by Diana (see page 16) – could be convicted for living off immoral earnings. Card girls – at least two operate in London – are immune from this offence since it relates to the activities of men. However, if they stuck the cards in the booths with glue or tape, both sexes could be prosecuted for criminal damage. Those who just insert them in a booth could be prosecuted for littering it. The

Metropolitan Police's Eight Area vice unit brought 281 such prosecutions in 1992 against card boys and girls.

Some card boys and girls work for several women and can earn between £30 and £70 per prostitute per day. It is claimed that students and pensioners as well as the unemployed are increasingly turning to such jobs to boost their income.

The House of Lords rejected an attempt by Westminster City Council in 1992 to make unauthorized advertising in booths an offence with a £400 fine, stating that national rather than local legislation would be better suited to deal with the matter.

Contact magazines are bought through either mail order or sex shops, or a few are on newsagents' top shelves. Most vice squads have copies of the various publications and use them to keep an eye on who is doing what on their manors.

The more explicit magazines have adverts accompanying small, amateurish photographs of women, usually dressed in underwear and posing provocatively in their living rooms or bedrooms. Others have rows of adverts containing saucy messages along the line of: 'Julie, exotic model enjoys water sports and being photographed. TVs [transvestites] welcome'. Transvestite prostitutes and clients also advertise for specialist services in the magazines. Box numbers or telephone numbers are printed for replies.

Each magazine will have a disclaimer near the booking form, saying something like 'all personal adverts are accepted for publication on the understanding that they are placed for pleasure and not for financial gain'. Others are more direct and say no adverts can be used for the purpose of prostitution. This protects the owners, publishers, printers and sellers of the magazines from prosecution under the 1959 or 1964 Obscene Publications Acts.

Contact magazines have existed in one form or another for centuries. The high-class Greek *hetairae* often used an Athens cemetery garden, Ceramicus, as an ancient equivalent. Each courtesan had a stone on which she would leave messages and a client would write compliments on it to her, along with a suggested meeting time and fee. The *hetaira*'s personal slave would convey the message to her and she would meet her client in the garden at the agreed time.

Eighteenth-century forerunners of the magazines came in the shape of directories which detailed women's talents. 'A List of the Sporting Ladies', dating from about 1770, saucily sells the game girls:

> Miss D.G. . . . is a strapping wench, and from her experience and high training, is possessed with every charm to render an Amour with her delightful.
>
> Miss Rattletrap, from Pall Mall; . . . the rider must be very careful of her as she starts at good speed.

PAT

'Mature, cuddly lady' is how Pat describes herself in the advertisements she places in today's contact magazines.

Readers who ring to discuss a price and book an appointment are told that charges start at £35 an hour for a porn film and sex in the front room of her Birmingham terraced home. Those who cannot contain their pleasure and want a repeat performance – of the film – have to stump up a further £20.

Pat, 42, has worked 'off the phone' for the last three years after deciding street prostitution had become too dangerous. 'There's a lot of robberies of punters and the girls and I thought, that's it. I didn't feel safe out there.'

Clients drawn from the magazines are generally 'more middle-class' than the typical street punter, says the dark-haired mother of two. 'I tend to see them when I know bills need paying. Otherwise I don't do so much. I've had a few American and European tourists who have seen me in the books while they've been visiting London. If they want sex, it's on the lounge floor. I don't let them use my bedroom. Quite a number don't have sex these days, a lot will just want to play around, probably because of AIDS.

'I am happy and live from day to day; I don't think ahead. Prostitution is what I've always done. I quite like the excitement of it all though you have to become hard and cut yourself off from it otherwise it would drive you mad. I treat it as a business and think about the money.'

Pat sets to work on a client while he watches a film and lounges in an armchair with a drink. 'It can be a bit nerve-wracking because I don't know who is coming until he is in my house. I always get the money first and tell them it will last an hour, but usually they're over and done with in

20 minutes. It's a bit of a con but you've got to know what you are doing and get them to come while they're watching the video. Everything is done with a rubber, even hand relief.

'I never do anal or kiss. Some ask but I tell them I don't do it; there's no involvement. They like to tell you their life stories. The older ones are more civilized and some reckon they haven't had sex with their wives for 20 years but I switch off as I don't want to know. I'll say, "Oh yes, it's a shame," but deep down I think what a bleeding shit-head.'

She has had regular medicals for years and proudly states that in 20 years she has never had 'a dose' (venereal disease) – only a bout of fleas from a punter. 'If I do three or four a week that suits me now. On a good week I can make £160 to £200 then other times it might be down to £80, but I don't sign on.'

Despite being a prostitute for nearly 30 years, the gently-spoken Pat says putting on an act is her way of overcoming her natural shyness. For her that is achieved by transforming her appearance and disguising her true self with different coloured wigs and heavy make-up. 'When I go out I like to be myself, go somewhere decent and not mix with prostitutes. I am very shy but doing prostitution is ten times different from sleeping with someone you like. I'd have to have a drink if I was going to do that, but if it's business I don't.'

She speaks hesitantly about her work. 'In the beginning it was hunger,' she says, explaining why she first dabbled with prostitution at the age of 13. 'My dad was a very ill man. Half the time we starved or if not, we pinched. An older woman told me about the game and I started doing a bit. My mother thought I had a pub job. I went to live in a room at 14 and worked from then on around Balsall Heath.'

Pat, a single parent, has always worked for herself. Money has been the only motivating force, to support her parents and siblings, and then help raise her two children – before they were taken from her. 'Social services told me to get a proper job. My kids were starving so I went to get help from a charity. I hated it, felt really embarrassed and vowed never to do it again. I was given a choice by the courts to pack in working or have the kids taken off me. My daughter was 12 when they took her. But both my kids are great and I still see them.

'I've done prison for not paying bills and I'm not sure how many convictions I've got, but I know it's a lot. The police don't bother me these days, not since I hit a woman copper three years ago. I was walking down the street to the pub when she thumped me in the back, God knows why, and I hit her back. When it went to court I was told if I didn't plead guilty they would put everything against me and I'd go to jail. I thought I might as well admit it and get it over. The magistrate fined me £50 and winked at me as I left court.'

Plans to decorate her house, particularly the front room, are on hold. 'I'm not doing the place up while ever I am working. This carpet is good enough for the punters,' she says, pointing to a well-flattened beige pile. Retirement does not beckon for the foreseeable future: 'I've seen poverty since childhood. Prostitution is not an easy life. But I'd sooner have money in my pocket than nothing at all.'

CHAPTER SIX

Protectors and 'Protected'

ROY

'There are four main ways of getting a girl on the streets – and keeping her there.

'Hitting her is the first one. I never had to do much of that, usually a back-hander across the face was enough, but it was often the only way to get them out. Some need to be hit because it's the only thing they understand. You have to make sure you don't hit them so they can't work or on their faces, after all a girl with two black eyes won't earn as much as one with none.

'Apart from hitting 'em, you get 'em out by being nice to them, playing one against another, or getting 'em into drugs.'

With a chilling casualness magnified by his gentle voice, Roy reveals how he kept dozens of prostitutes under his control as a professional pimp for 20 years, and lived off their earnings.

Pimp, ponce, protector, hustler, manager, controller, boyfriend: these are the different words used by those involved in the sex trade for the same 'job' – controlling one or a group of prostitutes, usually by violence or coercion.

If prostitution is deemed to be the world's oldest profession, then pimping must be the runner-up.

Many prostitutes never work for a pimp. Others do for a period, but as they grow older and more experienced they manage to get away from him, though often not without years of harassment. Young girls, often runaways from home or in care and vulnerable to exploitation because of their histories, are pimps' favourite targets, as Roy admits.

Casting an eye over a passing female is not done out of fun for Roy – he prefers men – but as an occupational habit. 'I don't look at women and think how pretty they are. I see them in terms of whether they'd be good earners.

'Some women were born to be prostitutes. They are amoral and see having sex with men for money as a means to get what they want. To find that sort of woman is every ponce's dream.'

White, slightly built, grey, balding, gaunt-looking – and gay – he is the antithesis of the stereotypical ponce. In a career which started at 13, guarding the room where his prostitute sister worked, he went on to operate a string of brothels, rent out flats for business at 1,000 per cent above going rates and live off street hustlers' earnings.

Violence is an accepted part of many pimp/prostitute relationships. (Within the trade, these terms are rarely used; instead, ponce or hustler are favoured for the pimp and hustler for the woman.) Roy says many of his women expected him to lash out occasionally. 'If I didn't hit a particular one once a month, she thought there was something wrong. I'd seen my dad hit my mother for years and my brothers all hit their wives so it was normal for me to hit women.'

Hilary, an ex-prostitute and friend of Roy's, nods in agreement. 'You want their praise and respect, to have your self-esteem boosted by them. If they hit you, that's proof they're bothered enough about you to do it. It's like proof of ownership. You think in return for giving him your money, he's going to protect you. Ponces offer a degree of security, regularity, in your life. Roy was one of the better pimps. He was a good-looking bloke and always dressed smartly. Girls take a lot of pride in that.'

Jane Mezzone, a sociologist who helps run the Praed Street Project for working girls in London, said because prostitutes tend to see their relationship with the pimp as the most stable thing they have, they want to hang on to it and stay with him for security. 'If you are totally ostracized by the society you live in, it is very difficult to turn your back on any affection shown to you, even from a violent man,' she said.

The second ploy used to control a prostitute is to be kind to her, according to Roy. 'Speak nicely to them, maybe buy them something like a cheap bottle of perfume and it pays dividends as they'll go out and work twice as hard for you.

'Sleep with her occasionally – not too often. That bit is not too important to the women as they're having sex all day, it's everything else, looking after them, pretending you care even if you don't. You haven't got to be too nice, otherwise they'll think you're going soft on them and you won't want them to work any more – which is the last thing you want.'

Prostitutes keep sex in personal relationships distinct from 'business' by a variety of techniques. A common one is not using condoms for sex with a partner. Other methods include adopting false working names, not kissing punters, only doing business on top of a bed if in a room, and taking as few clothes off as possible. Many do not remove any clothing at all; some will just take off their panties, or even pull them to one side. If a punter wants to see the woman naked, he will have to pay. Wilier women have been known to put a price on each article he wants removing!

Though research has shown the majority of working girls opt not to wear condoms with their lovers, some do not have a choice in the matter. 'You always insist a punter wears a rubber, but you'd never dare ask your black man to put one on for fear of a slap or beating. He'll think "So what, it's only a white girl",' said ex-prostitute Pat. It was a view voiced by many prostitutes.

Some women who have black pimps are forbidden by them to do business with black punters. A West Indian writer suggested this was because the pimp would be worried that the women might enjoy the experience too much.

The third means of exercising control over a prostitute is by playing on her vulnerability and insecurity or, as Roy puts it, playing one prostitute off against another. 'This was a favourite of mine, worked wonders,' he recalled. 'A girl gives you £50 and she might slag off another of your women, but you casually mention she earned you £80 and the next time you can bet the other will set out to get you more. If, on the following night, she brings in £80, you praise her for having a good night, so when she brings in less it is instilled into her by hints that you are not happy with that. They are in no position to do anything about it apart from shout and scream – and then they get slapped.'

Some pimps operate women in different cities. The distance offers no safeguards, as he will have 'friends' who keep a watch on the women and the amount of business they are doing. It is not unknown for a pimp to work two women within yards of each other, but neither will be aware of that as many are ordered and threatened not to mix with other prostitutes.

Mandy, who like Liz suffered years at the hands of a vicious pimp, explained the thinking behind the ban. 'If you're chatting with them you could be losing work. The guy won't want you blabbing his business or you finding out too much about his. Also the women are very protective about their guys and often won't say who he is. Women describe them as boyfriends and say, "Oh, he's not that bad. He only hits me now and then and let me stop work while I was pregnant (usually with his child)." But he's a pimp. It's just they don't want to admit it. Many ponces will tell you how much you have to earn that day – and you do or you do not go home.'

Liz, whose story is outlined in Chapter 5, has borne two of her three children to her ex-pimp. He, like most of those in Leeds, is black: 'The few white ones here have usually been brought up with blacks and want to be black,' she said. 'It's mainly the younger girls who have pimps as the older ones won't put up with them, but the guys will always make sure they have a main prostitute who can regularly bring in the money. Fear of being battered or losing their pimp to another woman allows the men to have these women in their grip. They're forced on the streets through love.'

Being used emotionally, physically and financially by pimps is an acceptable price to pay for a love relationship for those women with few other options. 'If nothing else, life in the sex business taught them all forms of love had their price,' says the author and ex-prostitute Nickie Roberts.

Roy's friend, Hilary, explained why. 'There's an unspoken pressure, a sense of obligation, that you have to work. You think, he spends a lot of money on me, buys me clothes [even though it is money she has often earned] and will protect me if I have any trouble. A woman always makes money for her pimp first and if she does not bring enough in to satisfy him, he will play on her guilt.

'If you've made £30, you might say you did three at £10 rather than six at £5, for pride's sake. It's easy for people to wonder why we don't leave these men. But, we wouldn't just abandon them, we'd have to give up our home, friends and lifestyle.'

Pimps are known to cruise around beats to check on their women. They frequently use rental cars, hired in another name and often from out of their locality, making it more difficult for the police to keep tracks on them. Often, pimps collect women's earnings as they stand on the street, in case a punter should rob them – that is the excuse they give. The women know that is the last they will see of their earnings.

In return for their giving him money, the pimp supposedly offers protection to his women from clients and other prostitutes. But this is a myth, says Roy. In reality, a pimp exploits the woman's need of and dependence on him, which a clever ponce will have developed when they were lovers.

The only protection Roy gave was in the form of condoms which he supplied to the women he ran. 'Sure, you might sit in the next room while they're doing business, but you rarely have to do anything. If a punter turns nasty, he's slung out. If there's any trouble between the women, I'd just have a quiet word with the other woman's pimp and ask him to sort it out at his end.'

As in any trade, strong competition can exist between many prostitutes and they are often initially suspicious of a new face. The women tend to have their own patches by which they become known; for example, they will talk of Mary who stands on Smith Street. They are very protective of their territory, as regular punters get to know who works where. Any rookie prostitute who strays on to an established woman's patch without her or the pimp's permission will be quickly turfed off. Cardiff is a perfect example of a street set-up. It has two city centre beats which are separated by a busy main road and a few hundred yards. Yet the women who work in one of the areas rarely stray on to the other.

Drugs are the fourth way of getting a woman to work. A pimp will often encourage a woman to dabble, particularly if he is a dealer. Roy, 43, tells of three sisters he knows who all work for the same heroin-dealing pimp in Manchester. 'Their money is used by him to buy drugs but if they want any he don't give it to 'em – they have to do another punter to buy it. He got 'em on drugs in the first place. Often, a guy will get a girl to try the drugs and when she becomes hooked on more serious stuff, he makes her go out and work to pay for her habit.

'Drugs and prostitution have always been linked. When I started poncing in the 60s, there was a lot of Irish guys and some Scots doing it. The black guys followed us onto the scene. Now they control the drug scene – and consequently the women.'

Cafés and pubs are favourite recruiting grounds used by pimps to hook their female prey. 'You can always spot them, looking a bit scruffy and in need of a bit of money and friendship,' says Roy.

'They're known as mysteries – because that's what they are and all you know of them is that they're running away from something or someone. From the outset, they are at a disadvantage because you know exactly what you want from them whereas they know nothing.

'You chat her up, persuade her to stay at your place – and that's your first job achieved. Then you start taking her out, showing her around and buying a few bits for her – nothing over the top, you don't go mad.

'Introduce her to a friend who already has a woman working and she might be well-dressed or always seem to have a few bob. Drop a few hints that she's a prostitute and that's how she can afford to have nice clothes.

'Leave matters for a few days and just mention you're having a few money problems, paying bills or something wrong with the car, and if she wants to keep up the lifestyle you suggest she goes out to work with your mate's woman. A favourite line is "Can you help?"'

A pimp always makes sure a new girl is accompanied by an experienced prostitute for her first shift who will show her the ropes and tell her the prices. She would never be allowed to go out on her own, for fear that she would run away.

'They might have dabbled a bit on the streets and think, "Well I've already done a bit, no sweat." The unspoken takes over and it becomes less and less emergency money and more for everyday things. They'll think, "I'm earning £10 for myself and I'll give him a bit extra to stop any trouble." If they decide not to go out one night, you sulk and she'll think, it's not worth the aggravation, I might as well just go.

'Of course, you impress on her that if she doesn't like it, she can give it up.'

They rarely do.

Pimping is mainly centred around street prostitutes who work full-time. A minority of those who work in commercial parlours and saunas are put in them by pimps. The casual prostitutes – who work occasional days to pay quarterly or catalogue bills, for example – tend to be independent.

Roy is one of a handful of white men accepted by the more numerous black pimps in the notorious red light district of a large northern city. Pimps are virtually non-existent in several cities with thriving red light areas. Prostitutes in Cardiff, Edinburgh and Glasgow say one or two occasionally appear but never for long.

In many areas such as Bristol, Birmingham and Leeds the majority of pimps tend to be Afro-Caribbean, but it can vary in cities with a specifically strong ethnic community. Bradford, for example, which has a large Asian population, has at least one brothel staffed by Asian women who serve their own community.

London is the exception, with pimps of all nationalities. The Metropolitan Police's Charing Cross-based vice unit smashed a brothel run by Chinese men with links to the Triads from a detached house in a select north London suburb. Women were being flown over from China on three-month rotas purely to service Chinese men.

The West Indian author Ken Pryce, commenting on Afro-Caribbean lifestyles in Bristol, says hustling in the ponce's eyes 'restores his sense of pride and feeling of mastery and autonomy. He is in control again. This is especially the case if it is a good hustle; the hustler can live like a king, and move "cool", clean and well-dressed without any means of visible support. Poncing is ideal because it is the very antithesis of "slave labour" [by this he means legal work in this country], fulfilling all the hustler's wishes. Not only does it give him a good income, it also allows him to play the role of stud . . . and in doing so, expresses a reaffirmation of his sense of machismo and manhood, lost in "slave labour".'

He also emphasizes how racism in British society restricts the black workers' abilities to improve themselves. 'In rejecting the work ethic,' says Pryce, 'the hustler is reacting to at least four aspects in this situation: poor pay and lack of opportunity for self-improvement; threats to his manhood and conception of himself as a man; white supremacy – a situation where the white man is permanently the boss and the West Indian permanently the menial; and rebelling against a genuine lack of opportunity for self-growth and self-realization. The hustler response demonstrates a refusal to accept the ascribed sub-proletarian role defined by the official society.'

Poverty is a powerful motive to better one's circumstances, but it can never be an excuse for a pimp to use violence against a prostitute and Pryce's explanations would find little sympathy from the women who are at the receiving end of a pimp's fist.

Discussing the place of the pimp in the history of the prostitute, Nickie Roberts says: 'Pimps generally came from the same social background as their whores and therefore faced similar problems of poverty and lack of prospects. They could, however, play on what little power patriarchy afforded them by exploiting the sexual labour of women. Pimping was one of the few ways a man from a poor background could achieve upward mobility, or at least a higher standard of living.' Included in that list should be status among his peers.

At his peak, Roy controlled an average of 21 prostitutes from three adjoining terraced houses, working them seven days a week, 24 hours a day.

His career began in his home town in Lancashire. 'My sister used to do the Pakis, go to one of their houses on a Friday night and see about six. I'd go with her, sit on the floor outside the room where she worked and as one left, I'd let the next in. Sometimes I'd collect the money from them before they went in.'

He did this for three years, around three times a week, when his parents believed he was at school – until he was arrested.

'We were sat in the car waiting to go into one of the houses when we were surrounded by police. My sister was charged with soliciting and I was going to be done for living off immoral earnings until they found out I was only 15.' His mother was called to the police station and Roy was let off with a caution.

He and his sister decided it was too risky to work in their home town and went mobile. Travelling around Yorkshire and Lancashire, they never varied their routine – find the nearest pub, buy a drink and wait until somebody struck up a conversation. Again, Asian mill and factory workers were a regular source of income. 'A lot didn't have their wives in this country like they do now, and we'd do a few in a house.' Again he would act as doorman and, in return, his sister bought his clothes and occasionally gave him spending money.

He moved to a rented room in a house in a red light district at the age of 16. An attractive black prostitute, Charmaine, already lived and worked there and Roy let a friend of hers use his room for business in return for ten shillings a punter.

'I decided that if I worked it properly, instead of getting part of her money I could have it all. I moved to a house with two rooms and put a bed in the kitchen and had the two women working.' Within months he had expanded to five rooms, including a bed in the bathroom, and let the Asian owner collect his rent in kind.

By the age of 20, Roy was an established ponce, had bought a terraced house and organized a rota of eight girls working in every room during the day and another eight at night. He was given half of the money earned by every girl who used the house except Charmaine. She was his 'number one' woman – and gave him everything.

Today, pimps still have 'number one' women, a position which prostitutes regard as a status symbol among the stable of sex workers the pimp might operate. In effect, it means he will keep his clothes at the number one prostitute's house, sleep with her most nights and she might have his children – even if he already has a wife.

The women usually sat on the garden wall to hustle for trade. If they did not attract enough business or missed a couple of shifts, Roy would turf them out and replace them within hours.

Occasionally he was called on to perform extra duties. 'Quite often, a punter asked if I would go with one of the girls while he watched and a few wanted to have sex with a man while the girl watched. It wasn't a problem as I was bisexual then, into everything at that time and it was just part of living. My lifestyle was so high, I'd do anything to keep it like that. When the police raided the place, they found something like 29 pairs of trousers in my wardrobe – all with the price tags still on.'

He received plenty of money in the five years he ran the brothel. 'It was spent as quickly as it came in. I've never had a bank account and it all went on booze, gold, cars, and clothes.'

When police raided the house in 1971, Roy pleaded guilty to keeping a brothel and was fined £25. He asked for and was given time to pay the fine – something he has never done.

He closed the place – and waited a week before setting up business again. 'I acquired three terraced houses and put in linking doors. But this time I decided to do things differently and rented each of the 21 rooms out to girls for £50 a week, though the average going rent was about £4. The girls were charging £5 a trick then, so anything they made after that was profit and we claimed the rent in benefits.'

After several years of running his operation, hassle from the police and clients became too much and Roy got out – but not totally. 'Everything had moved up a stage by this time. Robberies, violence and muggings were more commonplace, even the clients had got harder.' He moved to a council house and allowed a prostitute to work 'off the phone' from there, while he again picked up money from her.

Ironically, he believes that if the gay scene was as open then as it is today, he would have worked instead of pimping. It was not until the mid-80s that he worked for a time from a flat, seeing transvestites. He gave it up after a punter attacked him with a knife.

Today he manages a pub in the heart of the city's drug and prostitution trade. Having lived in or around the red light area for nearly 30 years, he says little has changed in the workings of the trade. Age has made him wiser, but has not dimmed his eye for the main chance. 'I don't feel guilty about what I did. These days, the pimps only seem to run a couple of girls. I think it would be hard to work on the scale I used to. I would start up again tomorrow but I was told that if I was caught again I'd end up in the nick – and that's what stops me.'

Under section 30 of the 1956 Sexual Offences Act, unless a man can prove the opposite, he will be presumed knowingly to live off immoral earnings if he lives with or is constantly in the company of a prostitute or if he exercises control, direction or influence over her movements in any way which helps or forces her into prostitution. This section of the act could be applied to any man – be it husband, boyfriend, son, uncle or grandfather of the woman in question.

The offence is one of the few in British law where an accused has to prove his innocence in court, rather than the legal system prove his guilt. Once the Crown Prosecution Service can show a man to be frequently in the company of a prostitute, the burden to prove innocence shifts to the accused. It is up to him to clear his name by showing how he affords his lifestyle. As with street prostitution offences, it goes against the basic principle on which the legal system operates, that a person is presumed innocent until proven guilty.

The evidence of a prostitute alone will be insufficient generally and, according to Butterworth's Police Law, it is recommended that plain-clothes police observations of the man's activities over at least four days should be offered in evidence. The police handbook goes on: 'Prove that the woman is a prostitute, that the man lived with her or was frequently in her company and that he appeared to be directing or controlling movements. It is also helpful if it can be shown that the man had no other source of income, or if he did, that he lived well above the standard that his income would have allowed.'

Anyone found guilty faces a large fine and/or a jail sentence of up to seven years in England and Wales, but only two years in Northern Ireland.

However, critics of this law say it can stigmatize and criminalize a perfectly honest relationship between a prostitute and a male family member or friend because the offence can be applied to any men with strong links to working girls. An adult son, for example, could be criminalized simply by sharing a household's running costs or if his prostitute mother helps him out financially. It assumes that the male, whether he has any involvement or not with the woman's work, is considered to be exploiting her simply by being under the same roof.

Organizations such as the English Collective of Prostitutes and the Walsall-based Soliciting For Change believe there is no need for the pimping law, as other charges, such as blackmail or assault, could be used against men who force women to go on the game. Such campaign groups say the immoral earnings offence further segregates and stigmatizes prostitutes, and pimps who use violence should be treated in the same manner as any man who inflicts violence against a woman.

Unlike other European countries such as Holland and Italy, and many Third World countries, organized pimping in the United Kingdom is not syndicated and is still very much small-scale, a cottage industry, with most pimps operating two or three women on the streets. Those like Roy, who organized prostitutes to work from houses, receive money from a greater number of women, though possibly not as large a share of their earnings compared to pimps who control street women.

The police admit to great difficulties in being able to bring the professional pimps to justice. To the unprofessional eye, pimping is the unseen, hidden aspect of the trade. Some women deny they work for pimps, shrugging off why they have no money by saying they share it with their 'boyfriend'. It is difficult to know where to draw the line between partner and parasite. Brutality, while abhorrent, is a dangerous measure to use. After all, pimps do not have the monopoly on domestic violence and many non-prostitute female victims of domestic violence are just as reluctant to pursue matters in court as the working girls.

Ireland has convicted two men for living on immoral earnings in the past ten years. However, stringent new legislation was introduced in its Parliament, the Dail, last summer, which set out wide-ranging changes in relation to the prostitution laws. Under the Criminal Law (Sexual Offences) Bill, those who actively 'manage' one or more prostitutes face up to five years' imprisonment or a £10,000 fine.

A separate offence of living on immoral earnings is aimed at a person who lives on a prostitute's earnings but does not actively manage or control her activities. However, so that a prostitute's children or other dependent relatives are not criminalized by this, the revised offence can only be committed where the person living on the earnings also aids and abets that prostitution.

Prosecutions of pimps have been on the decrease over the past decade, with a total of 1,318 adult men found guilty between 1980 and 1991 in England and Wales. The annual totals are as follows, with figures in brackets for men under 21 who were sentenced to spells in young offenders' institutions:

1980 – 143 (1)	1986 – 93 (7)
1981 – 162 (5)	1987 – 74 (1)
1982 – 159 (2)	1988 – 75 (5)
1983 – 154 (7)	1989 – 101 (7)
1984 – 117 (6)	1990 – 62 (1)
1985 – 110 (4)	1991 – 68 (1)

These low figures, say the police, reflect the difficulties they face. Inspector Dave Dawson, chief of Nottingham's anti-vice squad, says they have one of the highest conviction rates for pimps, with successful prosecutions ranging between 17 and 38 a year since 1986.

The Metropolitan Police's Eight Area Vice Unit, which covers Westminster Borough, has also had some success in this field, with one pimp recently being jailed for 14 years for rape and running ten prostitutes. But, compared to the 2,905 arrests for soliciting, they charged just 28 men with living off immoral earnings in 1992.

To achieve a single prosecution can take many man-hours and it can all be lost if a prostitute decides to withdraw her complaint. The pimps and police know this and Eight Area Vice Squad goes to great lengths to protect the women once an arrest has been made, putting them up in hotels or guarding their homes.

One of the greatest safeguards is for the alleged pimp to be remanded in jail, but even then a prostitute is not totally safe, said the Met's Sergeant Grenville Bint, whose years spent policing indoor sex emporiums have given him extensive inside knowledge. 'The guy has plenty of friends on the outside and he just has to tell them to apply a bit of pressure,' said Sergeant Bint.

'We had one woman who was going to prosecute but two men took her to Shepherds Bush market, held her over a meat mincer and told her it was them or the mincer.' Extreme measures, but then some pimps have much to lose. One received more than £1 million – all tax free – over ten years from three or four women he ran, said Sergeant Bint.

CAROL

'I must have about 250 convictions, maybe more, and been to prison seven times for not paying fines. I never paid fines and would get 21 days for owing £2,000 fines and serve about two weeks. It was like boarding school and a rest from work. I didn't give a damn about anything then. But now I try and keep out of trouble.'

Like many Midlands prostitutes, Carol often spent weekdays working in London. At 19, she was a regular at King's Cross. 'I could earn up to £1,500 for five days' work, but I'd average £700. Bayswater was another haunt and Park Lane around by the Hilton Hotel. The money was good – £50 for straight sex back in the mid-80s – but the police were red-hot. I was arrested and put in a cell and this copper asked me if I did oral. I said no but then he said, "Give us a look at your tits if you want to get out of here tonight." I had to but I've never been back there since.'

Today she says she is working harder than ever. 'I work usually noon to 5 pm, see about six punters a day and make about £140. It's £20 for straight sex and £30 for oral and sex but most punters give you an extra tenner. I don't do Asians unless I know them as they're always trying to bargain with you. Most are regulars, businessmen. Some are OK. I talk dirty to them so they'll come quickly – that's experience. If you lie there like a bag of spuds, they'll take ages.

'I also do all this domination, humiliation and corporal punishment stuff with a friend at her house. She's bought this £70,000 place, blacked one room out and made another into a fake gas chamber. She never has sex with them and drafts me in if a punter wants it. I get about £60 an hour for that.

'I don't work at night on the streets as I'm too scared and I'm seeing a man who says I am too good to be staying out there. I'd like to try and make a go of it with this bloke. I don't want to be doing this when I am old.

'My parents know what I do. They have nothing against the work but can't understand why I do it and why I have nothing to show for it all. I've been written out of their will because they didn't want their money getting into the wrong people's hands, like my ex-fella's. I don't know what it is with me . . . my lifestyle gets so boring. Sometimes you just want to get out of the house and work can perk your life up. I am wised up now. If my daughter told me she was going on the game I'd advise her to do it the right way, not like me.

'Women are simply buying love when they hand over their money to the pimp,' she says. 'You want to please him and think the more you give him, the more he will think of you. Few admit that though. Because the women are normally so frightened of these men, they have great difficulty breaking free from their hold over them.

'I look back now and think why did I do that and the only reason I can give is that I didn't give a damn about myself.'

It is not just men who can control and exploit prostitutes. Women, in a number of guises, do the same. Madams are best known, but there is another position which can be equally omnipotent – the maid.

Her position varies from all-powerful to a friend earning a bit of extra cash on the side. They are often the 'power behind the throne', the eyes and ears of the owner of the premises; among their duties is the keeping of a tally so that the boss knows exactly how much has been earned.

Some ex-prostitute maids often own a room and, having retired, rent it out to younger working women. There is little they do not know about the business and they exploit their knowledge fully. The maid might set the fees and the prostitute will have to agree to them and the amount she has to give her from each client before starting work. The maid might also provide a range of uniforms and equipment, such as canes, and if the prostitute wants to use any, she will have to pay each time for each item.

'These maids never admit the extent of their power and try to put across this image of little old ladies working for tips, but that's rubbish,' said Sergeant Bint.

Visitors to Soho can see handwritten signs advertising 'beautiful young models' on bits of cardboard stuck on scruffy-looking doors which often lead to sparsely-furnished tatty rooms. Maids, or the often faceless bosses, can make hundreds of pounds a week from these places as the going rate to hire them in parts of London is up to £200 a shift. But the prostitutes have to work hard to make much profit, as sex can be bought for as little as £15 and competition is plentiful, with more than 100 'call flats' in Soho, Earl's Court and Paddington.

Maids have been central figures in prostitution for centuries. Apart from her basic responsibilities, it is often the maid who shows a new girl the ropes and explains tricks of the trade, such as how to 'chat' a customer out of more money. It is not unknown for her to go home with more money in her pocket than the prostitute.

Like madams, women who operate as maids face being prosecuted under Section 31 of the 1956 Sexual Offences Act for controlling prostitutes. The charge carries a maximum penalty of seven years' jail and/or a fine in England and Wales, though only two years' imprisonment under Northern Ireland law. Anyone who answers a prostitute's telephone, places her advertisements in shop windows or newspapers, or plays an active part in the running of the business can be accused. Proving it is another thing. In 1992, Eight Area Vice Unit, which patrols Soho, charged just six women for this offence.

Nationally, only 127 women between 1980 and 1991 – an average of about ten a year – were found guilty under Section 31 which, in full, states that it is an offence for a woman for purposes of gain to exercise control, direction or influence over a prostitute's movements in a way which shows she is aiding, abetting or compelling her prostitution.

If a maid is employed by the prostitute or property owner, she could be charged with running a disorderly house or assisting in the management of a brothel by helping to negotiate prices.

The Criminal Law Revision Committee of 1985, chaired by Sir Frederick Lawton, offered in its report 'Prostitution: Off-Street Activities' extensive criticism of the laws relating to those who control and exploit prostitutes. It also went on to recommend changes – none, unsurprisingly, have been acted upon.

Sir Frederick Lawton acknowledged that the present laws penalized men in a wider range of circumstances than women. 'Under Section 30, a man is guilty if proved to live on prostitute's earnings, whereas a woman is guilty only if she exercises control over a prostitute . . . [and it] fails to identify what we consider ought to be the main thrust of the criminal law, namely to prohibit the organization of prostitution.'

SHEILA

Most days Sheila is too busy answering clients' calls to worry about the possibility of police raids.

Putting on a polite telephone voice, she says, 'Well, sir, we've got a lovely young lady working today. Crystal is a blonde model with a superb figure and we offer massage and video for £10.'

She goes on to tell him of two other girls who are available – but they are not and never will be, as they do not exist. It is a ruse to make the client think he has a choice of women. Once he is in the flat it is a case of his choice being unavoidably and suddenly called away – but luckily the blonde model is free to see him.

Sheila works Monday to Friday for Linda, a madam who runs her brothel from a rented flat in Wandsworth. On the days Crystal, the 'new girl' whom we have already met, does not work, Linda, whose real home is several miles from the area, will.

Although Sheila is friendly with Crystal, and explained the working set-up to her, her loyalty lies with her boss, Linda. Sheila keeps a daily tally in a child's exercise book of clients seen, what they had and how much they paid, which she reports to Linda every evening.

Sheila's responsibilities are usually over when the client steps into the bedroom, but occasionally she is called on to perform extra duties. 'We get odd ones who'll want me to go in and watch and I get an extra £10. It tends to be those who like a whacking and I have to sit there. I daren't laugh though or he might not come back.

'Last week we did 13 punters. The first and last week of the month is always busy with the 'monthly payers' – guys whose salaries have just gone into the bank. Otherwise we either get them in really early or between 5 pm and 7 pm when they are on their way home. Most of our punters have straight sex rather than the kinky stuff.'

A 36-year-old mother of three, Sheila started on the game four years ago and has worked at several of Linda's brothels. 'She asked me if I wanted to answer the phones for £30 a day. At that time she had several women working for her at a cottage in Lewisham before we moved to another place in Croydon,' recalled Sheila.

'One day a customer came in and said he wanted me because he liked big bums – and that's how it started. We were really busy until we got raided. Linda closed the place down and I got a job in a record shop. I earned £109 a week for a lot longer hours. So when Linda rang to say she had set up here and wanted me to come back I gladly did.'

Many men like larger females, says Sheila, whose measurements are 40-28-40. 'They like to see big women in basque and stockings. I had four regulars and would make about £200 a week from them. I don't mind having sex with them. I think of my husband when I'm doing it, otherwise I don't think I could perform.

'When I was at my busiest, it did put me off having sex with him for a while. He knows I answer the phones but he's never known that I've worked. I think he'd leave me if he found out. I've never cheated on him and I don't class this as cheating. I haven't got the guts to commit a crime but we're in debt. I only started 'cos we needed the money. My husband gets such poor wages, they just can't keep us.

'Domination is my favourite as it makes me feel that I can get the better of them. I think this goes back to me being a battered wife in my first marriage. It's not the punters I'm hitting, it's my ex-husband.'

Sheila is happy maiding while she recovers from an operation, but she is considering doing some business once she is well. 'I would be worried if we were raided, but only because I can't afford to be fined. Other than that, I don't care what people think.'

119

It is clear, from conversations with Roy and others in the sex trade, that the pimps' and controllers' favourite prey is young runaways and girls in care. Sir Frederick Lawton, the chairman of the CLRC, believes more should be done in terms of 'moral education' for these young people. This country's courts and police forces carry out a practice of cautioning teenage girls for soliciting – even though many are not legally old enough to consent to intercourse. The Metropolitan Police holds the dubious honour of cautioning a girl of ten – the earliest age at which a child can be dealt with by police and the courts for any crime.

Figures released by the Children's Society show the number of police cautions issued to schoolgirls for soliciting in England and Wales (see table below).

The police force which cautioned the greatest number of teenagers was West Yorkshire, which, in 1991, gave 33 official warnings. Second on the list was the Greater Manchester force, which cautioned 29 in the same year.

Age	1988	1989	1990	1991
10	1	0	0	0
11	0	0	0	0
12	0	0	2	1
12	0	0	2	1
13	2	3	3	5
14	4	9	13	10
15	23	32	19	34
16	75	60	99	111
Total	105	104	136	161

The Children's Society has voiced its concern at schoolgirls being cautioned by police rather than being treated as victims of sexual abuse.

'Some of these children have been sexually abused and are acting out their pain and feelings of worthlessness. Their friends may be prostitutes and so they stand and watch. They get drawn in,' said Ian Sparks, the society's director. The police approach depends on where the sex act takes place. If it is in the home or school, the adult male faces serious charges of statutory rape or having intercourse with a minor, and the juvenile is viewed and treated as a victim of abuse or sex attack. When the street is the backdrop, on the other hand, the girl faces being branded as the criminal and it is highly likely that the male will drive home scot-free to his wife and children.

Many people, irrespective of age and profession, are impressed by status and image. It is easy to understand how young people can be taken in by someone who appears to have money, respect within their community, fashionable clothes, a nice car, takes them to pubs and clubs and – best of all, maybe – shows interest in them. One 16-year-old prostitute spoke proudly of her new boyfriend being the 'hardest guy in Chapeltown' and of the 'flash car' he drove.

Professor Norman Tutt, a member of the United Nations Standing Advisory Group on juvenile crime and a former director of Leeds Social Services, outlines the predicament faced by agencies dealing with vulnerable girls. 'A "boyfriend" in a sports car is always far more appealing than a social worker. There is also the lifestyle in what seems to them to be an exciting sub-culture. What on earth does a social agency do about the attractions of earning £100 a night? One can't ascribe their involvement solely to money, however. There is the trade's network. I know of no 15-year-old who can walk out of a home and set herself up in a flat. There must be an infrastructure of people behind her. Once involved in this network, she is pushed on to other people and further drawn in. People involved in recruiting these children are extremely successful in hiding them. They have strong reasons to, as the girl will bring in money to sustain them.'

Professor Tutt says there are two main reasons why strong links exist between children in care and prostitution. 'A number of youths who come into local authority care have been sexually abused within and outside the family – a higher proportion than we at first realized. Many young girls have had some experience of sexually satisfying a man. It will often be their first sexual experience – and thus an important one. For them, this would have been translatable almost as prostitution, even if it's a local neighbour or shopkeeper saying, "Play with me for five cigs". Children are no fools and if they are on the streets with no money and know they have something to fall back on, whether it is prostitution or knowing how to break into houses, they will use it.

'The second reason which might explain why girls turn to prostitution could be due to the extremely mixed population of children's homes. We care for a wide range of kids for various reasons. Some will have come from homes where the mother is a prostitute. Children talk to each other, share their experiences and informally recruit others. "I know how we can make £20". When they run away, prostitution is an immediate answer to getting money to live. If a girl goes on the run for weeks or months there is going to be a great deal of discussion on her return about how she survived. To other youngsters, she is a success because she got away and she might glamorize life on the streets.'

Despite police, social services and the prostitutes themselves repeatedly stating that more and more under-age girls are appearing on the streets, little is being done for these young people.

In an industry where the majority of the workforce is hidden, this section, unknown in its size or breadth, is the most hidden of all, yet there are no more than a handful of organizations in the country which offer practical help and counselling for young girls.

Imagine being raped up to seven times last night by seven unknown men and then turning up for school and being asked why you haven't done your homework, says one. That is the pressure teenage prostitutes face daily, Meg Strong comments.

She is the joint co-ordinator of ACE (Action Choice Empowerment) which deals with those aged under 17 involved in or at risk of prostitution in Bradford. Its first year's funding came from West Yorkshire Police's urban crime fund and staff were seconded from Bradford Social Services. Aimed at offering a lifeline to young prostitutes in the region, it had made great inroads when funding dried up and its future, sadly, hangs in the balance.

In the first six months of 1993, ACE saw 64 girls aged under 17. At least 50 per cent had worked as prostitutes on the streets and indoors in the preceding 12 months. ACE coined the phrase 'third party abuse' instead of using the term 'juvenile prostitute' for the young girls they see.

Ms Strong explained why: 'Prostitution is usually associated with the sale of sexual services for money, clearly indicating a level of gain. For young people involved any gain is rarely financial, more often it is one of sheer survival. To the under-age young girl, prostitution is just another form of abuse and we define it so:

first party   – young woman

second party – pimp

third party   – punter

'Many young people who become involved in third party abuse have suffered other forms of abuse, either physical, sexual or emotional. This leads to low self-esteem, a sense of isolation and a lifestyle where sex and violence are viewed as "normal". Unsupported and alone, these are the children most likely to be exploited and snared into further abuse from unscrupulous people who have no qualms about doing so.'

The team operates from secret premises in Bradford and has a flat which the girls are encouraged to treat as home. They can sleep there, call in to wash their hair, for a hot drink or a chat. Counselling and advice is offered and, unlike most social workers, the team is not obliged to act on details the girls tell them. The young people can see any information kept on them and staff pass this on if they permit.

'We don't condone or condemn. Our aim is to increase their self-esteem and worth, help them make informed choices and take control of their lives. We give them a chance to be young again and take them to the cinema or ice-skating,' said Ms Strong.

Of the 369 prostitutes arrested in Bradford in 1992, 47 were under-age. One-third of 26 juveniles cautioned in 1991 were in care. This tallies exactly with local police estimates that one in three of known young prostitutes is from care – a figure which does not include those living with foster parents. The first time a girl is dealt with by the police she is referred to ACE but the next time she is cautioned – and thus considered an offender and not a victim.

ACE staff have been able to build up a picture of the network involved in teenage prostitution. Ms Strong outlines how it works: 'It starts off low-key with a young man/boyfriend getting to know the girl.

She is then pushed further along the chain to a tougher, often more violent man and the first boyfriend goes off to recruit another girl. Or they might use a young girl who is heavily involved in the network and order her to bring a girl to them. She obeys as it is a way of achieving some status.

'A girl becomes embroiled in a very short time. She gets a buzz out of life if someone comes along, says he loves her and takes her to pubs and clubs. The fear is, "If I stop doing what he wants me to do, I am back to nothing." She believes some attention is better than none and prostitution is the only way she sees to keep or attract a boyfriend.'

Some taxi drivers are known to operate a service providing young women for punters in Bradford and other places. Drivers and 'boyfriends' have been known to turn up at schools or local authority children's homes to collect girls. Social services staff who have refused to let them go have been subjected to threats and violence from pimps angry that their source of earnings has been denied to them.

Derelict houses are also used for business. On the pretext of looking around an empty property, men get the keys from estate agents, have copies made, put mattresses in every room and punters are brought to the girls in the house.

The Children's Society and National Children's Bureau (NCB) have pointed to a strong link between poverty and teenage prostitution. An estimated 10,000 16- and 17-year-olds leave care every year to face life on their own, according to the NCB. Within months a great number are homeless and within a year most have no social services support at all. Nearly one in seven of these young women already have a child or are pregnant by the time of their discharge.

Further problems are caused by 16- and 17-year-olds not being eligible for benefits if they refuse or are not on training schemes. In 1991, there were between 45,000 and 50,000 young people without jobs, Youth Training placements or income support. The social security system is based on the assumption that young people can look to their families for help until they reach the age of 25, when they become eligible for full rates of income support.

Professor Tutt has harsh opinions about the present care system. 'It does not do enough to stop young people getting into prostitution and drives children into trouble. The government has an ideal view of the family which even those of us who are in relatively OK families find difficult to recognize.

'Our ability to control our own lives is down to our upbringing. Parents who encourage give children the self-confidence to take control of their lives. But if they have a chaotic family background and parents not in control of their own lives, the youths do not get that training. A lot of children in care feel they are failures – they are not going to get a job, may be in jail by the time they are 25 and this negative image is clearly allied to their being recruited into prostitution. We have got to be able to offer something positive enough for them which counteracts what they see as the benefits of prostitution.'

Many young prostitutes have been in situations where it seems better to run away and live on their own wits. Prostitution gives them a chance to make friends and money. No one asks questions or hassles them.

But at the end of the day one point must be remembered. There are men – in the role of either punters or pimps – who are prepared to use these girls, no matter how damaged they are.

SALLY

She, Roy would say, was a classic 'mystery', recruited into vice from one of the 'training colleges' from which many prostitutes have graduated – children's homes.

A Leeds prostitute branded the city's council-run homes as 'schools for sex'. But Leeds is not unique in that sphere. The petite auburn-haired street-walker's path to going on the game is one many in similar circumstances have trodden.

'I just wish I could turn the clock back to when I was 16 and have known then what I do now. I wouldn't be where I am today,' reflects Sally, who at 30 has spent exactly half her life on the game. For when Sally's rebellious teenage behaviour proved too much for her Birmingham parents to cope with, she was put into care.

By the time she was 20, she had met and had two children by her Rastafarian lover. 'My parents knew I was street-walking but they set me up in a nice house. The biggest mistake I ever made was letting him move in with me. I'd been going to London to work for three or four days at a time and when I came back one day, a friend said she thought he had hit the baby and called social services. They said he had picked her up by the leg and banged up against the wall. The kids were taken off me and put into care and I moved into a room. They were later adopted. I did contest it but the family really wanted them and in another three years the eldest one will be able to come looking for me.

'I met another man, Sammy, and we were together for years. I had two children to him. I was working all the time because he was a pimp and social services told me I was putting prostitution before the kids. But I wasn't – I was putting prostitution and my man before them. He was the only man I ever loved; I'd have done anything for him. His mother would look after the two youngest while I'd go out to work. I might not see them for a couple of days as I'd be out to 3 am and then maybe go on to a blues club.'

Sammy had a ring of prostitutes working for him but Sally was known to them as his 'main girl'. 'He only ever went out with working girls. He was probably seeing others while I was working but I stood for it and wasn't allowed to mix with them or have friends.

'He has never had a job in his life and though he never demanded it, I always handed my earnings to him. I used to think the more I earned the more he would be pleased with me. When I look back now I think I must have been thick. I wouldn't do that now. One girl I knew used to hand over her earnings to her pimp on a plate. I feel I want to advise young girls how pimps target them, but they wouldn't listen – I never did. I saw two pimps fighting over a girl and one shouted "You can have her for £1,000." It's slavery.'

Her years with Sammy, a jealous drug-addicted alcoholic, were marked by constant violence. Beatings, whether by hand or objects such as billards cues, could be triggered off simply by seeing Sally talking to another man. 'He's spat in my face, stubbed cigs out on my chest and punched my face so much it looked as if I'd been in a car crash. I moved to Telford to get away from him as I became severely depressed but he found me and burst my head open with a dog chain.

'I fled to the police station and was later rehoused. But I took him back and had another daughter to him. He never hit me in front of the children. I suppose he did love me in his own way. I don't know why he beat me, that's just the way he is, trying to control people. He beats all the girls he sees. He's found another woman and though he still bothers me occasionally the difference is I'm not frightened of him any more.'

While Sally says she has always been mature for her age, it was not until she was placed in a secure unit at 15 that she became initiated in selling sex. 'My parents are comfortably off and I had a good upbringing. I was never hit. Dad's a foreman and they've always been careful with money. But I was 13 when I started rebelling against everything. I was forward and had sex at 14 with a boyfriend. I always mixed with older girls at school and wanted to be going to the ice rink or disco with them. My parents always refused but I just used to go.'

Persistent truanting was at the root of her first involvement with the local authority. A court hearing decided she should be put into the care of an assessment centre in Birmingham, where she stayed for three years. 'I'd keep running away so they put me in a more secure place. But that didn't stop me so they sent me to a school in Coventry. I buggered off from there – and that's when I got into prostitution. The girls in the home would talk about it and when two of us ran away, she did a punter to get the train fare home. The girls in the home, some only 14, had pimps. They'd say they were their boyfriends, but looking back they were just pimps.

'It looked such an easy way to get some cash so I started doing it. We went to Ladypool Road, then part of the red light area of Birmingham, and the women all seemed to have money and it was exciting at the time. I suppose I was easily led.'

Her first arrest came at the age of 16 and – after giving false details to the police – she found herself in prison. 'I'd told them I was 17. Suddenly I was behind bars in Risley and I stayed there for three months. When I came out I began working regular and was really busy, doing eight or nine men a night in the car, for about a fiver each. I didn't think it was bad and enjoyed my lifestyle.'

Sally has paid dearly for her lifestyle. But she has set a target of five more years on the streets so she can get a comfortable home together for herself and her two youngest children. 'In a few years the other two can come and look for me,' she mutters quietly.

CHAPTER SEVEN

Walking the Streets, Working the Windows

Docklands and ports have traditionally been areas where prostitutes are guaranteed to find work. When Cardiff docks were at their prime, street women were known to get shipping lists and plan their work around those. It is a practice which has died with the demise of the docks in recent years.

It was pretty much standard practice for the British navy to invite prostitutes on board ship as soon as it docked in the nineteenth century. In fact, some captains ferried boats full of women out to greet their men.

As military authorities became increasingly concerned with sexually transmitted diseases, Parliament introduced a series of Contagious Diseases Prevention Acts in 1864, 1866 and 1869. The first gave control of prostitutes and regulation of brothels in 11 designated military and naval cities to the Admiralty and War Office in an effort to prevent 'contagious diseases' spreading around military and naval stations.

In those 11 cities, any woman thought to be a common prostitute by the police or an informer could be ordered by magistrates' courts to be examined at a local hospital. If she refused, she could be forcibly detained. Any person harbouring a prostitute known to have venereal disease could be fined or jailed.

A twelfth area was added to the original list by the second act. It also established a register of prostitutes from which a name could not be removed without going through a formal procedure. It legislated for regular medical inspections, and women who passed them were given a certificate indicating they were free of any contagious diseases. Infected women could be detained six months without a court hearing, which was extended to nine months by the 1869 act. Six more towns and cities were added, to bring a total of 18 areas under the acts. They were Aldershot, Canterbury, Chatham, Colchester, Dover, Gravesend, Maidstone, Plymouth and Devonport, Portsmouth, Sheerness, Shorncliffe, Southampton, Winchester, Windsor and Woolwich, and in Ireland, The Curragh, Cork and Queenstown.

To enforce the law, a special squad of plain-clothes police officers was formed, whose responsibilities included mixing with the poor with the aim of ensuring every prostitute was known to them. Blackmail and intimidation thrived and, inevitably, almost any poor, wretched and illiterate woman was branded a prostitute.

It took the Victorian reformist Josephine Butler two decades of vigorous campaigning before the acts and what she called 'state-regulated vice' were repealed in 1886. Mrs Butler (1828–1906) tirelessly crusaded to improve the rights of prostitutes. Her involvement grew after meeting some in Liverpool workhouses when her husband was principal of the city college.

Her beliefs that prostitutes were victims rather than offenders, and that making adult prostitution a criminal offence was an affront to personal freedom, were ahead of her time. Today, her campaign is carried on by a small but enthusiastic membership of the Josephine Butler Society.

MARIE

After 47 years on the game, Marie is recognized as the undisputed 'Queen of Balsall Heath' by her colleagues.

At 62 – an age when retirement looms for most people – Marie cannot envisage the day when she will finally hang up her basque and discard the leathers. Probably one of the best known prostitutes in Birmingham, she works in what many consider to be the country's most notorious red light district. Daily she dons her working gear and walks the several hundred yards from her terraced home to the local 'beat'.

Plans to retire gracefully or otherwise are not even on the agenda for this mother of five and grandmother of 11.

Marie is a common prostitute. Not every prostitute is tagged with this archaic and degrading label. All male prostitutes and some female ones are excluded. This dubious award is given only to the legions of street women who walk up and down their various beats across the United Kingdom awaiting the clients.

The women often call themselves working girls. To the courts they are common prostitutes, to police in London and Manchester they are Toms, in Birmingham they are referred to as brass, while in other areas they are known simply as tarts. It is, understandably, a term many strongly resent. 'I get really annoyed when the police and courts call me a common prostitute. It's a disgusting term. I'm a prostitute but I'm not common. I prefer to consider myself as a pavement hostess,' said Pam, a Cardiff street-walker.

No matter what laws have been introduced, prostitutes have walked the streets for thousands of years and have always been the most visible symbol of their trade.

Historically, street-walkers were considered to be at the bottom of the pecking order. That attitude remains today. In a society where women's respectability is measured by wealth and status, there is a far greater stigma attached to the low-paid street hustler than the high-class call girl.

There are three main types of street prostitutes, according to police:

1. 'Professionals' who work full-time for a living and may be controlled by a pimp.

2. Those who work to feed a habit, be it drugs or drink.

3. The others – part-timers, mums who work to feed their children or pay bills or debts, the homeless and victims of other kinds of social deprivation.

In fact, there are as many reasons why women turn to prostitution as there are prostitutes. Think of all the reasons why you and I work and the same applies to these women.

Ash-blonde Marie has, like many of her colleagues, at one time or another fitted into all three categories in her lengthy career. These days, she classes herself as a part-timer.

Work gear is dictated by clients' demands and the environment. If she is street-walking, she opts for either a red leather mini-dress and thigh-length boots or black four-inch stiletto-heeled shoes, stockings and suspenders. They are carefully positioned to show just below the dress or a black stretch skirt which barely skims her thighs. Accompanying the skirt will be a lacy, gravity-defying basque which attempts to encompass her magnificent bosom.

Apart from the usual services, the versatile ex-secretary and waitress offers other specialities including 'playing aunty', entertaining cross-dressers and transvestites (TVs), posing for men who want to take photos before having sex, water sports (the women have to urinate on the men) and bondage ('leathers a must then, lovey').

'I advertise in a few monthly contact magazines as a sexy, mature lover, 46-30-40 and get business from all over – Scotland, Ireland, Isle of Wight, even France. The first two weeks after the magazines come out are busy, but then it drops off. I do a lot of cross-dressers. They either bring their own clothes or dress in mine. I usually chat with them before they get dressed up then we have sex while they're in the gear. Sometimes they come to the house with basques and undies on under their own clothes and that seems to turn them on. They like to live out their fantasies. It's very common, you know, though they usually have normal sex. But I'll tell you something, in all the years I've been doing them – and I've had hundreds – I've never been able to fathom it out why they do it. It's a funny old world, isn't it?'

One regular TV she has is a sergeant-major in the army. 'He used to bring a case full of beautiful clothes and wigs and had £200 false breasts specially made. All I had to do was insist he was a girl and he would say

"No, I am a man" and then I'd have to insist he was a girl. We'd go on like that for 90 minutes or so and he'd give me £180 for that. I have a dildo for the TVs. But the more they want the more I charge. I also do quite a lot of photographic work. My ad in the contact mags shows me lounging on a bed with my bust exposed.'

These days, Marie mainly works weekdays either on the streets or 'off the phone' between 11 am and 3 pm. Nights and weekends are kept free to spend with her family or enjoy the occasional evening out at the local bingo hall. Despite years on the game and decades of drug and drink addiction, Marie looks a good ten years younger than her age. Her soft voice, gentle manner and clear skin, coupled with her well displayed voluptuous bust, ensure a stable of 12 regular punters – more than many prostitutes half her age could boast.

One client has visited her every week for 30 years and she admits to working hard these days to ensure they always want to come back. 'I think the one who's been coming for 30 years is in love with me. He's married and can only see me when he is on certain shifts. He started off having straight sex and now likes to be beaten, treated as a slave and peed on. You should be here when he is. You can hear me kicking him about.

'When I'm playing aunty, I'll say ever so gently, "Come and sit down next to aunty." Then I'll lift up my skirt to show my stocking tops and coax them, "Look at aunty. Shall aunty make us tea and biscuits?" as I stroke my thigh. They pretend to be little boys and will tell you about an aunt who touched them up when they were little. I don't know whether it's true. I have a tea cup specially for punters. It's kept separate and never ever used by me or my family.

'In the past I've had two clients from contact magazines who I had to write letters to. Each would pay £50 for a letter and all I had to do was tell one his school fees were due and give him a list of work to do such as lines or an essay on a place he had visited. Another I just had to write dirty letters to. Some want you to send knickers to them. I charge £5 a pair. They don't know if they're mine or not.'

Her punters are aged between 17 and 70 and many find her age an attraction, she believes. 'They all like the bust. But the younger ones probably look to me for experience while the older ones think I am more patient. The younger girls are probably wham, bang, thank you ma'am but you've got to learn to be nice to the punters. Some of the older ones are a bleeding nuisance, they can't do anything apart from rub against you. They're pathetic, but then I think most men are pathetic. Some of 'em are dirty rotten sods. In all these years not one of them has ever turned me on. Sex with them doesn't mean a thing. You don't have to be in the mood for it. In fact, I'm never in the bloody mood for it! It's not like proper sex. I clench my teeth, look at the ceiling and think of England. The less physical contact the better. I hate being touched intimately by a punter but if they pay for it you have to let them.

'In my younger days when I'd do a double with another girl, we'd be discussing what we were having for tea while the poor sod of a punter laid there. Now I appreciate that if you tell a man to hurry up he isn't going to come back and I want them to. You've got to be a con merchant to be successful in this game; be persuasive to the punters. I've never robbed a client. If he leaves his wallet here, it will still be here when he comes back. I've got a drawer full of punters' underpants from when they've left them. I always put them in the wash and leave them upstairs in case they return.

'My punters come from all walks of life. I've had a few school-teachers. One took me to Amsterdam. I think he wanted the company and to take some pictures. Like most girls, I won't do anal but if a man asks I will agree and trick them into thinking we're doing it by holding his willy against my back and say "ooh, aah". But I'm careful who I do this to otherwise some would get angry and string me up from the ceiling. If I think I've got a dodgy punter, then I'll tip a neighbour £5 to sit downstairs while I'm doing the business.'

Marie's fees start at £15 'for a quickie' and £25 for strip and sex. Though she managed by sheer willpower to break her habits, massive chunks of her earnings over the years went on financing her cocaine and alcohol addictions. 'I suppose I've been an alcoholic for as long as I can remember, all my life. I started drinking heavily when I was 35 and was well hooked by 40; brandy, whisky – beer was a chaser. I'd want a drink as soon as I got up on a morning and I've taken drugs since I was young. I sniffed coke in London but things became much worse when I moved to Birmingham. I'd easily knock back a bottle of brandy a day but when I took amphetamines as well they made me feel as if I could drink for ever. It never seemed to hit me. I've tried crack and you can keep it.'

The only child of respectable working-class Surrey parents who, Marie says, 'never went inside a court-room for so much as spitting on the pavement', she encountered her first prostitute while waitressing for 35 shillings a week at a London café. 'On a morning I used to serve these girls and wonder where they got their big, crisp £5 notes from. We got talking and they asked how much I earned and then one said, "You'd make a lovely brass" and asked me to meet them in a pub. I did and had a few drinks with them and we were all chewing tubes of Benzedrine. I felt great and we all trooped off down to Piccadilly, by Lyons' Corner House.

'There was a line of taxis and people were going up to them and being turned away. There were punters inside and one of the girls pushed me into a cab. It took me twice around St James's Park, the driver gave me a brief [condom] and I earned meself £3. I wasn't totally naive about sex as I'd lost my virginity at 14 to a boyfriend. Being a hard-faced bitch I started working from then on. I went to a "black dance" at the Paramount Dance Hall on Tottenham Court Road and met a guy. He took me to his flat and locked me in it for two weeks. The only way I was allowed out was with another woman who kept her eye on me. He told me if I went to the police he would have me put in a home – and I probably would have been in those days.

'I was with him for nine months in that flat and he pimped off me. I'd have to work three weeks and he let me stay off the week I had my period. I finally got rid of him when he went to Manchester.

'I got a flat in Bayswater Road and worked Hyde Park – ten bob against a tree, more if they wanted it lying down. I got done for indecency after being caught without my knickers on with a punter on a park bench. By the time I was 18 I got my first fine, £25, for brothel-keeping. I moved to Camden Town and became a call girl for 18 months. I was on the books of five women, among them a lady, a film director's wife and a boxer's wife. I'd ring them on a morning to find out if they had any bookings for me. The clients were amazing. One was the head of a brewing family and I'd go to the Dorchester Hotel but he'd get too pissed to do anything, crash out then go and pick up some rough birds from Piccadilly the next morning. Another was some Indian prince who I've have to sit and drink cocktails with.'

Marie fled London for Manchester after she failed to attend court for breaking a probation order. 'I knew I'd be sent to prison so I pissed off up north. I bought a two-up two-down and worked Moss Side and the streets around the Piccadilly Arcade. I got nicked a lot and did three months in Strangeways for running a brothel when I was 24. But I stayed in Manchester for 14 years and was off the game for five years when I married a cook and had two kids. I got a job in a factory but we couldn't manage on the money coming in so when my husband went off to work I'd do a bit on the side. He was so mean and when he found out what I'd been up to he hit me and burnt the money. I was 28, really depressed and one day I just got the kids, left him and came to Birmingham.

'I started doing the beat around Balsall Heath, standing on the doorstep or in the windows. I met someone. He was a pimp and I think I was brainwashed about him. I was with him five years and gave him half my money, but he did look after us. He got jailed for wounding someone and I was on my own then.'

Despite Marie's illustrious career, landing her with more than 100 convictions, a string of fines and spells in prison, she cheerfully admits she cannot see a time when she will give the game up. 'No two days are ever the same. It's a job and like other people I work for the money. I couldn't live on benefits. I've got a son unemployed and it's hard to see him go without when I know I could earn a bit of cash on the way to post a letter.

'I suppose I see about 30 punters a week. If it's sunny I might go out at 10 in the morning and stay out all day but if I'm not in the mood I might not work for weeks. The only things I don't get fed up with are my children, grandchildren and cooking. I'm really close to my kids. One's at university and she and her close friends know what I do. I've promised and promised my children I'll give up but I get fed up. I know the day will come when I will look too old,' she reflected as she donned her coat to saunter back to the beat, 'but there's always plastic surgery.'

Many street girls prefer working outdoors, as they can generally choose their working hours, view a client before agreeing to business and refuse to provide services they consider offensive. However, they have no anonymity, are more likely to be arrested, are vulnerable to violence from pimps and punters, and open to abuse from the public.

Marie and fellow street-walkers in England and Wales are prosecuted under the 1959 Street Offences Act which was born from recommendations made by the 1957 Wolfenden Committee. Section 1 (1) of the act states: 'It shall be an offence for a common prostitute to loiter or solicit in a street or public place for the purposes of prostitution.'

The estimated 30 street prostitutes who operate in Northern Ireland, mainly in Belfast city centre, have a choice of three acts by which to be prosecuted – all created well over a century ago. The 1847 Town Police Clauses Act, the 1845 Belfast Improvement Act and the 1854 Towns Improvement (Ireland) Act set down fines and jail sentences as penalties in the region.

Before the 1959 act, police in England and Wales were limited to the 1824 Vagrancy Act, Section 3, which made it an offence for a common prostitute to wander in a public place or highway and behave in a riotous manner. Though the act has little application today, it is still used occasionally. Scotland is more up to date, with male and female prostitutes being dealt with by the 1982 Civic Government Act. Because of the way data is collected by the Scottish Office, it is impossible to know exactly how many women were found guilty of soliciting. However, annual totals of women found guilty of prostitute-related offences between 1983 and 1992 range from more than 1,000 to 443. A large share of these would have been for soliciting.

A total of 234,400 crimes were committed by women in 1991 out of an overall 1,070,800. Street-walkers made up 9,565 of the total of women convicted in England and Wales. Between 1980 and 1991, the number of women convicted in the United Kingdom for soliciting and loitering has roughly trebled (see table opposite).

A major reason why the number soared in England and Wales between 1982 and 1983 was because jailing of prostitutes for soliciting was no longer permitted under the law. A change in Northern Ireland's method of keeping statistics accounts for the massive increase in the same period.

The average fine increased from £28 to £53 between 1980 and 1991. Fines are still the most common form of punishment but the going rates varied tremendously before the unit system was brought in. Apart from this scheme, there never has been and still is no Home Office policy on fine levels and it is left to each individual bench to set the amount. Official figures revealed that in a league table for fines, Teesside magistrates were bottom, with the lowest in the country outside London at an average of £14, while Luton colleagues were top at an average of £227, and some inner London courts doled out just £10 fines. Fears were expressed – and

	England & Wales		Northern Ireland
	1959 act	1824 act	
1980	3,321	15	n/a
1981	4,125	2	3
1982	5,799	5	7
1983	10,438	4	34
1984	8,595	10	44
1985	9,159	2	39
1986	9,091	7	35
1987	8,171	12	50
1988	8,829	10	53
1989	10,153	6	52
1990	10,020	4	60
1991	9,559	6	43

n/a = not available

will no doubt be voiced again now the old system is back in place – that some magistrates deliberately imposed heavy fines knowing the prostitute will be unable to pay and, in defaulting, will be jailed.

According to the Crown Prosecution Service, the average cost of bringing a defendant before a magistrates' court is £277. As one solicitor quipped: 'It would be cheaper for the police to give the girls out on the streets working £50 each and send them home!' Based on these figures, up to £2.5 million of tax-payers' money was spent bringing these women to court in 1991.

Prostitutes were one of the few groups of people to benefit overall from the unit fine system introduced in the 1991 Criminal Justice Act. Magistrates had to take into account a defendant's ability to pay and, as most prostitutes were on benefit, they were usually fined a maximum of £40, a manageable sum for many. With the ending of this system in September 1993, fines reverted to being based on what the bench of the day decides.

The jailing of prostitutes as a penalty for a third or subsequent conviction was introduced in the 1959 act and abolished in 1982. However, the practice has never really stopped, as they are still imprisoned if they default on fines. Most are sentenced to two or four weeks and serve an average of six days. The Home Office does not publish separate figures, but it is estimated that a couple of hundred prostitutes are jailed each year for fine defaults. To a woman branded a common prostitute by society, prison serves little deterrent purpose, with most viewing it as a chance for a rest rather than as a punishment.

Inspector Roger Smalley, who heads King's Cross Vice Unit, says fines fail to deter trade. In the first six weeks of 1993, they made 124 arrests for soliciting or loitering. 'The going rate at Clerkenwell court is between £20 and £25 – one trick for most of the prostitutes.'

What has become a routine practice for many prostitutes has become known as the 'revolving door' policy – prostitute arrested, prostitute fined, prostitute goes back to work to pay her fine. The same faces appear in the same courts before the same faces on the bench. Prostitutes are given time to pay their fines and everyone knows what they will have to do to pay them. But the futile exercise continues to be practised daily at magistrates' courts up and down the land.

The positive effects of such punishments are non-existent. Indeed, they might even undermine a woman's attempts to practise safe sex. If she has massive fines and the threat of jail hanging over her head, the temptation is great to accept a punter's offer of £50 extra to have 'bareback sex' (without a condom). If she does not succumb, she will have to stay out longer to see more clients in order to pay the fines.

The term 'common prostitute' seems to sum up how society treats these women. Used for centuries, the phrase serves little purpose except further to stigmatize and isolate prostitutes. Though it has no statutory definition, the women are called it by the officer who charges them, and again when they appear in court. It is also written on their criminal records. Male prostitutes are charged with 'importuning' as opposed to soliciting for the purpose of prostitution.

The courts have for years accepted that a prostitute is a woman who offers her body commonly for sexual intercourse or acts of lewdness in return for payment. It is not necessary for an act to take place before a prostitute can be arrested. 'Acts of lewdness' are acts other than intercourse which involve sexual acts between a man and a woman, such as masturbation or mutual whipping for pleasure. Since sexual intercourse is not required as proof of prostitution, a virgin can be prosecuted.

Two matters have to be proved – that a prostitute offered herself generally and that she was paid for this. Even if it can be shown that she does all these things, a woman is not prosecuted because she is a prostitute (that is not illegal), but because being a prostitute she has broken the laws as set out in the 1959 act.

Evidence needed to prove that she solicited and loitered includes that, on at least two previous occasions, the woman was seen accosting men in the streets and that she was seen to leave the area with them. Avon and Somerset Police Force guidelines say that a prostitute should be observed loitering over a 30-minute period, or officers should note three separate sightings at least ten minutes apart.

Loitering is the easier of the two offences to prove, as all that has to be proved is that she is a 'KCP', known common prostitute, and that she was seen dawdling in a red light area. The need to prove that a prostitute annoyed others, set out in various 1830 and 1840 statutes, was dropped by the 1959 act. Only Northern Ireland's aged laws still require the offence to amount to an annoyance of a resident or passers-by.

The offence of loitering for the purposes of prostitution has been repealed by a new Sexual Offences Bill currently going through Parliament in Ireland. But fresh powers have been given to the police which will allow them to order a person suspected of loitering for the purpose of prostitution to leave the street or public place. The person does not have to be seen to solicit or importune another person. The offence applies to prostitutes and clients and an offence will only be committed if the person does not comply with the officer's order.

Only 11 prostitutes have been found guilty of soliciting in Ireland over the past ten years. When the new bill becomes law, those found guilty of soliciting, whether as prostitute or punter, face three months' imprisonment and/or a maximum £1,000 fine. The previous fine was £2.

Unlike clients, prostitutes in England and Wales can be arrested immediately and convicted solely on the uncorroborated word of a single police officer. Because no proof of annoyance is needed, the law is used against the street-walker who touts for business away from residential areas.

The same offence applies in Scotland but because of the degree of corroboration needed, two officers have to observe the woman. However, it is not an arrestable offence and the woman is issued with a summons to appear in court the next day but if, as in England and Wales, officers consider she might not attend, she can be detained overnight in the local station cells.

According to English law, a woman can loiter on foot or in a slow-moving vehicle. The police officers' guidelines, *Butterworth's Police Law*, explains: 'Loitering by a common prostitute does not need to be for the purpose of her making approaches to men; it is sufficient that she loiters for the purpose of being approached by men.

'Soliciting need not be by words and can be carried out by all of the accepted forms of non-verbal communication. Movements of the body, arms, hands as well as facial expressions and gestures can be equally compelling forms of solicitation. A deaf and dumb prostitute solicited by making grunting noises accompanied by a gesture with a folded right arm being bent and straightened. Her meaning was never in doubt!'

Other forms of solicitation include tapping on house window-panes, leaning out of windows with signals to indicate price and signalling the position of the entry door with the fingers.

Butterworth advises: 'The test to be applied should be, "Is it clear to the reasonable man that he is being offered sex for money?"' No one has ever achieved a suitable definition of the 'reasonable man' but one can speculate that the law assumes it is someone who would never visit a prostitute!

Before a prostitute makes her debut court appearance, she will have been given at least two official cautions in England and Wales, three in Scotland. These were introduced at the same time as the 1959 act by the then Commissioner of the Metropolitan Police as a safeguard to prevent innocent women being arrested as prostitutes. Their other purpose was to give the women a chance to reform by putting them in touch with services which might help steer them off the game. The scheme was supported by the Home Office and adopted as common practice nationwide.

How the police apply this rule varies from force to force. Some allow prostitutes to be cautioned twice within a year before charging them, others will press charges irrespective of how long ago the two cautions were issued. More generous ones will start afresh with the cautions if a prostitute has not been dealt with for soliciting in the past year. The system is open to abuse and women have been given two official warnings in the same night, even within the same hour, by officers.

To be cautioned, two officers will have observed a woman allegedly loitering or soliciting. They inform her she has been suspected of the offence and ask her if she is willing to be put in touch with a welfare, social or probation worker.

If she is suspected a second time, the same procedure is enacted. All cautions are recorded in an official caution register kept at police stations. If she is seen a third time, an officer has the power to arrest without a warrant and charge her. One vice officer boasted that the station record for arresting a prostitute, processing her details and releasing her was 12 minutes.

Most stations within red light areas have records of prostitutes working in the area: one in the south of England keeps details of arrested women going back to the 1970s. One could argue that today's police already operate an unofficial registration system.

The women play on the system and know how to get round this. Those without family ties might receive two cautions in Wolverhampton and then move to London to work. If caught there, many give false identifications. 'Caution circuits' or 'runs' exist: for example, Leeds–Newcastle–Manchester is a known one used by northern women.

The Chief Constable of South Yorkshire, Richard Wells, considers that the prostitution laws are illogical, effective only on the margins of the trade, and admits that enforcement is riddled with discrimination. 'Bias occurs at three levels. Firstly, an individual commanding officer decides whether to give prostitution policing a high priority or not. His ruling is issued down rank to senior divisional officers who also have a voice in the degree of enforcement, and finally to the local bobby who actually patrols the area and has to decide which women to arrest.

'Does he arrest one prostitute on that patch, or all? If a sub-divisional boundary cuts through a red light area, girls on one side of the street could face regular arrests while on the other they might never be bothered. Wherever you get such freedom or discrimination, then corruptibility is an issue. Officers have in the past had sexual favours from the women who want to buy off a possible prosecution. That danger is still there.

'People have tended to turn a blind eye in the past, including the police. We could do nothing and leave matters as they are, but the present policing system is spasmodic, arbitrary and often in response to a rising crescendo of complaints.'

In most cases, the police investigate a crime after it has happened; in prostitution the perpetrator is arrested beforehand. With an average of, according to Home Office figures, one in four crimes being solved, street girls are an easy target for police officers who want to push up their figures of arrest, whether in answer to residents' complaints or to show they are doing something to 'clean the streets' of this 'evil'.

When a prostitute's case is before the bench, it is not necessary to mention the cautions. But the conduct which led to her receiving these would probably have to be described to prove that she is a common prostitute.

Hence, prostitutes are among the few, if not the only, sections of society to whom the basic tenet of British justice – innocent until proven guilty – does not apply. The prostitute is prosecuted for illegally preparing to offer a service which is legal.

In the 1984 report of the Criminal Law Revision Committee, a majority of its members called for the cautioning system in its present form to be axed after agreeing that it had not fulfilled one of its original purposes. 'Its most practical function nowadays is to ensure that when a woman goes to court for the first time, the prosecution has evidence that she has been cautioned . . . so that if she denies being a prostitute, the cautions can be put in evidence to gainsay her denial', they noted. What was introduced as a means of protection and help for the women has thus been turned into a tool for the police and courts to ensure that she is criminalized.

Prostitutes say some police abuse their powers by arresting working girls, many of whom live on or near a 'beat', as they do their shopping.

Pam, the Welsh street-walker, said that when she was arrested while queuing in a fish and chip shop she took her wrapped-up meal to court the following day as evidence! Dawn, who has worked in Bradford and Leeds, says the young constables are the worst. 'They come up and say, "We're warning you, we're nicking you tonight." Some will wait until you've done your first punter if you ask them nicely.'

Most prostitutes rarely plead not guilty, say support workers, because they know if they do it would mean the officer involved would have to go to court and afterwards would make their lives a misery. Many women also believe magistrates would never believe their word above a police officer's.

For an offence to be committed, it must be done in a public place. That has never been defined but generally the courts have accepted that a public place is one where members of the public go, whether they have a right to or not. This includes houses, particularly those used by Birmingham's notorious 'window women' – prostitutes who sit scantily clad in the large windows of the terraced houses in the city's red light area.

SAMANTHA

Samantha is one of the select band of infamous girls who 'work the windows' in Balsall Heath. The unique sight of women plying their trade afternoon and night from houses in Cheddar Road and Court Road has stirred various organizations into branding the city England's answer to Amsterdam.

In an already infamous area, these two small streets have gained a notoriety of their own. Certainly it is a brazen display, and fascinating. The bay windows are perfect frameworks for the girls to display their assets and allow plenty of space for a comfortable chair, which many girls lounge on, and space for items such as a lamp (some complete with red bulb), telephones, plants or ornaments. Because the windows adjoin the street, the women are prosecuted in exactly the same way as those who solicit on street corners. At least one window girl has been successfully prosecuted by the council on the grounds that she did not have planning permission to use her home as a business.

Of the 61 houses in the two controversial streets, only about a dozen are used by prostitutes. Most work in basques or bras and French panties coupled with stockings and suspenders. They signal their fees with their hands to passing drivers. Birmingham Council officials fear the area is fast becoming a tourist attraction for men and other sightseers who travel from across the Midlands, not to avail themselves of the services on offer but to window-shop at this unique site.

The Cheddar Road houses fill just one side of the road and face green fields as well as a recently built children's nursery and play area. While it is not the ideal place for a kiddies' playground, Cheddar Road is perfectly designed for kerb-crawlers, who can gaze at the fleshy displays on the way down and plump for one on the way back. The lay-out – with a dead-end turning circle at the end of a 200-yard stretch – also helps the police. When a crackdown is in force, officers stand behind the end house and nab drivers as they turn to travel back up the road. Excuses which pour forth strain credulity: 'I was looking for my niece. She's become a prostitute and I want to save her'; 'I'm on my way to collect a take-away'; and the most popular one, 'I'm lost'.

In the past decade, Court Road has had new homes built yards away from the notorious windows. The new residents complain about the women, the police have to react and rows blow up. The window girls are one of a number of reasons why the city council, along with Nottingham, is looking at implementing 'toleration zones'. This idea, modelled on the Dutch city of Utrecht, would entail moving the red light area to a designated zone such as an industrial estate, where prostitutes and punters could meet without fear of arrest.

But, as detailed in the final chapter, the proposal has had a mixed reaction. In the meantime, business tends to get going at about 2 pm in Balsall Heath, with the window girls proving a popular draw.

Samantha works evenings at her house in Cheddar Road and rents the room out for £60 a day to girls who do the afternoon shift. At 32, she is in her fifth year of doing the windows and her 14th on the game. Depending on how many punters she has seen, she'll stay in the window from 7 pm up to 4 am. Like some of her prostitute neighbours, she employs a sitter, in her case Margaret, an ex-prostitute, who acts as a safeguard against difficult punters.

Unlike her colleagues, Samantha prefers to wear a blouse over her skimpy underwear. 'I'll show my tits but not down below. That's just how I am, I suppose it's because I feel ashamed of what I do. Some of the other window girls show their pubic hair and just about everything else and I think it's revolting. Some of them think they're above the street girls but we're all doing the same thing,' said the divorced former factory worker.

'It's bad enough being a prostitute but you have to have some respect for the innocent residents on the road. My next-door neighbours are brilliant. They never complain about me but I make sure they have no reason to and if their kids are out playing I'll keep an eye on them from the window.'

Samantha admits to years of duping her punters. Though she sees several hundred men a year, she has sex with hardly any. Only they do not know that. 'They think they're having sex with me but it's the way I hold them.' Grabbing a plastic oblong lighter, she explains, 'Pretend this is a willy. Well, I hold it at the base and I put the palm of my hand at the tip so it bangs against that and doesn't go in me. I tell them I'm holding it to keep the Durex on. One in every 20 will realize so I'll put KY jelly on it and do the same but he'll usually just say, "Oh, that's much better".

'I do the same with oral. I put my head down and make sure my hair is covering my face so they can't see anything and slowly run my hands up and down his dick. If they ask to see me doing it, I tell them I can't perform if they watch. The only time I got caught was when the punter asked me a question and I replied! He thought it was quite funny.'

Faking has been practised for centuries, whenever women felt they could get away with it. Adroit prostitutes who recognized the money to be earned from customers eager to sample a virgin whore in the late 1880s would feign as often as possible the breaking of their hymen. Strategically hidden bags of pigeon's blood, combined with tightening the vagina by applying potions of astringent, was a popular ruse; having sex during a period was a simpler one. The price of a 'maidenhead' in a top nineteenth-century London brothel could be anything from £5 to £25.

Samantha rattles off her prices – £10 for hand relief, £15 to £20 for straight sex, £20 for oral, £25 for oral and sex or strip and sex, £30 for strip, oral and sex, and those wanting to spend 30 minutes of their time with her will have to fork out £40. But, she added: 'They're just basic rates. It basically boils down to what you can con out of him. I do black men but not Singhs [Indian men], no matter how desperate I am, as they're too rough. They grab your tits and dig into and twist them. Pakistani men seem to hate prostitutes yet they still go with us.'

If the police are in the area, she sits away from the window on the single bed in the room, which is covered by a sheet. 'Sometimes I feel embarrassed when I am sat in the window. My own home is six miles away in quite a posh area. I like to keep that part of my life separate from this. I never mix with other working girls.'

Samantha returned to the business in 1988 after a four-year break while she was married. Though she started selling sex when she was 18, she could not build up courage to go back on the streets and went into Cheddar Road instead. Many of the older prostitutes say the level of violence around 'the Heath' has scared them off the streets. 'Even though there's more business to be had out there, I feel safer indoors, particularly as Margaret is with me. I'd work on my own during the day in the house but not at night. I'll never go back on the streets, not because I look down on it but because I don't have the guts to get in a car with a guy. Here, I feel I have more control over how I operate.

'We get a lot of men who are kicksters who'll just drive up and down the road looking at us. The best punters are the walkers, as nine times out of ten they want business. A few have told me their wives know they come here but prefer it to them having an affair. Last year I was doing £200 a night but it's gone quiet, partly because of police crackdowns after some girls aged about 14 were found down here. Some evenings I might only do three men.'

Like many working girls, Samantha shaves off her pubic hairs to reduce the risk of catching 'crabs' (lice) or other infections. 'You get a lot of punters saying they will pay you more if you don't use a condom and a lot of the girls who are 'crack heads' will do it without.'

Samantha grew up in Coventry's red light area. After years of rowing 'like cat and dog' with an alcoholic mother, she left home at 18 and went to live with a friend who, unbeknown to her, was on the game. 'She had this chap round and he wanted me to join in. I looked young and he paid me £40 to get my tits out and lay there while he had sex with her. After that me and two pals decided to be prostitutes and hitch-hike to Birmingham. We told this fellow who picked us up of our plans and he gave us £10 each for a play around before dropping us off in Balsall Heath.

'That's when I started on the streets. I had nowhere to live and knew fuck all. Within weeks I'd met a Pakistani and was with him for six years but he turned out to be a right bastard. I had fallen in love with him before he started hitting me but he was a pimp – no other word for it. He would beat me just about every day. Even when it was snowing I had to go to work in a pair of sandals, armed with nothing more than £10 and some Durex. Most girls have pimps at one time or another.

'I would eat, work and sleep. He was well into smoke [cannabis] and would go out to blues clubs. If I didn't make enough money or back-chatted he'd beat me with sticks and wires.'

To escape him she moved to Kettering, where she wed a young Asian man within one month of meeting him in a café. 'I suppose I did it to get away from the other guy. I thought I was safe.' They bought a house, she got a job in a meat factory and gave up prostitution for four years. But within 12 months, he too started beating her and lashing out verbally with cruel taunts about her past. 'I left him and returned to Birmingham five years ago. Money was tight and I started working again. Like they say, once a prostitute, always a prostitute. You'll always go back to it if it's your only means of making money.'

As with many prostitutes, Samantha's baby son was taken from her by social services because of how she was earning her living. 'He's 12 now. They wanted me to sign him over for adoption but I refused. I'd never do that. I suppose then I could have given him money more than love.'

MARGARET

The 'window girls' are not a new development. They have been a part of Birmingham's red light district for several decades. All that is new is that today's women wear fewer clothes than their predecessors.

Margaret regularly did the windows during the 24 years she was on the game. Like hundreds of single mothers today, she only ever turned to prostitution when faced with big household bills or to pay for essentials for her three children. 'As I've always said, if you want a roast dinner, you know you have to peel the spuds,' she chirped in a still strong Cockney accent.

'I've raised my kids on my own, more or less, and if they needed stuff I'd go out to work. I'd do three or four days a week and worked from a room rented from a friend. If I made money, I did. If I didn't, I didn't. I might not work for a year then go back maybe to pay for a new carpet. I never claimed benefits for years, didn't know how to, until a social worker told me what I was entitled to after I'd been to court one day.

'When I did the windows, we'd wear low-neck tops and mini-skirts. Some of today's lot look disgusting, showing their hairs down below. They're just taking the piss out of the law, aren't they?

'I gave up the game seven years ago because I wouldn't do what a lot do now – and it got too dangerous and nasty.'

For the past four years she has been involved in the window trade again, albeit from a different perspective. Margaret, 52, now works evenings as a 'sitter' in Cheddar Road for her friend Samantha. Her duties are totally different from being a maid. She has no financial dealings with clients, there is no phone to answer and no time is given to social niceties such as handing out drinks. She is there primarily to give the prostitute added safety. Many women who work on their own employ sitters who are often ex-prostitutes or friends wanting to earn a bit of cash. But Samantha and Margaret leave themselves open to brothel charges, with the latter possibly having to prove that she does not offer sex.

Margaret remains out of sight of the punter. 'A client negotiates a price with Samantha. When he comes in the front door I slip into the back room and he never sees me. If he is in too long with Samantha, I'll shout through and ask if she is OK so he knows she is not on her own. If he is rowing – usually because he can't discharge [have an orgasm] – or refuses to pay, then I go in and help get rid of him. A couple of times we have had to call the police to deal with a difficult punter. Some of them think they should get bed and breakfast for their money,' she joked.

The old-timer, who went on the game at 21 after losing her factory job, has some harsh opinions on today's working girls. 'Things have changed drastically in Balsall Heath. Years ago there was a higher class of prostitute; we had moral standards and seemed to stick together. We wouldn't budge from our charges. Now some will do it for £10 – that's because of crack. Just a few women did gams [oral sex], now most do because they have to. I only ever offered straight sex. When punters asked me to do oral I used to tell them I was vegetarian or I'd say, when my mouth is a piss hole I will let you know. I was always dead straight with them. I think that's another reason why I never had any regulars.

'I never did coloured [black] men. Bengalis and Indians wouldn't wear contraceptives so we'd put a lump of surgical sponge inside and arrange with a friend to disturb you just before he came. When I brought a punter back, I'd never lie straight back on the bed as that was too intimate. I'd sit on the edge, the punter would kneel on the bed and then we'd lean back slightly.

'We wouldn't allow young girls to hang around and would call the police because we didn't want to encourage them. Now there are far too many youngsters down here. We could never be seen with a coloured fella, not even sit in a pub with one, otherwise he'd be done for living off immoral earnings. We never had any hassle with the neighbours years ago. When they walked by, we would just step inside the house.

'I was having a drink one night in a pub with four other prostitutes when a punter came in and said he wanted to have a word with one of my friends in private. She told him to say his piece in front of us and he shouted, "You've given me a disease." She turned round and said, "I've given you nothing – you bought it!" and with that we carried on drinking.

'In my day we had more respect for the police, but that's all stopped. Yet, you've got to have respect for them – no ifs, no buts. I always had big gaps between my convictions. I got a two-year suspended sentence and never worked throughout it as I knew if I was caught it would be prison.'

A few members of the 1984 Criminal Law Revision Committee were critical of using the words 'being a prostitute' as part of the criminal charge, believing the presence of the words was prejudicial and made it difficult, almost impossible, for a defendant to get a fair trial.

Sir Frederick Lawton's report noted: 'These words offend against one of the fundamental rules of our criminal law, namely that, save for good and special reasons, previous criminal conduct is irrelevant to the proof of the offence in issue.

'In their opinion, soliciting is a public nuisance offence and it is the activity of soliciting that should be penalized rather than the woman for the fact that she is a prostitute.'

While voicing sense on the one hand, Lawton went on to say that these criticisms underestimated the integrity and ability of magistrates, and few prostitutes ever challenged the allegations. 'The majority of us', wrote Lawton, 'consider that the answer to this line of criticism lies in what the present law is designed to do, namely stop prostitutes plying their trade on the streets. The fact that the alleged offender is a prostitute is what gives her the potential for making what she does a nuisance. . . .

Were the court to be denied this knowledge, its task of reaching just and fair decisions would be severely hampered.'

They also considered replacing the phrase 'being a prostitute' with the word 'persistently' before 'loitering or soliciting', but felt it would weaken the law if persistence had to be established in every case. Thus, what is deemed fair for the kerb-crawler is not for a prostitute – yet another case of double sexual and legal standards?

The committee recommended by a majority that the 'only practical way of stopping prostitutes plying their trade in the streets is by retaining the present offence under section 1(1) of the 1959 act': obviously a recommendation which has overwhelmingly failed.

Inspector Dave Dawson is one of a few police officers to state publicly that the present street prostitution laws are ineffectual and should be abolished. In their place he would like to see new public nuisance laws, by which prostitutes and punters would both be prosecuted if complaints were made, for example, by local residents or traders.

As head of Nottingham Police Force's anti-vice squad for the past two years, he admits that they have tried every possible scheme to end street prostitution – and all have failed. 'Existing laws do not allow us to control prostitution to the full satisfaction of street vice area residents. We can maintain a level of acceptability but cannot eradicate the trade.

'People who don't live in vice areas have little idea of the problems facing those who do. Therefore, there is a general lack of public support for those who do. We have tried every initiative going but it reaches a point where you can't do any more. Yet I still have to put resources into a problem which I know I can't resolve. Girls have told me that no matter how many times we arrest them, they won't stop working. I don't think the public would ever want to go back to the Draconian punishments of jailing prostitutes – so we need to look at alternatives.'

New anti-social behaviour laws are one option. 'We would not be policing sex but behaviour which would be offensive to the public in the same way as drunkenness is. Several women could work from a house or the street and that would be fine so long as they or their customers didn't disrupt other people's lives. But if they did, then they would be severely dealt with under the law. This would take the onus off the police and on to persons taking part in that activity.'

Policing prostitutes is low on Inspector Dawson's list. 'If I rank [my priorities] one to ten in importance, it comes tenth. Top of my list are paedophiles and obscene publications.

'The police are in a no-win situation over street vice. Sometimes it feels like we are going around in circles and unless changes are made, the situation will remain the same for another 30 years. We spend thousands of pounds a year policing prostitution – money which could be channelled into more serious issues.'

The city's vice trade used to flourish around its busy city station ('trains and tarts always go together', according to one old-timer) until an army base was set up outside the centre during the Second World War – and the women moved to where the trade was.

Many prostitutes lead fairly transient working lives, taking off by choice to the other end of the country because they have heard of a particular brothel where good money can be earned, or if the street scene is booming in another town. Some prostitutes describe how their pimps have on occasions kidnapped them and made them work in other parts of the country for a time.

Flexible hours are one reason why many women prefer working the streets. Some prostitute mums work in the afternoons and most red light areas quieten down between the end of the school day and mid-evening. Some women never work nights. Others get the children settled, make their tea and probably watch their favourite soaps before starting on the evening shift.

One street girl banks all the money she earns Monday to Thursday to help pay for an engineering course she wants to do, and Friday's takings are spent enjoying the weekend.

The trade is as susceptible to the laws of supply and demand as any other. It is not rare to find up to 50 prostitutes walking Birmingham's streets during a night and countless more working indoors. Competition is brisk and prostitutes are aware of those with drug habits, who will offer sex for as little as £10.

ZOE

Zoe lives in a neat terraced house owned by a 65-year-old man. Jerking her head towards a shuffling, stooped figure, she said, 'He's been hanging around prostitutes for 20 years or more. I pay my rent in kind, as often as he can get it. I couldn't get anywhere like here to stay otherwise. I try and ration it to once a week, but he takes bloody ages and I have to share his bed but he don't touch me. He's OK, good to me, cooks my meals.'

To her credit and with the help of medical and professional support workers from a local drugs scheme, Zoe has drastically reduced her drug addiction from a £1,400-a-week habit to one costing £300. She works every night, starting at 8 pm and staying out until up to 4 am, usually standing alone at her regular street corner 'patch' in Bristol's red light area of St Paul's. 'You can have a laugh with the other girls and it's more fun on the streets than inside.'

For several years, every penny she earned – up to £200 a day at one point – went on heroin. 'I've always been a smoker, never an injector. You know why so many hookers take heroin? It takes away your sexual feelings, leaves your body feeling numb so you don't have an orgasm. I've cut down and spend about £40 a day now on coke and smoke.'

Her battle to keep her bleary, drooping eyes from closing and her strangulated speech from seizing up was sustained by a can of lager as she looked back on the three years she has been hiring her body out to pay for her habit.

She proudly boasts of offering a more professional service than most street girls. The dark-haired 27-year-old says she enjoys her work, and sleeping with many of the 24 to 30 punters she sees a week. 'Guys say I switch into them and they say that's what is different about me.

'I enjoy sex with different men, always have done. I've always been a bit of a slag. It's nice if you fancy a punter and I have had orgasms with some of them but I can even get off on the repulsive ones after a while, there's almost a pleasure in it.

'A lot of the time they want to talk about their rotten sex lives with their missus. They love their wife but the sex is crap. Generally, she has her kids and won't let him have it any more and that's why they go to whores.

'I charge £20 for straight sex or I might go by how much is in the guy's pocket. I want them to feel they are giving the money for a good job and not being ripped off. I like my job very much because I can use all the skills I am best at. I am a good actress and like analysing people. Every punter is different.

'The clients I keep are those who want more of a play around and a bit of name-calling, tell me I'm a dirty whore while I call them fucking bastards for what they are doing. They often want to play totally different roles, ones they can't do with wives at home because that's not what they have built up together. I think that's why a lot of men like it with me on top. Others want to be shy boys who don't want to be touched down below while I dominate them.

'The whole idea of the game is that they touch you as little as possible while they think they are getting everything and more. I get them to tell me exactly what they want. If they want beating I use whatever's about the house as I don't have any equipment. A punter stole my vibrator and you wouldn't believe the amount of knickers I have had stolen.'

Zoe was one of the few prostitutes interviewed who admitted she occasionally offered anal sex. 'I had a go but it hurt and I wouldn't inflict pain on myself unless they paid me more than £100 to make it worth my while. They want to do things like this to demean you, that's why I don't do it so often,' she said.

Anal sex is a taboo subject among sex workers. Few admit to doing it with clients. Of 1,157 client meetings recorded by Birmingham Safe workers, only five involved anal sex. It is believed that the incidence is much higher. Research by Birmingham Safe in the late 1980s revealed that many prostitutes were more knowledgeable about HIV risks than medical students from the city's university!

Though obviously bright, Zoe left her Portsmouth school with no qualifications and spent the next couple of years hairdressing. 'I found school childish and started to rebel. I suppose if I had opened my eyes a bit I would have been cleverer.'

Her first taste of drugs came at the age of 15 when she smoked 'hash', but her life began careering off its comfortable middle-class course when she met and joined a group of travellers and set forth around the country, running the occasional second-hand market stall, before settling in Bristol.

'I'd dabbled in heroin for a few years but had always managed to escape getting hooked. I was using £20 or £30 a day and doing some illegal shop work or shop-lifting to help pay for it. But my habit got bigger and I was bored with the work. One of my friends had started on the game and within a month I could see all the money she was getting. I thought, "Sod it", and I went out.

'Drugs led me to this business. I was smoking one thing and taking another and gradually got more and more heavily involved. It's got me into all sorts of scrapes. I got paid £2,000 for smuggling drugs out of Morocco for someone, but that money soon went.'

Her parents know what their only daughter's occupation is. She told them, to avert the danger of anybody threatening or blackmailing her. 'I regret getting into drugs as heavily as I did. The way I see my future is that I have another four years at the most on the game and I want to make the most of it, become a better quality prostitute.'

CHAPTER EIGHT

Old Habits, New Threats

LIZ

'Look, see these,' as she hoists her skirt up to reveal deep holes either side of her groin set amid black panties, stockings and suspenders, 'that's where I inject.'

Two cavities the size of an adult's thumbnail were testimony of the hundreds of needles Liz has plunged into her body. A desire to lose weight led her to try 'speed' 12 years ago. In the ensuring period she lost those pounds – roughly 70 – and continues to see thousands of pounds of money disappear in the struggle to satisfy her craving for heroin, Temazepam and amphetamines.

'I don't see a future for myself. Life is just going around in circles. Last night, I did a guy aged 60 in a hotel, a man aged 40 at the flat and a car punter. I made £150, scored my drugs, paid £10 for a taxi home and by the time I'd got my cigs I was left with about £20.'

Liz's life is a vicious merry-go-round of drugs and prostitution. She works every day – she has to in order to feed her £120-a-day habit – and often stays out until 5 am to catch any trade from punters who have struck lucky at nearby casinos.

'Temazepam makes you forget what you're doing, not that you want to remember anyway, and it numbs the brain. I inject my first of the day usually before I start work as I'm quite shy but smack [heroin] makes me feel brazen, gives me confidence to approach the punters. I have worked without taking drugs but I felt dirty and hated myself for what I was doing.'

She can only go home when she knows she has money (usually six punters cover her costs) for enough drugs to see her through until her next score. Heroin, also known as H or scag, is bought in small plastic bags or wraps, costing a minimum of £10 each or £70 a gram. It can be smoked, snorted or injected and the effects – emotional numbness or a peaceful drowsiness – last several hours. Temazepam's nicknames include 'beans', 'bongo', and 'jelly' because of the jelly-like capsules in which it can be bought for as little as £1 each. They can be swallowed, heated or injected three or four at a time for a warm, relaxed feeling which can last hours. It is often used to help induce sleep after the use of stimulants. Liz injects both types of drugs at regular intervals during day and night.

Most Glasgow prostitutes work a stretch of several hundred yards in Anderston, a busy area with multinational companies based alongside hotels and casinos. Come midnight, traffic can be nose to tail. The women mainly buy their drugs from dealers who loiter around the nearby bus station. Around midnight, Liz buys and takes her second score and pockets a third which will be taken after finishing work at about 5 am. She then sleeps most of the day, until it is time to start work again.

Large cities generally command top rates for goods and services. But the rule applies in reverse with prostitution, particularly if the place has a strong drugs culture. Hence, Glasgow and Birmingham street girls will offer sex at some of the lowest prices to be found in the United Kingdom. Those who need to feed a habit costing anything up to £500 a day, more if they support a partner's addiction, know they have to raise the cash somehow and £10 from a punter is better than nothing at all.

Liz says going rates 'down the drag' (the red light area) in Anderston start at £10 for hand relief, £15 for oral, £20 for sex; £40 to £60 an hour for a hotel visit or business at her flat, and £100 to £150 for an all-night stay. Business had been good this week. She had done two 'all-nighters' and it was only Wednesday. Hotel clients tend to be English or Scottish businessmen, some wanting sex, others just company.

Drugs, in one form or another, have been around Liz from her childhood. Her father died from drink when she was five, her mother is an alcoholic, her brother died aged 27 from drugs and is buried in a pauper's grave, and her older sister, 'a speed freak', turned to the streets for funding before drugs also led her to an early death. Liz grew up in a children's home and, on leaving school at 16, became a shop assistant, not far, ironically, from where she now touts for business.

When Liz swapped speed for heroin to shed weight more quickly she had to fund her expensive diet and followed her sister's path – street-walking in London.

She worked 'the Cross' (King's Cross), where in between spending £70 a day on heroin she would pick up punters and take them to a bed and breakfast in Argyle Square. Within a year, she moved back to Glasgow and became involved with a drug dealer by whom she had two sons, now cared for by others.

Her youngest child (and only daughter), aged three, was fathered by a punter. 'He burst the Durex deliberately on me while we were doing business in the car. I always touch their private parts to check if the condom is on, but I kid on it's because I want to. I felt his hand go down and I never thought anything but he had come. He told me he had pulled it off and I was soaking. My boyfriend didn't know I was on the game and thought I was shoplifting. But he was in jail when I caught on with her and so it was obvious she wasn't his. I only did the punter that once and have never seen him since – but I'd know him straight away if I ever set eyes on him again.'

Despite the attention Glasgow has attracted for its concentrated street prostitution and drugs trade, Liz says punters still offer 'an extra fiver' for unprotected sex. 'No way. If I'm going to die it will be through drugs, not AIDS.'

Hardline prostitute pressure groups insist the 'junkie whore' is a myth. It is not. One only has to trawl the streets of Glasgow, Manchester, Birmingham and other cities to find habitual drug users who have drifted into selling sex.

Arguments have abounded in the past over which came first – prostitution or their addictions? Undoubtedly, some working girls find solace and Dutch courage in having a few drinks or taking drugs in order to cope with having sex with numerous men.

But for others, prostitution is simply the most profitable way of raising the massive amounts of cash needed – up to £2,000 a week – to feed their habits. The street is the favoured place for most because the sex is basic and turnover is quick, though not easy. Once they become embroiled in the sex trade it is difficult to break free, as one habit is intrinsically linked with the other. Social workers in Glasgow say practically every one of nearly 1,000 women who have used a city drop-in centre are injecting drug users.

Many prostitutes never touch drugs. Working girls do not have the monopoly on being addicts, just as pimps are not the sole licensees for sponging off or being violent to women. Nevertheless, because of the known overlap between drugs and prostitution, it is the habit-addicted prostitutes who are often viewed as a major source of sexually transmitted diseases or AIDS. A number of HIV prevention and research schemes were set up around the country to look at the two groups. These were the first sex worker-designated schemes, and for the first time in the United Kingdom the scale of the prostitution trade began to emerge. Research by some of these academic studies strongly supports the view that instead of scrutinizing the prostitutes, the spotlight should fall on their clients with regard to HIV transmission.

One project is worth looking at in detail, not just for the information it provides about drug-using prostitutes, but also because of the massive level of commercial sexual activity it reveals which occurred in one night in one city in the United Kingdom.

A total of 68 women were interviewed by Neil McKeganey and Marina Barnard, of Glasgow University's public health research unit, to assess HIV-related risk behaviour among street prostitutes. The two noted: 'In the minds of many people, there is a simple, though largely erroneous, belief that female prostitution is associated with the spread of HIV infection. . . . The view of prostitutes as a reservoir of HIV and other infections also resonates with the moralizing stance frequently adopted in relation to sexual matters in general and AIDS in particular. Indeed, it is arguably the case that it is this stance rather than anything approximating scientific data which underpins depictions of prostitutes *per se* as a risk activity.'

The women they questioned were aged 16 to 51 and had been on the game between two weeks and 30 years. On average, they worked five nights a week and did business with 7.1 clients a night.

Of the 68, 49 were injecting drug users. The same number had private long-term relationships of several years' standing and 32 were working to fund their partners' drug habits as well as their own. 'Contrary to popular images of prostitutes as having numerous sexual partners in their private lives, many appeared quite conservative,' said the academics.

A large number of the 49 injecting prostitutes had undergone HIV tests and, appreciating that they considered themselves at risk of infection, regularly monitored the situation. About half admitted sharing injecting equipment, mostly with partners rather than friends.

Detailed reports were received from all but two of the 68 women of their previous night's work. Oral sex topped the list as the most bought service, totalling 200 out of 405 transactions. Vaginal sex accounted for 147 exchanges and masturbation for 58.

Prostitutes across the country say oral sex is increasingly requested, possibly because the client sees it as a way of reducing risk of infection and many punters say their partners are reluctant to perform it.

The academics worked out the weekly volume of sexual services by these women, to reveal some staggering statistics. On average, 764 acts of vaginal sex, 1,040 of oral sex and 301 of masturbation, giving a total of 2,105 sex acts, were bought from just 66 prostitutes over a five-day week. 'We have estimated there may be as many as 1,050 women working the streets of Glasgow over a 12-month period. The sheer amount of commercial sex taking place may then be quite remarkable,' commented McKeganey and Barnard.

Remember – this figure of 405 is for one night in one city and a small number of women. Multiply the number of nights by 365, the number of towns and cities by a few dozen and the number of women and clients by the hundreds and we might have a vague idea of the enormous scale of the prostitution trade. Food for thought for any lawmaker, surely?

No prostitute, whether drug-using or not, will admit these days to offering or giving services 'bareback' (without a condom), as they know they face verbal and possibly physical attacks from colleagues. Most have been offered extra cash, ranging from a few pounds to a couple of hundred, to have unprotected sex.

The unit's report concluded that it was unlikely that street prostitution in Glasgow was associated with significant heterosexual transmission of HIV infection. Its authors proposed clients should be targeted for education on the risks of unsafe sex in an attempt to stop them requesting it: 'To include clients in such initiatives will require a shift in attitudes and an open acknowledgement that the women who sell sex comprise only one-half of the prostitute equation with the other half being those men who purchase sex.'

All the women interviewed insisted that working after taking drugs did not hinder their efforts to work safely. But some of the substances used, Temazepam in particular, are associated with lack of control and awareness. Anyone who has suffered a hangover appreciates how one's faculties are dulled. Prostitutes are no different. Their ability to negotiate and effect safe sex properly must diminish as their drugs intake increases.

TINA

'You're chasing the perfect stone every time you inject. You can never achieve anything like your first stoning, but that's what I pursue. All junkies do. The best stoning you can get is an overdose.'

It is a pursuit which costs Tina a minimum of £80 a day. Veins on her arms, feet, groin, even her neck – where a plastic one replaces an over-used collapsed artery – have been injected in her tireless efforts for the perfect stoning.

The Inverness paratrooper's daughter says having 'jelly' makes her feel as if she can take on Goliath. Instead, she takes on willing punters who pick her up from a street corner in Anderston, Glasgow.

Petite, with dark hair and a bright personality, Tina started on the game four years ago at 18 and has come to terms with the life in her own way. She has teamed up with Liz, and at the end of every night they pool their earnings to buy drugs. 'I don't save any money. I suppose it's an addiction to money as much as drugs. I sometimes think it would be harder to give up working than stop taking stuff. It's a wee community here. The lassies tend to stick together more in Scotland than in England, probably 'cos there's little pimping.' Saying that, she was nursing a broken nose after two jealous colleagues, who had done no business the previous night, attacked and robbed her.

Restless to leave home, Tina moved to Glasgow and stayed at a hostel for the homeless, after being told that was the quick way to getting a council house. But she met and moved in with a man who within weeks began encouraging her to work to fund his habit.

'He was a junkie, on heroin, downers, whatever was going. He beat me up, put me in hospital a few times. I was suffering from depression and the doctor prescribed Valium and Temazepam. I got hooked within four months and when he stopped prescribing them, I began snorting and injecting speed [amphetamines] and have done for the last three years.'

For Tina's first attempt at prostitution, her boyfriend escorted her to Anderston and showed her where to stand, but she could not do anything. 'I felt sick about it and when I went home, he battered the fuck out of me and said if I didn't get any cash the next night he'd bounce me off the walls.'

She managed to shake him off once she started working regularly. 'I have a lot of regulars, mostly local men. I've had a few Scottish footballers. Punters are scared of drugs so I make sure I take enough before I start work to keep me going. I'll have another fix when I'm finished.'

Tina worked on the streets of Southampton for a year. 'A police officer pulled up with three others with him in the car and said if I wanted to work here, I'd have to do them favours – sleep with them whenever they wanted.' It was enough to send her back north. She worked in a Glasgow sauna, where she was careful to hide the injecting marks and bruises on her arm. But paying the bosses £25 a punter ate into her drugs money and she returned to the streets of Anderston. Many massage parlour managers will not employ drug-injecting prostitutes and some women have been forced to strip and endure examinations by bosses to check for signs of injecting.

Glasgow, Aberdeen, Dundee and Edinburgh are the four main cities in Scotland with sizeable prostitution trades. Glasgow appears to have a much higher proportion of drug-injecting street prostitutes than other cities in the United Kingdom, noted the researchers Neil McKeganey and Marina Barnard. They estimate that 70 per cent of the city's streetwomen inject drugs, heroin, Temgesic and Temazepam being the main ones.

The lengths of desperation drug-addicted prostitutes will go to for money were brought home to me during a visit to Glasgow. An excellent drop-in centre for prostitutes, run and funded by a team of women from the city council's social work department from a side street off the 'drag', has proved well-used and highly popular.

In many parts of England and Wales, a lot of working girls were, understandably, reluctant to talk about their work. Just a few were happy to be photographed. But so desperate were the Glasgow women for any extra cash that 13 crowded into the drop-in centre, some almost begging to be interviewed for a few pounds. A couple even suggested they be photographed. 'Take my picture, I'll speak to you for a tenner,' they pleaded. Any money earned from an interview meant one less punter to see before they could score.

The Glasgow centre, which was set up in 1989, is open weekdays 7 pm to midnight. A doctor or nurse works each evening and a lawyer or welfare rights officer might also be available. Facilities include needle exchange, advice on safer sex and working practices, hot drinks, snacks and a bathroom where the women can shower and change. The staff, selected partly by the prostitutes, see an average of 40 women a night and forbid drugs on the premises.

Substances used vary regionally. Crack, a lethal cocaine derivative, is in plentiful supply around King's Cross, Balsall Heath and Bristol. 'Dealers hang around the streets and even if a girl wants to come off drugs, she is surrounded by temptation,' said a Birmingham working girl. Amphetamines and cannabis are the most used substances among Cardiff women, though the younger ones opt for Ecstasy.

In many cities, the drug dealer has become more prominent and to a degree has usurped the pimp, Bristol being an example. Outreach workers say all but a handful of the city's street prostitutes are crack addicts. In other places, the role is combined, with the pimp also being the provider of drugs. There is more money to be made from drugs than from pimping.

Crack is either smoked in a pipe or with tobacco in a joint known as a 'rock'. From 1 oz of crack (roughly the size of a golf ball), around 140 rocks can be made, selling at between £25 and £50 each. Dealers often mix the crack with other substances such as baking powder to make it go further. Across Britain, the amount of crack seized by police and Customs officers in 1992 more than doubled to 4,200 grammes – enough to make around 17,000 rocks. The effects of a rock are brief, maybe only lasting eight to ten minutes, but they are intense and prostitutes might smoke as many as 15 to 20 a day. Quite a few women support their partners' habits on top of their own. A prostitute who does not earn enough will often be given drugs on credit on the understanding that she pays off her debts the following night. It is a vicious circle.

PAM

Fridays are Pam's favourite day for working to earn a bit of cash for the weekend.

She works in one of Cardiff's two main street prostitution areas. 'I won't work in the day. I'm a bit too old and my age shows up then,' she says. 'Sex is £30 in my flat, £15 in the car and if they want the fuck beating out of them that's extra. I don't mind as it gets rid of my aggression.

'I only do straight sex, nothing else. I've tried twice to do blow jobs but it makes me feel sick. I've never had an orgasm with a punter but I've only ever had two in my life anyway. Street girls don't need to get turned on for business. Sex for us is like waving a pencil about in the Albert Hall.'

Pam, 44, chatters incessantly. Tall and slender, she shows the years of drug abuse clearly etched on what was once an attractive face. She started on drugs when she was 14 – around the time she accidentally discovered she was adopted – and has never stopped since. 'I first tried heroin when I came here. A friend was heavily into it. I had a go, liked it and injected as much as I could afford for years. I went on a methadone programme and loved that even more.

'I'd work absolutely stoned. I realized one Friday that I would die if I didn't stop soon. I did cold turkey on my own, it was hell but I got through it. I'm back on dope [cannabis] and get whiz (amphetamines) on prescription now. I won't touch E (Ecstasy), as I'm too old and if I liked it I'd want more. Drugs have kept me on the streets. I can't stand out there dead sober. I need something in me to make me feel more confident.'

Pam was adopted at birth after her natural mother became pregnant during a brief affair while her husband worked away. Unable to keep Pam, she had her adopted by a Cheshire couple. 'My adoptive father was wonderful but I didn't get on with my mother. When I found out about the adoption I screamed at her, "You are not my fucking mother," and she said, "You'll end up like her, a fucking whore."

'Not long after that we were shopping and she pointed to a delicatessen's and said, "There she is." I had shopped there every weekend for years and my natural mother had talked to and served me loads of times. My real sister worked there too and she was the double of me. I went home, took an overdose and was put in a children's psychiatric unit at a local hospital. I was there for five months and wouldn't speak to anyone.'

On leaving the hospital, Pam also left school and became involved with a group of beatniks from Rhyl. 'I'd go off for the weekend with them and smoke dope. My parents didn't care and the beatniks were kind to me.'

'I ended up penniless after clubbing in Liverpool one night and had chatted to a couple of girls who said they'd been on the streets and there was nothing to it. I was plastered and this guy pulled up and asked if I did business. He asked if I had a Durex and I didn't know what one was as I never had any sex education. Anyway, we did it and he gave me a fiver.'

She met a half-caste man at a Toxteth club she used and courted him until she became pregnant at the age of 19 and he ditched her. History was to repeat itself as Pam gave birth to a girl and handed her over to a cousin, a university lecturer, and his teacher wife. 'I was well into drugs and couldn't bring up a child. They wanted to adopt her but I refused and they are her guardians. She's 25 now. I still suffer a load of guilt and it's always depressing at birthdays and Christmas but I wanted my freedom. I suppose I was still a kid myself.'

She moved to London and got a job in a trendy Carnaby Street boutique. 'I posed in a Sunday newspaper wearing a fashionable see-through blouse with a red bus painted across my bosom and my parents went crazy and demanded I return home.'

That, with hindsight, was the worst move she made. 'I couldn't stick it, moved to a squalid bedsit in Liverpool's red light area and started on the streets. I was drinking a lot, cider mainly, and doing speed, dope and acid [LSD].'

She worked in Huddersfield and Middlesbrough before arriving in Cardiff with her vanity case and a carrier bag of clothes for a weekend stay – 22 years ago. 'I left a house and a fella and never went back. I liked it here, it reminded me of Liverpool. My pal and I got a taxi and asked the driver to drop us off at the beat. We did two punters and that paid for somewhere to stay. We worked around the docks night and day and with what I earned I'd buy heroin.'

After 24 years on the streets, Pam knows all the tricks of the trade and says she has developed a sixth sense for picking out dodgy punters –

but at a cost: 'I picked up one guy, said he was in the army, and went with him in his car. My bottom half was naked when he suddenly put something metal to my head and said he had a gun. He then gagged me, tied my feet but as he set off I threw myself out of his car. I can still picture him today. Now I never get into a car if a punter is wearing gloves or if they don't look direct at me.

'You're a psychologist, probation officer, marriage guidance counsellor. You need all these skills to be able to get yourself out of a situation if a punter is coming on heavy. If you can't talk yourself out of it, you'll end up hurt or killed.

'I'm not ashamed of what I do. If people ask, I tell them. Some of the younger guys can be a bit condescending but the older ones are more understanding. I've never given much thought to the moral aspect of my work, I suppose I've blanked that out. I've no regrets.'

From the mid-1980s it became apparent that the HIV infection posed a new and serious threat to public health. It was also noticeable that there was a lack of knowledge on the subject. Various schemes and projects were set up to tackle this, such as the Glasgow research project we have already looked at.

One of the best-structured and thriving of the practical schemes is the Birmingham Safe HIV Prevention Scheme, now in its seventh year of operation and headed by one of its original founders, Hilary Kinnell. Out of a £200,000 budget, of which two-thirds comes from Birmingham Health Authorities, all but £40,000 goes on salaries for a research officer and a team of outreach workers who specialize in the sex industry and the drugs culture. A worker also attends a magistrates' court in the city on a Monday morning, when most of the prostitutes appear for soliciting or loitering.

Safe has built up good relations with most of the street girls and many of those indoors. The latter are the hardest to target, leading as they do more isolated and discreet working lives. It is assumed that among this group, and particularly the more expensive prostitutes, safe sex and HIV awareness will be understood and practised. But very high cubicle or window rents often mean that some women are unwilling to leave the premises and miss potential clients to attend a clinic. Outreach workers say that these workers and the high-class sector of the trade are the very ones who need to be reached, as many dare not attend NHS clinics for fear of being asked what they do for a living. Similarly, many do not claim benefits because they fear their children might be taken from them if their work was discovered.

In addition to HIV infection, sex work also puts the women at greater risk of suffering syphilis, gonorrhoea, hepatitis B, scabies and thrush. Prior to projects like Safe, the health needs of prostitutes were hardly being met by the NHS. The women were suspicious, often justifiably so, of how they would be treated because of their work. Hilary Kinnell explains: 'The whole social attitude to prostitution is so unpleasant that these women feel excluded. They do not want to access services they have a right to if they believe they will be insulted. Sometimes services respond in an appalling way to prostitutes. We offer a service to a section of the community very much deprived of services or access to them. We help the women make informed choices about their health so they can minimize the damage caused to their bodies by sex work.'

The Safe team, which employs ex-prostitutes, has converted an old ambulance into a mobile drop-in centre. One evening a week they take the van around the red light area of Balsall Heath, and chat with the girls while giving out information, advice and condoms. 'Our presence is a reminder for the women to look after their health. They are flattered that someone is trying to provide a service for them. Giving out condoms breaks the ice, you have something to chat about with them. But it has still taken us years to get to this level of confidence,' said one of the outreach workers. Employing ex-prostitutes breaks down suspicion, as the working women often know and trust them, as opposed to non-prostitute women whom many view as 'do-gooders'.

As health groups and outreach workers gave condoms to brothel and street girls to use for work, some police were using the large number of condoms in a woman's possession as a reason to arrest her. The English Collective protested publicly and successfully and many forces have stopped the practice. But the presence of condoms on a woman would still be used as secondary evidence by police should she decide to plead not guilty to soliciting or loitering. 'It's a bloody farce,' said one Birmingham madam, 'the Government through its health authorities is supplying us with the tools to break the law.'

Jane Mezzone, a sociologist who works with London prostitutes, believes such policing methods have a negative effect on their health care: 'The way these women are marginalized and punished makes them difficult to access. Prostitutes are seen as a deviation away from the norm. Most women would be horrified at the thought of becoming a prostitute – it is not sexually correct and they are more disgusted about it than men. A sex trade which was not castigated would be more beneficial to punters and prostitutes from a health perspective alone.'

With the help of nuns from a local convent, Safe runs an excellent activity centre one day a week for the women. On offer are classes ranging from literacy to basic driving skills, as well as some help with household skills such as budgeting. A creche is available for the children and for many of the women it is the only time in their pressured lifestyle that they get to themselves.

There are similar schemes working around the country, though Safe is one of the largest. They were set up on an individual basis and any links with other schemes were made by the workers involved. It is lamentable that it took hysteria over the AIDS virus before the Government and health authorities were stimulated into action to provide some help to these workers. Today the schemes have all-round benefits in terms of health and personal safety, while previously unknown information on the clients and their needs has grown extensively, probably to the chagrin of some. 'Knowledge gained from working girls cannot be cast aside, they have a lot to offer,' said an outreach worker. 'They see sexual sides of people that most of us never experience, or want to.'

One wonders, when the Government or public become jaded with the topic of AIDS and its surrounding risks, as seems to be happening, how many of these projects will survive. Already some have had funding reduced or even axed. With Home Office figures showing prostitute arrests on the increase, now is the time when every town and city with a red light area ought to have a Safe project. Drop-in centres should be housed near the local 'beats', offering advice on sexual, legal and welfare matters. When it seems that every other type of criminal has support systems to help them ease back into society, the prostitute remains the ignored poor relation.

DEBBIE

'I'll do it for a tenner, don't mind admitting it. A lot of working girls say they won't – but they do. Look, if I've been stood in the rain all night, made sod all, got to pay for a taxi home and a babysitter as well and I've got the chance to make a quick £10 then of course I'm not going to turn it down.

'But if I've made money and they offer me £10, I tell them to fuck off.'

The Birmingham Safe team have been extremely supportive of Debbie. 'I use them for practical and domestic problems as well as medical matters. The good thing is, I can go to the clinic they run and know no one is looking at me thinking "you dirty bastard".'

The 28-year-old single mother has been a prostitute for two years. 'I didn't want to do it – not at this stage in my life, but I had nowhere to live, nothing to my name and the social wouldn't give me any money.'

She works part-time and fits it in around her young daughter. After taking her to school, Debbie travels across Birmingham to work afternoons on the streets of Balsall Heath. Weekend evenings usually find her travelling to Coventry or Northampton to work their beats. 'You can't make any money in Birmingham as there's too much competition and too many "crack heads" hanging around to rob you.

'I don't have regulars as I don't work set days. I might be out three days and then not go out for three weeks. Some days I might only make £40. But if I've been stuck in the house for two weeks, I quite like going out to work. I also advertise in contact mags but that can be difficult as I won't have punters in the house while my daughter is up.'

Having broken free from years of heroin addiction, Debbie turned to drink. 'I only started knocking it back heavily when I was working regularly. I think I did it because I was scared and it gives confidence to talk to the punters. I hate them but if I have a drink I make more of an effort to chat. I can do nine or ten cans of strong lager a day. I know it's become a problem and realize it's dangerous as punters will take advantage of me if I'm drunk.'

Debbie, who grew up in a quiet Welsh coastal town, traces her drugs habit back to when she became involved with a dealer. During an eight-year relationship he fathered her child. 'I left home when I was 15 as I wanted more freedom. I lived with some girls and we'd do shop-lifting to get by. I started on cannabis when I was 16. He was into heroin and I got into it.

'We'd travel to Manchester or Liverpool to buy it in bulk. Sometimes we'd almost dive into the bags of stuff. We'd pay £1,000 for an ounce but we knew we'd double our money by selling it. At my worst, I was spending £150 a day on it. Then I turned to crack and for two years whatever money I got was spent on that. That's how it goes.

'I was still shop-lifting and finally jailed for six months because of all my previous [convictions]. When I got out of Styal [prison], my boyfriend had sold our house for £40,000 and spent all but £12,000 of it on drugs. I'd had enough, left him and came to Birmingham.'

Debbie took a lodger in her new home to help make ends meet, but he was into drugs. It was not long before she fell back into old habits – and crack – and his rent was being paid in rocks. But his brutal death finally brought her to her senses. 'We went to Manchester to buy some heroin and two guys put a gun to his head and shot him. He was dead but all I could think about was that I was desperate for some crack. I went in hospital and then a rehab centre for nearly five months.

'I came out to nothing so I sent my daughter to my family and I started working. I met another guy and he suggested it. I moved in with him, not through choice but because I had nowhere else to go. The first night he took me down to the beat and I can remember him looking at me, smirking as if to say, "I've got you." I hid behind a tree for a while but I eventually made £90 that night. I gave him a lot of my money but since I left him the pressure to go out every day has gone. When girls haven't got a man a lot lose enthusiasm to work regularly.'

Debbie says she is getting her life together now, having moved with her daughter to a council house away from Birmingham's red light area. She has no set working pattern, going out when bills need to be paid or if she fancies a night out.

Last summer was spent in Bournemouth, where she worked the genteel town's beat for several months. 'It didn't look like a beat as the streets were tree-lined and not rough. The clients were different too, mainly elderly, and paid well – £30 on the street or £60 if we went to a room.

'I did a spell in a brothel in Torquay, a converted barn. It was long hours and I made money but I had to give a fair bit to the owner. I prefer street work. Northampton's not bad but Coventry is only slightly better than Balsall Heath.'

With ten convictions to her name, Debbie says she would work in a toleration zone if she thought it was safe and she would not be arrested. Like many working girls, she has had a narrow escape with a vicious punter. After picking her up in Balsall Heath, he drove to his house in another suburb. 'We'd agreed on £40 but when we got there he gave me a glass of whisky and said he only had £10 and wanted me to stay an hour. I got annoyed and he hit me across my face.

'After that I don't know what happened, even to this day I can't remember a thing. The police found me the next morning unconscious with black eyes and marks on my legs on a grass verge next to the A45 to Coventry.'

KAREN

It was prostitution or shoplifting. Karen was sick of being jailed for her copious theft convictions, so she decided on selling sex 'down the drag' in Glasgow.

She spends a minimum of £150 a day on drugs, usually 'smack' or methadone, bought from her regular woman dealer at the bus station.

The 29-year-old, quietly-spoken blonde explained: 'I got fed up being inside. One year, I did three spells in jail with just a few days in between. I dried out each time I was inside but started again as soon as I came out. At least prostitution keeps me free so long as I pay my fines – and I try to.'

An addict since 1983, she was introduced to drugs by her then boyfriend. 'I snorted some smack to see what the big deal was. I didn't take anything for another six months and then I just got into the scene.'

Karen does most of her business in punters' vehicles or their premises, down a lane or against a wall for those on foot. 'I know it's risky, but I always tell another lassie where I'm off to.'

She worked until she was seven months pregnant and still injected drugs. 'My baby was taken off me as I'd injected into the veins of my stomach when it was big. I've injected everywhere.

'A question I ask myself – and can't answer – is why I go back on the drugs. It's a craving for a hit. Most nights I don't have a bean left. I'll stand outside until I know I have enough for my drugs. There's been times when I've been freezing, but I know I have to stay there. I'm usually out until 3 am and see about six punters. If I've only made £80 then I'll buy drugs for that amount and try to make them last.

'I can't see any future for me unless I break my habit. But if I don't take anything, I don't know what to do with my life. It's become so that it is more of a habit having a habit.'

CHAPTER NINE

The Bright Red Lights

King's Cross is perhaps the country's best-known and possibly seediest red light area. A total of six sergeants and 25 uniformed constables make up the vice squad, patrolling a square mile of busy streets where they estimate a maximum of 100 women aged between 20 and 38 work and 100 drug dealers peddle. Along one wall of the unit's base is the 'frequenters' board', where mug shots and details of 45 of their most regular female clients look down.

The vice business around the north London district is unique in several respects, says Inspector Roger Smalley, who heads the unit. The three mainline stations, six underground lines and 50 bus routes which converge on the area draft in hundreds of potential customers every hour.

'The trade operates 24 hours a day, 365 days a year. Depending on the time of day, there's between 20 and 30 girls working the streets. Some are out early to catch the commuters,' says Smalley.

'A lot are single parents, a lot are druggies. Some are running drugs between punters and dealers. Not many have pimps but it is difficult to distinguish between them and the dealers.'

Going rates for straight sex are the same as the average fine at the local Clerkenwell Magistrates' Court – between £20 and £25. Oral sex is high on the list of punters' requests, says Smalley, with nearby yards off run-down streets being the favourite haunts for the action to take place.

There is a clear division between those selling sex to pay for their drug habit and those who do it purely for the money, added Inspector Smalley: 'The drug users stay out a long time. Many need up to £200 a day to feed their habit, usually crack, heroin or cocaine.'

Mayfair, home to some of London's most aristocratic and wealthy families, is one of the few areas in the country where well-dressed prostitutes solicit pedestrian men for sex from their cars – kerb-crawling in reverse. The area tends to have a more attractive, higher-class prostitute, who can earn £300 or more for a couple of hours with a rich resident or tourist staying at one of the nearby five-star hotels, according to police.

Mayfair street-walkers are usually arrested every day and are fined an average of £25 by the courts, said Inspector Richard Powell, of Charing Cross Eight Area Vice Unit. 'They [the fines] prove to be of little deterrent value and certainly do not dissuade them from continuing with this way of life. In fact, many look on it as an unofficial form of taxation,' he said. Women who work in Mayfair and dabble in drugs favour heroin, if anything.

A lot of 'Awayday' prostitutes – women who travel from their home town to London for the day or during the week – work around Mayfair. The areas in front of and behind the Hilton Hotel are known popular spots. Some women will tout for business around nearby streets, with rates starting from £50, and take a client back to a room or flat they have rented. One former Hilton employee said some prostitutes were known to tout for business along the corridors of the famous hotel.

While most major British towns and cities have a single area where prostitution is practised, London has seven, according to the Metro-politan Police, ranging from up-market Mayfair to the zone branded by many involved in prostitution as 'the lowest of the low' – King's Cross. The others are in Paddington, Bethnal Green and the Commercial Road area of East London, Tooting and Streatham, Stamford Hill and Stoke Newington and the most famous of all – Soho. In reality, sex for sale exists in every borough of the capital.

The Metropolitan Police formed the Vice and Clubs Squad in the 1930s in response to what was seen as a growth in organized prostitution. It now employs nearly 80 officers in several permanent vice squads to deal with the capital's sex trade. Temporary units are occasionally set up if an area is to be purged.

Eight Area Clubs and Vice Unit is staffed by one inspector, three sergeants and 20 constables who deal with street prostitution and brothels in Westminster, where three of the seven red light areas are situated. More than two-thirds of the street prostitutes arrested in London in 1991 were from the borough – 3,045 from a total of 4,475.

Eight Area is one of the country's largest designated vice squads and is based in the station at Charing Cross. Organized brothels and pimping, rent boy rackets, juvenile prostitutes, sex bookshops, strip clubs and the clip joints all come under their umbrella.

Officers in the 'Tom Squad' are responsible for policing street prostitution across the borough. Apart from dealing with the traditional prostitutes who tout around the city, they also have to police the country's best-known sex district.

Soho, along with the West and East Ends of London, has been linked with sex for more than 200 years. Today it is trading on past glories, its reputation as the sinful square mile of the capital established in the 1950s and 1960s. Sexy Soho is now another myth. True, it has the famous Raymond's Revue Bar, peep-shows and sex shops, but the very commodity it boasts plentiful supplies of – sex – is in reality exceedingly thin on the ground.

The 20-plus female and the handful of transvestite prostitutes who dawdle, often in pairs, around the streets from 10 am onwards are regularly arrested by Eight Area Vice Squad for soliciting. Yet few ever have sex with the punters, preferring to 'clip' them instead.

Clipping is street parlance for fleecing and is performed on the streets and in the sex clubs in different ways, but with the same result – filching the would-be punter. A woman who dawdles along Soho's narrow streets approaches or is approached by a possible client and makes arrangements for sex. She gets her fee from him supposedly for a deposit on a hotel room, about £20, but this can vary greatly depending on how much she reckons can be wheedled out of him. She arranges to meet him at a named spot at a set time, after she has booked a hotel room. Not surprisingly, the woman disappears from the scene and the would-be punter has seen the last of her and his money.

Sergeant Richard Watling, of the Eight Area Vice Unit, expands on some of the ploys the clippers use: 'Occasionally punters are known to return to Soho and another prostitute offers to search for the original girl for a few pounds. They too, not surprisingly, do a runner.

'If the original one is spotted, she will just tell him that she was at the room but the time ran out. These women are very good at their job and will gauge how wealthy they think the guys are before settling on a price.'

Although these women do not have sex with punters, they are still prosecuted under the 1959 act, as the police deem them to be loitering for the purpose of selling sex. 'I don't know any of the street girls who do sex. Quite a few get offended if you call them prostitutes and prefer to be known as clips,' said Sergeant Watling, 'whereas the genuine prostitutes who work nearby say the clips give them a bad name.'

But a far more menacing method of clipping is experienced in the supposed sex clubs, where sightseers are lured in by garish adverts boasting exotic dancers, strippers and sex shows. In reality, few offer anything better than a soft drink served by tired-looking women in tatty cellars, and a fleecing.

Japanese men are favourite targets for clipping, as they have a reputation for being wealthy and clean; Americans are next, and non-London tourists are third on the hit list. The known record amount 'clipped' from one Japanese man by a club is £900, but it is believed a few tourists have lost several thousands of pounds by this scam.

Following Westminster City Council's efforts to clean up the area in the 1980s, it restricted the number of licensed sex shops and clubs. But the 25 'clip' clubs, nicknamed 'near beers' within the trade for no known reason, know how to play the laws. For example, there are no restrictions on drink prices and the clip clubs exploit this to a ridiculous level. The luckless punter invariably ends up with no sex, no sex show and no money – after stumping up extortionate prices for soft drinks, often with assistance from well-built 'security guards'.

The clubs are on the margins of prostitution. Though many boast of offering sex shows and saucy dancers, few have an entertainments licence and even fewer have a drinks licence. Because they sell non-alcoholic drinks they are not subject to licensing regulations and this greatly reduces police powers.

Women are often placed at the doorways of these establishments to entice customers in with hints that something or someone sensual awaits them inside if they pay a few pounds' entrance fee. The door girls are paid a percentage of the night's takings or a fixed daily rate. Occasionally they are charged with obstructing the highway by stopping passers-by.

A visit to one of the supposed 'better' clip clubs took me to a reasonably sized basement where patches of black and red paint peeled off the walls. Six chipboard tables covered with thin paper tablecloths were empty. On a 'stage' – a slightly raised section at one end of the room – stood a camp bed which had seen better days and plenty of use at some time judging by the sagging, paper-thin mattress. 'We don't dance or nuthin', just do a few exotic poses while the client enjoys a drink and a chat with one of our beautiful girls,' explained the blowsy manageress.

Two attractive foreign women, both no older than 20, lazed about clad in skimpy outfits while the manageress brazenly attempted to defend the club's prices, far more expensive than many of the city's five-star hotels.

After paying a £5 entrance fee, a punter is shown to a table and approached by one of the hostesses, who asks him if he would like her to sit and chat with him. Unaware that he is paying for this pleasure, he will be encouraged to buy her a drink from the menu. He appears to have quite a choice, starting with lager, beer and soft drinks at £4 a half or £8 a pint. House wine is £10 a glass or £45 a bottle, while those wanting to splash out on champagne, usually fizzy grape juice, will pay £15 a glass or £95 a bottle.

For those with exotic tastes, a range of cocktails including a Lolita or Harmony is available priced £12 to £55. While the choice appears ample, they are in reality all the same mixtures of fruit juice and soft drinks, the only difference being the price. One clip club manager told a vice officer that from an 80p bottle of Tizer, he could make up to £2,000, the cocktails being no more than a mixture of that and fruit juice. Ribena and water are another commonly used combination.

Extras on top of drinks include a hostess fee of £25 and a 27.5 per cent service charge. At the very bottom of the clip club's drinks list, it states: 'All drinks are de-alcoholized by law'.

Shows are rarely performed and trouble often erupts when the punters are presented with the bill. Amounts of £200 to £300 are common. It is not unknown for 'security' men to escort stunned customers to cash machines or bureaux de change to pay the bill. This is the club that charged a Japanese tourist £900 for three soft drinks. Though he reported it to the police, there was little they could do as he was flying home within days and a prosecution would have been difficult and expensive to bring. This is a common stumbling block for the police – and the clip clubs know that.

'It is a problem we face all the time. The people who own and manage these clubs have got it down to a fine art. If someone does not pay a bill, the heavies are brought out. If it is reported to us, they just shift the men to another club or keep out of sight for a while,' said Sergeant Watling.

The set-up is totally legal, unless violence is used by club staff on a customer if he refuses to pay the bill. The police have prosecuted for assault and demanding money with menaces.

One of the clubs at the bottom end of the range in Soho is little more than a dingy cellar, with two cheap sofas beside a coffee table. At the top of the stairs leading down to the room is a neon-lit sign advertising striptease acts. Just inside the entrance, nearly hidden by a door, is a sheet of A4 paper curling at the corners. It is easy – but expensive – for customers to pass by without giving it a second glance. It states: 'Seated covers with a hostess warrants a hostess fee of £120. Acceptance to buy a drink for the hostess is done with the understanding that the customer is going to pay.'

Customers are also faced with a 30 per cent service charge on non-alcoholic drinks costing up to £90. At the very bottom of the drinks list, it states: 'This is not a sex establishment'.

Last year, a hostess from this club was jailed for nine months for blackmail after charging a Turkish airline pilot £265 for nothing more than a chat and a soft drink.

The women who work at these clubs are nearly always young and foreign and earn a percentage of every drink they can encourage the gullible customer to buy. Often a notice states that a minimum charge has to be paid and this allows the customer to have three drinks of his or her choice.

Former prostitutes who have worked as clip hostesses said it was up to them if they wanted to have sex with a punter. Club bosses were only bothered about getting customers to buy the drinks.

Nevertheless, sex is a thriving business for some Soho people – but increasingly at the expense of ordinary tradespeople, who cannot afford the £1,500 weekly rent demanded by some of the area's property owners.

The area is valuable in retail terms. One of the biggest landlords is the multimillionaire soft porn publisher Paul Raymond, who owns at least 100 Soho freeholds and is one of the country's richest men.

As many established traders have had to shut up shop in the area over the past few years, unable to meet rents of £60,000-plus a year, space has been made for the vice merchants who can afford to move in.

Peep-shows which break the law are raided regularly by Eight Area officers. Under the law, the women – for whom viewers pay £1 for a few seconds to peer at them through a hole – have to be clothed and cannot move in time to music. If they dance or strip, they would need licences, or risk breaking the law.

Police know most peep-shows break the law and as soon as they shut a place down it reopens within days with new people fronting the business. 'These people know when they have stepped over the line and usually just take the day off before starting up again,' said one vice officer.

The nickname 'near beers' could become official terminology this year if, as expected, a bill currently going through Parliament is passed. The London Local Authorities (No. 2) bill has a specific section to deal with 'near beer licensing' and could signal an end to the present dubious operations of the clubs.

A host of strict conditions could be imposed on a licensee, including restrictions on hostess fees and drinks prices. Failure to meet them would lead to the near beer licence being withdrawn and the closure of the premises.

The third region which Eight Area polices is Paddington. 'This is mainly frequented by women who could be described as being from the "bottom end" of the market. King's Cross is the next rung down. Business is normally performed in clients' cars, nearby garages or even gardens. Payment tends to range from £20 to £30 for full sex,' said a vice officer.

'The women frequently run up large amounts in unpaid fines which inevitably leads to their imprisonment. Some are quite openly working the streets while suffering from AIDS, HIV, hepatitis and other sexually transmitted diseases.' The officer did not say what proof he had of this. There is an estimated regular core of 150 women who work the three beats. Although a number had worked regular patches for ten years or more, most are transient and aged between their late teens and late 30s. 'Each of the three areas attract a distinctly different type of prostitute. It would be rare to find these girls moving about the different areas within Westminster,' commented the vice officer.

Apart from Soho, where business is ongoing throughout the day, most soliciting gets under way from around 10 pm and continues through the night. Prostitutes have been arrested while working at 9 am. Up to 15 are arrested on average every night by the 'Tom Squad'. Force guidelines suggest uniforms are worn, but they always work in plain clothes as uniforms hinder their evidence-gathering observation duties, they say. Teams of ten constables, headed by a sergeant, usually patrol in pairs in unmarked cars, vans or on foot. 'We watch a prostitute from a vehicle or, if on foot, from a vantage point until we have enough evidence to arrest her. All we have got to establish is that she is there for prostitution, she doesn't have to approach a car.

'It depends on a prostitute's record as to whether we keep her in the cells overnight. A fair amount of them immediately go back to work once released and that puts us in the position of deciding whether to take her in again or look for one who hasn't been arrested. I feel it is more worthwhile to do the latter,' said a vice officer.

CHAPTER TEN

Their Bodies, Whose Business?

Prostitution is a hot potato for politicians. Many dare not become involved in campaigning for legal changes for fear of being branded the 'hookers' MP' or in case they are tainted with the 'guilt by association' theory. Unless the subject becomes fashionable or gains public support, as with green issues, we can expect little change, as there are few votes to be gained by it.

An interesting illustration of MPs' reluctance even to discuss the subject was experienced during research for this book. Letters requesting interviews on the subject of prostitution and their opinions of the laws were sent to the Home Secretary, the Rt Hon. Michael Howard, the Shadow Home Secretary, Tony Blair, and the Liberal Democrats' Home Affairs spokesman, Robert MacLennan.

The latter replied first with an apologetic note, saying he was booked up and could see no opportunity to meet for several months. Mr Howard also turned down the request and went on to add that the junior minister responsible for this area of the law was also unavailable. However, I submitted a list of questions on the Government's position, to which the Home Office duly replied, and these are set out below. As you will see, for a Government which has repeatedly supported deregulation on every aspect of our lives from industry to care in the community, the Conservative Party is mightily unwilling to relax the rules on prostitution.

QUESTIONS BY THE AUTHOR TO THE HOME OFFICE ON THE LAWS OF PROSTITUTION

Q. 1. Why can two consenting adults not buy/sell sexual services without breaking the law? I know the Government argues about 'public nuisance', but the law arguably goes much further and takes a moral stance. Should it?

A. A woman can work as a prostitute without breaking the law, just as a man can use the services of a prostitute without breaking the law. The aim of the law is to prevent serious nuisance to the public caused when prostitutes ply their trade in the streets; to discourage women from becoming prostitutes; and to penalize pimps, brothel-keepers and others who seek to encourage, control or exploit the prostitution of others' bodies for financial gain. The Government believes it is right that the law provides such protection for both the general public and to prostitutes. As for the central moral question which you pose, it is fair to say that the *criminal* law has always concerned itself with the nuisance that may arise from prostitution, rather than the activity itself.

Q. 2. Why, when the Criminal Law Revision Committee's 1984 and 1985 reports said the term 'common prostitute' was pejorative, do the Government and courts still use it? Are there any plans to dispose of it?

A. The term 'common prostitute' appears in existing legislation and is, therefore, still applicable. Whilst noting the CLRC's comment that the term might be considered pejorative, the Government has no present plans to amend the law specifically to meet that concern.

Q. 3. Have you any plans to get rid of the caution system? Comments on its value would be welcome.

A. The Government has no present plans to change the law in this area. The cautioning system was considered by the CLRC and you will see from its 16th report that this is a difficult area in which there is no real consensus of opinion.

Q. 4. Considering prostitution itself is legal, how can the Government justify outlawing all forms of practising it? I have in mind women who work discreetly indoors, either at home or in massage parlours.

A. See answer to 1 above.

Q. 5. There is a growing band of opinion that the brothel laws prevent women working safely and off the streets – something the Government and courts want to see. Many believe two prostitutes should be able to work together free from prosecution. I would appreciate comments on this.

Are there any moves to change the laws as set out in the 1956 Sexual Offences Act?

A. The argument that the law should be relaxed in this area and that brothels should be legalized was considered by the CLRC but rejected. It considered that legalizing brothels would be likely to increase their numbers, increase the demand for the services of prostitutes and attract more girls into prostitution. The Government has made it clear that it agrees with the committee's conclusions and it has no plans to relax the laws in this area.

Q. 6. How does the Government justify accepting prostitution as a legal trade for tax purposes on the one hand and then on the other criminalize the practitioners for carrying out such work?

A. The law does not make prostitution a criminal offence.

Q. 7. Critics say the kerb-crawling laws are unfair compared to the female prostitution laws because it has to be proved that a man 'persistently' solicited a prostitute. In reality few have to, and so are safe from prosecution. Police and residents of red light areas say the men are often more of a nuisance than the prostitutes, yet vice squads openly admit that they target the women as it is easier. What is the Government's opinion of the 1985 act and is it considering any future changes?

A. The CLRC, in its 1984 report, recommended that kerb-crawling by clients should be made a criminal offence. This was made a specific offence for the first time by the Sexual Offences Act 1985, and the Government is keen to tighten the law further in this area, by removing the present need to prove persistence (or nuisance or annoyance) on the part of the kerb-crawler. A Private Members' Bill to achieve just that was introduced with full Government support in 1990. Unfortunately a small group of MPs deliberately prolonged the debate beyond the point where the measure could reach the statute book. The Government has since made a commitment to re-introduce the measure as soon as a suitable legislative vehicle can be found.

Q. 8. Men who use brothels to buy sex do not commit any offence, yet the people who sell it to them do. Again, this strikes one as discriminatory. Why is this? Would it not be better to scrap the brothel laws?

A. The law in this area seeks to penalize those who seek to encourage, control or exploit the prostitution of others' bodies for financial gain. The Government agrees with the conclusion reached by the CLRC on the point you raise. [It states that the majority of this committee was not in favour of extending liability to the client. 'The person primarily responsible is the person keeping the brothel and if such person is convicted the brothel will usually be closed down. Involving the client . . . will not help the process of closing down.'] The Government has no plans to legalize brothels.

Q. 9. From my research, it seems that many women become involved in prostitution while at a young age, with children in care seeming particularly vulnerable. Would the Government consider putting more funds into preventing females becoming involved in prostitution in the first place and helping them exit it, should they wish to? With many schemes in place to help much more serious ex-offenders, there are only odd ones dotted around the country for prostitutes.

A. The Government provides funds to enable voluntary sector organizations to work in partnership with the Probation Service in tackling offending behaviour. The Government's policy is to devolve the majority of funding decisions to local probation services, to meet local needs and priorities.

Q. 10. The 17th CLRC report made recommendations about changing the 1956 act to make it easier to penalize pimps and women who exploit prostitutes. Nothing has been done on this – why, and are there any future plans to do so?

A. The Government considers that, with one exception (see Q. 7), the law works reasonably well in this area. It has no present plans to change the law.

Q. 11. A separate set of laws for prostitution stigmatizes an already stigmatized group, say many people. Why cannot they and their clients be prosecuted under, for example, the public order acts for nuisance, etc.?

A. Whilst it is possible to bring charges against prostitutes under the Public Order Act 1986, current legislation in this area deals effectively with a wide variety of specific nuisances associated with prostitution. The Government, therefore, has no plans to change the law in the way you support.

Q. 12. Recent calls for changes in the laws have centred on three main arguments – legalization, decriminalization, and the setting up of toleration zones. What is the Home Office's views on these?

A. The establishment of toleration zones would effectively mean disapplying the criminal law in a particular area. The Government has no plans to legalize the activities surrounding prostitution, either as a matter of general application or in specific geographical areas.

Historically, prostitution has been viewed as a 'women's issue'. That attitude appears to be with us today, at least within the Labour Party. Tony Blair, a barrister, was unavailable for interview, but suggested I contact Dr Marjorie Mowlam, the party's appointed spokesperson on women's issues. Mr Blair apparently sees prostitution as a female problem. Dr Mowlam agreed that prostitution was a very important issue and the legislation needed to be looked at. She then went on to admit that she was unfamiliar with details of the laws and the subject failed to rate a mention in the party's manifesto. Further requests for an interview with Mr Blair were rejected and when I emphasized that I wished to interview him as both Shadow Home Secretary and a barrister, one of his office staff declared: 'He actually specialized in commercial law.'

I tell this sorry tale of both Government and Opposition response as a way of highlighting the attitudes of the country's most senior law- and policymakers. But such a view is one apparently afflicting the vast majority of our elected Members of Parliament. A backbench MP who is a member of the All Party House of Commons Inquiry into Prostitution revealed Westminster colleagues' crass and out-dated response to the group: 'We get a fair amount of flak. Crude jokes along the lines of a nudge and a wink and comments like, "Where's your next fact-finding mission – Amsterdam?"

'MPs want to be loved, don't mind being hated but cannot bear to be ridiculed. Many are frightened to get involved with an issue like prostitution, because it makes you a figure of ridicule, and they like to steer clear of controversy. To some, it almost implies that you have a fascination with prostitutes.

'And then there is what we call the "moral majority" who write to us and say any solution you propose will encourage prostitution. We have even been labelled as sex perverts.'

The All Party Inquiry is the first of its kind on the subject and is headed by the Labour MP Diane Abbott. It has heard evidence from prostitutes, interested parties and residents and aims to put forward proposals for legislative change in this year's Parliamentary session.

It faces a long-drawn-out battle.

It has been ingrained in us over centuries that prostitutes are bad women and prostitution is an evil business. Why is this?

The stigma which envelops these women has always existed, yet rays of public sympathy and understanding have been glimpsed in recent times. Unfortunately, none seems to have shone on those who create and administer the laws.

Breaking down the stigma will take years, partly due to the vicious circle in which the working women are caught up. Very few prostitutes dare speak publicly for fear of reprisals such as having their children taken into care, benefits being stopped or police harassment. This allows for the myths and stereotypes – the dirty slag or nymphomaniac call girl – which have grown over centuries to flourish unchallenged. Often the only time prostitutes are given a voice is if they 'kiss and tell' in the tabloids or when the occasional celebrity hooker goes public.

Consequently, people are rarely allowed to peek through the veil of mystery cloaking prostitution to see for themselves that the women who practise the trade really are as normal as you and I.

Pat, a Birmingham sauna manageress, says people incorrectly presume that every man who visits a prostitute wants only sex. Some, as you will have read, pay for services and acts which their partners won't perform or they are too embarrassed to ask their partners to perform. Others might not have a partner.

Prostitution offers pleasure for men and work for women. While its practitioners might offend against the moral code, prostitution is not evil and it is not the Government's job to enforce what is regarded as morally correct behaviour. Until the demand for sexual services for money ceases, the trade will continue to thrive. As the Bishop of Liverpool, the Rt Reverend David Sheppard, pointed out when commenting about the Mothers' Union debate on legalized brothels: 'Sin and crime are not the same: considering changing the law would not mean condoning the sale of a person's body.'

Why should women be shamed and criminalized for doing what they have to do to survive – as well as performing a necessary and obviously greatly demanded service? When the two bodies involved willingly and jointly construct and enter into an agreement for sexual services and fees, why must the law interfere?

Though much of the present legislation was made only 40 years ago, a proportion of it was based on nineteenth-century laws and appears to have more in common with Victorian attitudes than those of a society nearing the twenty-first century. The sex laws encase prostitutes and prostitution in a time warp.

So just how far between the bedsheets should the law lords, politicians and police officers be allowed to clamber? Over the past 20 years, campaigns for changes in the sex laws have become more frequent, and though nothing positive has been forthcoming from Parliament, each lobby hopefully chips away at the public's general ignorance of the subject and the laws.

People are always eager to read about prostitutes, particularly if they are caught with a celebrity punter. However, only those who live in red light areas, along with the practitioners and police, have some understanding and appreciate the effects of the vice laws. Most of the calls for legal change centre around three main options: legalization, toleration zones and decriminalization. There is no clear-cut solution to this controversial subject. Most interested parties agree 'something should be done', but contemporary solutions seem to throw up as many problems as they attempt to resolve.

LEGALIZATION

Everyone bar the prostitute benefits under this legal umbrella, which has always found favour with the establishment.

Legalization would entail making all the current illegal working practices – soliciting, brothel-keeping and the like – legal. Because it would no longer be a crime, neither of the parties would be at risk of prosecution. Shame and ridicule would no longer be attached to the buyers and sellers of sex. Welfare, health and economic agencies would be on hard should a woman want to exit the trade. Financially, the state would benefit from revenue from the brothels, tax from the women and massive reductions in police and court costs.

Tax is already a controversial issue for prostitutes and in many ways is symbolic of the hypocrisy surrounding the business. On the one Government departmental hand (the Treasury) prostitutes' work is recognized for tax purposes, while on the other departmental hand (the Home Office) they are criminalized and further penalized financially by court fines for practising it. Of 9,559 women found guilty of soliciting or loitering in 1991 in England and Wales, 8,533 were fined an average of £53. Many working girls consider fines as an unofficial form of taxation.

It is a crime for a man to live off a prostitute's wages, described as 'immoral earnings'. But at what point in the prostitute's working life does this money change from being taxable income to corrupt cash? The Inland Revenue states that since a prostitute provides services for reward, her activities can properly be described as trade: 'Prostitution is not itself illegal. But the law is that profits or gains from activities which amount to the carrying on of a trade or profession are taxable, even though the activities may be unlawful. Earnings of prostitutes whose activities constitute a trade are taxed in the same way as those of any other person carrying on a trade.'

After seeing Lindi St Clair speaking on TV of her high earnings, tax investigators examined her brothel business and decided she owed £58,000 in lost tax and accrued interest. She and Leeds madam Sheila 'Goldie' Ford, who was said to owe £42,000 tax for massage and 'personal services', have both been declared bankrupt by the courts. Prostitutes known to be working can have their benefits stopped and are liable for income tax on all monies earned from sexual services. With so few women keeping records of their earnings, the Inland Revenue could estimate a prostitute's taxable earnings on her looks, age and number of years on the game.

Critics say women should not be taxed without having civil rights. They point to Germany, where prostitutes working in carefully monitored areas, such as Hamburg's Reeperbahn, are taxed at above the average rate of 56 per cent, yet the Government does not offer them any form of social security.

But there are advantages to legalization, argue supporters, who claim that state-controlled brothels would remove prostitution from the streets. The women would work in more comfortable surroundings and regular check-ups would improve their health care and keep diseases under control.

They would also be better protected from violent clients, exploitation, police abuse and pimping. The Chief Constable of South Yorkshire, Richard Wells, an advocate of legalization, says one of society's responsibilities is to control any commodity which has an element of danger in it.

'It is wrong that the legalization argument has become a police issue alone. There are too many vested interests – legitimate and illicit – for it to be a matter just for us. Wherever prostitution thrives, lurking close by is intimidation and the potential for financial gain,' he says.

'Sex for sale is permissible between individuals but, like alcohol and tobacco, it is open to exploitation. Just as there are restrictions on how and where the two latter products are sold, there ought to be places where sex can be bought under licence.'

Opponents of legalization list a host of reasons why it is not feasible, starting with the women who would be corralled into sex ghettos and further spotlighted as deviant second-class citizens. The sociologist Jane Mezzone says a lot of prostitutes appear to favour legalization because they wrongly believe it would 'get the police off their backs'. But legalization equals control, which equals increased regulation.

Do we really want to see the job of prostitute advertised next to that of an office worker or painter in the local job centres? It would make official the notion of women as sex objects, to be bought and used by men, and at the same time would drastically reduce, if not end, a prostitute's bargaining ability. Would the Government dare risk alienating massive numbers of voters by even proposing legalization, as, if it became a reality, the state would become a legal pimp?

Would a brothel worker be considered failing to fulfil her contractual duties and thus face the sack if she rejected a client or refused to perform services she considers distasteful? What if a woman wanted to leave prostitution? How would she explain her past career on her curriculum vitae or to a prospective boss? Legalization would deny prostitutes basic civil rights just as much as the present situation does.

State-run brothels would be designed and organized primarily to suit the interests of the controlling authorities and clients, not the workers. The health care argument is always put up as being in the women's interests. Would legalization lead to compulsory examination of a suspected prostitute? Research has repeatedly shown that most practise safe sex and it is the client who wants to take risks. One suspects he would not be willing to undergo enforced medicals. In the end, both parties are only as healthy and free from disease as their last sexual encounter.

It is a fallacy that legalization would clear the streets. European countries, such as Holland, which have introduced legalization illustrate that. It legalized brothels in 1992 and only 12 per cent of its known prostitutes work in them. The establishment of Eros Centres (apartment buildings for the exclusive use of licensed prostitutes) has failed to check street prostitution in Germany.

Many choose not to work in authorized premises, preferring the greater freedoms they have on the streets. Many brothel managers and madams refuse to employ women with drug habits. Some carry out body inspections on the prostitutes to check for bruises or scars from repeated injecting. A two-tier system would evolve, with those rejected from licensed brothels creating an underclass of sex workers.

The King's Cross-based English Collective of Prostitutes has campaigned for the abolition of all prostitution laws for nearly 20 years. It links the trade with poverty suffered by many women, particularly single mothers. Spokeswoman Nikki Adams said the ECP believed two million women are or have at some point been on the game. She admits the figures are seven years old and a guess based on the ECP's experience.

They vehemently oppose legalization, believing it would still leave prostitutes vulnerable to exploitation: 'The government, local authorities and police would be in control and make the profits. It would institutionalize working girls, they would have no choice about their personal details being logged on official registers which would restrict their chances of exiting the trade and getting another job, as well as leave them open to blackmail.'

She rebutted the safety arguments, saying that fierce competition and high rents could lead to pressure being put on the women to earn extra cash by practising unsafe sex.

Legalizing prostitution might raise the sex trade out of the same murky category as other criminals, but it would do little to enhance the social status of the prostitute. Being socially tolerated in legal terms is far from being socially accepted.

TOLERATION ZONES

Dubbed 'green light for red light' areas by the media, this option has been put forward as a strategy to tackle street prostitution in Birmingham and Nottingham. A toleration zone is a specific area where prostitutes are permitted to work set hours under conditions laid down by the local authority. Its strongest selling point is that by placing the zone out of residential areas, the nuisance factor is curbed.

Both cities have looked to the version which has been operating in the small Dutch city of Utrecht since 1984. It was designed by the city council, local police, and the social and health services. Although registration is not legally required, the vice squad encourages prostitutes to register before beginning work.

The meeting point is a 12-space specially constructed car park set in the commercial part of the city. Soliciting is legal within that area at set times and about 35 women work most nights.

Prostitutes solicit along a nearby designated stretch of the road leading to the zone's entrance. As a punter drives past, he signals to his chosen woman who then walks to and meets him in the car park. Fences separating each space offer some privacy and special bins are provided for the disposal of condoms, tissues and other litter. After business is completed, the client drives out of a separate exit and the woman returns to the roadside.

Prostitutes have to be aged 18 and over to work in the zone. They are forbidden to solicit in any other public roads or places. Working hours are 7 pm to 2 am, except on Thursdays, when due to late-night shopping, the start time is put back to 9.30 pm. A person booked twice within 30 days for breaking the rules can be banned from the zone for up to a week.

Pimping is banned. Police patrol the area twice an hour and encourage the prostitutes to report any incidence of violence. The local authority cleans the zone, car park and nearby areas regularly, ensuring the area is tidy and litter-free for the people who use the nearby commercial premises during the day.

A converted bus is placed close to the car park every night. It is staffed by outreach workers who sell hot drinks and condoms, offer a needle exchange, and give advice, information and support to the prostitutes. It also has a shower and a rest area where the women meet. Twice weekly, a GP runs a clinic on the bus. As the women gather in one area to do business, outreach workers can work far more effectively, resulting in a greatly improved health and welfare support service for the prostitutes.

Britain does not have the liberal sexual attitudes which the Dutch are renowned for and zoning is rife with problems, not least that zones would be created around residents' interests and not the prostitutes' needs.

Industrial estates and car parks are among the most commonly mentioned sites to place a British 'green light' zone, but this would undoubtedly stir up bouts of commercial NIMBY-ism. Factory bosses might object on the grounds that a zone near their business would lead to property devaluation and attract other types of criminals.

Would the reserved British male publicly queue to select a prostitute? Anonymity and the danger of searching the streets for sex are part of the enjoyment and challenge for many punters. These inclinations would not vanish with the introduction of zones.

Many prostitutes would not entertain working in a zone, as they do not want to be publicly identified or vie for business in such a small but highly competitive area. As street girls are the most susceptible to attacks and robberies, they feel safer working around well-lit public places, such as train and bus stations and residential areas.

If zones were placed in secluded non-residential areas with little policing or security, the women could possibly have less protection than they do now and the risk of attacks would still exist.

The ECP believes zones reinforce prostitutes' isolation instead of breaking down their segregation. 'Some propose zones because they can see the benefits of having women ghetto-ized. Such a concept bolsters the assumption that prostitute women are bad women,' said Nikki Adams. Yet Hilary Kinnell, of Birmingham Safe, says zones should not be totally dismissed and could ease the violence problem if they were policed and had bays equipped with telephones and panic buttons. 'I don't think the laws should necessarily be dismantled,' she said. 'If they were, it might lead to a flourishing pimp business which the police could do nothing about. That would give a clear message to men who do not want to risk becoming armed robbers that bullying prostitutes is OK. So long as completely uncontrolled pimping goes on, you will never get rid of street prostitution. There are few overheads and a pimp won't pay for advertising or a telephone line to be installed if a woman wants to work at home.'

Susan, the freelance mobile masseuse featured in Chapter One, says despite the risks she faces through her method of working, she would never work in a toleration zone or legalized brothel. 'I would prefer to work with another woman. But I wouldn't dream of working in a zone. Penning prostitutes in these areas is just another way of labelling us. I don't want that as I have my kids to consider and I definitely wouldn't register with an authority as one police chief suggested. It seems to me that those who want such changes in the law know very little about how the business works.'

DECRIMINALIZATION

This would see the abolition of all the existing criminal laws – including soliciting, brothel keeping and kerb-crawling – which single out prostitutes and other involved parties. Instead, all involved would be governed by general laws covering public order and assault. The women would be allowed to choose where, when and how to work. This would decrease the need for 'protection' by a pimp and thus weaken his power. It is the option favoured by the ECP and the Midlands-based pressure group Soliciting For Change, as well as other organizations such as the Royal College of Nursing and the National Association of Probation Officers.

Politicians probably think the public would not accept such radical measures. The powers that be might argue that women everywhere would set up as prostitutes or madams. That is rubbish! Did every lunchtime tippler become an alcoholic when pub opening hours were extended?

The ECP's Nikki Adams offers a possible explanation as to why so few MPs support the need for legal change. 'Many politicians see police crackdowns as vote-catchers. People who are vocally against prostitution are often "respectable residents" who are vocal in the community. We call them the vocal minority and in King's Cross the agenda is set by the police and this small section of the community.'

Champions of decriminalization say that such a policy would reduce police and court costs and free vice squads for other tasks.

They add that if the women were allowed to work in small groups from their homes, and were to be discreet in their daily work practice and advertising, it would lead to a near-abatement of violence and public nuisance. Self-employment would give prostitutes greater independence and control. They would have the freedom to work in comfort, when they wanted, and to refuse any clients' requests they were unhappy about.

'Why does the country need a special set of rules for prostitutes?' asks Nikki Adams. 'The only way prostitute women will be allowed the same civil and economic rights that others have is by abolishing the vice laws and making them subject to the same laws as everyone else. Our bodies and our money are our business, not the law's. What adults choose to do in private is their own affair, not the Government's.

'Sex work is very important. The present laws prevent working girls from defending themselves against verbal and physical attacks. Change has got to happen.'

Sir Frederick Lawton believes street prostitution can never be decriminalized or legalized because the law has to take into account the specific nature of the nuisance factor for residents and the public. He relates an anecdote revealing partly why the Criminal Law Revision Committee dismissed in the 1980s a proposal to permit legal brothels to operate in certain areas: 'We considered whether brothels could be set up on industrial sites and canvassed various site managers. They objected on the grounds that they would be a distraction to workers.

'I think we [the CLRC] got it more or less right,' were his final comments on the subject.

Anthony Scrivener QC is one of the country's best-known barristers and a former Bar Council chairman. He believes a cocktail of legalization and decriminalization is the way forward, but before any progress can be made, the public and politicians would have to discard what he sees as the hypocritical and moralizing stances which most people adopt whenever the subject of prostitution arises for discussion. 'Licensed brothels might get rid of street prostitution, but the nineteenth-century morals which regulate the subject – and which we pay lip service to, if nothing else – prevent politicians talking honestly on this topic and consequently any public acceptance of licensed brothels,' he said.

'Street prostitution and kerb-crawling are public nuisance offences and in so far as the law treats them so, it is on the right lines. Apart from that, I would have no problems with decriminalization.

'If the public annoyance element is eliminated by, for example, the participants committing the sex acts behind closed doors, then I have some hesitation in saying this should be an offence. That is private morality and not an area the law should venture into. Police resources are better spent on other things. Why should we waste state money on people who want to do these things?'

Mr Scrivener said he would keep the 'persistence' element in the kerb-crawlers' act but would remove the 'common prostitute' tag from the 1959 act. 'I object to that name,' he said. 'It is entering into the area of personal morality. Why call a man a complete womanizer, so what? One should not be condemned by the criminal law for sleeping around. Why don't we acknowledge what really goes on instead of being like a Victorian parent and brushing the subject under the carpet?'

Campaigners argue that because prostitution is a crime, its participants are pushed further underground and almost encouraged to associate with other criminals. Tarred with the same brush as robbers, thieves and every other crook, there is little wonder they become enmeshed in these communities. It also means they retreat further away from mainline medical services and so increase risks to health and personal safety. If the anti-prostitution laws were axed the mystery and stigma surrounding the prostitutes' job and working environment would be removed. Red light areas would not be as defined, possibly no longer needed, and it would be easier for prostitutes to report pimps and violent punters.

The status of the sex worker would be lifted and her services be recognized to the extent that prostitutes could be valuable assistants for sex therapists, counsellors and health educators.

Decriminalization would remove the whole force of moral judgment surrounding prostitution and a much more functional approach would be adopted instead. But Chief Constable Wells believes the opportunity for commercial gain would be exploited by large faceless companies – Sex for Sale p.l.c.s – through owning and running organized brothels.

'Part of me believes decriminalization is an attractive option. If you take away the stigma, you take away the women's fears of violence and public exposure. Take away those fears and you take away the potential for blackmail. But decriminalization is a dream which I am not sure the country is ready for. There are considerable anomalies underlying it and it is not the solution it appears to be. The trade would open up to macro-economic forces and lead to a different kind of exploitation. Just as alcohol and tobacco have been exploited by large companies, I wonder how long it would be before someone recognized there was a very lucrative and marketable product in prostitution.

'It will be the next millennium before decriminalization is – if ever – achieved. Legalization is the more practical of options. It falls between the spasmodic discrimination of the present system we operate and the pipe dream of decriminalization.'

In the meantime, the powers that be continue to come up with piecemeal schemes to deter purchasers and providers of sex, including instant cautions, letters to clients' homes, verbal warnings, high-profile policing with video cameras, and officers patrolling in marked cars, on horseback and even with dogs.

In recent years, police have joined forces with local councils to draw up traffic schemes, mainly aimed at blocking off routes around red light beats. Speed ramps and extended paving in the shape of light bulbs placed along the street corners of the main beat in Chapeltown, Leeds, mean that drivers have to slow down in the vital areas, and the prostitutes actually regard the measures as helpful for business. However, similar schemes have apparently had some success in Southampton, Luton and elsewhere. Though such programmes might reduce or displace prostitution, they will never eradicate it. Indeed, if the laws were effective, none of the above schemes would be needed.

Of course, there are those who believe that prostitution should be totally outlawed. However, this would be practically impossible as there are not enough police resources to enforce such a policy, which could also be deemed a serious infringement of the public's civil rights.

Whether or not prostitution is inevitable, negative ruling has failed, as history shows, to curb human sexual instincts or rid society of commercial sex. Prostitution is governed by market forces as much as any other large-scale service or trade. The business will only wither when the male's libido for commercial sex droops and women's financial needs are fulfilled in other ways. Until then, the sex trade continues to be a multi-million-pound industry and prostitution remains one of the few professions which has survived and thrived throughout the millennium.

Therefore we need to look at pro-active regulation of the trade which will protect the participants from violence and exploitation, the residents and public from nuisance, and promote effective health care to all involved.

No industry the size of the sex trade should be free from any regulation, but prostitutes should be governed by the same criminal, civil and commercial rules as both the crook and the law-abiding member of the public.

Licensing and monitoring would be the two main thrusts of the radical barrister Michael Mansfield's approach to new prostitution laws. His opinions of the present ones are as trenchant as his general criticisms of the British judicial system. 'They are completely wasteful, hypocritical and ineffective. I am not interested in cosmetic changes. They need to be abolished and replaced with decriminalization, regulation and a whole new policy of education,' he said.

'People need to be educated from school age to understand that we live in a society where members do different things – some of which might disturb us. Many people do jobs they don't want to because it's the only way they can earn a living. Prostitutes are no different but they are criminalized for having no alternative. The public needs to be made aware that prostitution is a way some people wish to live and be entertained by.'

He would like a practice of licensing similar to the system used by Westminster City Council to be adopted nationwide. Every working prostitute would have to register and be allowed to work at designated premises, whether at their homes, brothels or premises on recognized estates. 'It's not exactly romantic but this is not about romance. There will always be a proportion who don't want to pay for a licence but that doesn't mean we should criminalize everyone involved. You can imagine pimps threatening a girl not to register but the police would have to be prepared to tackle this.

'I don't see any stigma about registering as a prostitute. Quite the opposite, we would be saying you are a recognized profession. What's wrong with a legitimate career in prostitution? Give respect to women rather than treat them as entertainment. I would like to see a career structure as a prostitute. You should be able to leave school and make a choice between all sorts of possible careers.

'I link it to society and men's attitude to women. Women tend to be seen by men as sex objects, or as mother figures, and there is an assumption that they can be used this way. It is a power thing, to keep women in their place and deny them any degree of power. People's attitudes to women and their roles need to change. They have as much right to be in positions of power as choosing to be prostitutes. The only way to get the subject on the political agenda and in to the public arena is by talking about attitudes to women.

'Licensing and monitoring would protect those involved and the affected communities. Madams should be licensed and have to keep a register of women who work for them. Massage parlours and the likes should be regulated to prevent exploitation of women or children. The public health inspectorate would make regular checks to ensure the premises are satisfactory and a doctor would visit to give weekly check-ups to the women working.'

There are many women who are happy to work as prostitutes, but there is very little help for those who want to exit the business.

Once they are involved in the sex trade, society reacts to prostitutes in a very different way and marginalizes the women whether they want it or not. Professor Norman Tutt explains why: 'Apart from obvious stigmas they suffer, prostitutes gradually mould themselves into the stereotypical prostitute but it is an image given to them by outsiders. The working girls adjust their image and become defensive by saying they are exploiting the punter.

'If a prostitute is seen talking to a man, people assume he is either a punter or a police officer. I was aware of that whenever I visited the Islamic Centre near Spencer Place [in the heart of Leeds's red light area] and was always anxious in case any of the prostitutes who had been in care recognized me,' said the city's former director of social services. 'I don't know how I would have responded if they did but I was concerned about my loss of status should I be seen talking to these women.'

He agreed it was a rather shameful attitude and says this is typical of the kind of barriers which have to be broken down.

Deciding to leave prostitution is a massive step to take, as for many women it means giving up not just their job but their lifestyle. Professor Tutt says he is unsure whether the social services are the most suitable organization to help women exit the trade. 'If they have been in care or had children taken off them, these women would see it as a negative authority and might be reluctant to get involved with it again. The feminist movement has a strong appeal for women who want a new identity. Women's organizations offering education programmes may be the answer. They could offer connections with other women who have different lifestyles but share activities to learn a range of skills which might make them more economically viable and independent. Many prostitutes will have limited experience of seeing that women can be successful in other areas and can have non-sexual relationships with men.'

PAT

'Coffee and cream' was the nickname London police gave to Pat as she touted for business around Park Lane's five-star hotels. A handsome half-caste, she wears her 38 years, six children, two grandchildren, and years of hustling well. She had her first child at 14 after being raped during her first sexual experience by her 16-year-old boyfriend.

Pat's professional and personal experiences come in handy these days. She gave up the game a few years ago and is now employed by her local council as an outreach worker giving advice and support to working girls.

There is little she does not know about selling sex. She was brought up in a brothel, has hustled in top hotels and on the seedy streets of London, Cardiff, Bradford and Leeds, offering sexual services to every nationality and age group. She has conned clients, survived a violent pimp, a brutal attack by a punter, and grieved over a friend who was one of the Yorkshire Ripper's victims.

Like many embroiled in the vice trade, Pat had the seeds of selling sex first planted in her mind by teenage girlfriends she met while in council care. She never knew her real father, an African. Her alcoholic mother earned some money from hustling when she was not fighting or moving house with Pat's stepfather. By the time Pat left full-time education, she had attended nine different schools and was pregnant.

'I never told anyone and when the clinic wrote to me I hid the letter under the lino. I finally told my mum a few days before my daughter was born. When the ambulance came to take me to hospital she let me go alone and even waved me off. Days after the baby was born, I left her on a doorstep and ran away. The social services put me in a home and the manager used to beat me. I hit back one day and was sent to a remand home in Bristol for three months. I met Colleen and she used to tell me about all these black guys she'd slept with. I was transferred to a mother and baby home with a dozen others and I told them all these lies about the blues parties I went to and the men I'd been out with.'

It turned out to be a case of life imitating fiction, for when Pat was allowed to leave the home she quickly became enmeshed in Leeds's red light area. 'I was seduced by it. It was like Disneyland, going to all-night parties, dancing and talking to much older guys.'

After enduring four violent years with a man met at a blues party, Pat fled with her two children to live with two prostitute friends. She took up shoplifting but it was a matter of time before she began working alongside her pals.

'I worked round Yorkshire TV's studios in Leeds and had quite a few visiting celebrities and a newsreader. I have had orgasms with two clients and when I thought I was getting too involved I stopped seeing them. Some girls do fall in love with clients, or think they do.

'A lot of people think prostitutes will do anything. That's not true; each has her own limits. There's a bit of snobbery too. Sauna girls tend to think they're better than ones on the streets. But for a street girl to work indoors is like putting a labourer in an office.'

A new boyfriend, coupled with turning to the Rastafarian religion, helped her come off the game a few years ago. 'It took me months to finally do it and I moved out of the area. That was the best thing I did. I had a beautiful sex life with my boyfriend when I was hustling but now I am sexually fucked up. I bought a basque to wear for my guy but I didn't enjoy it as it reminded me of the past.

'I went on a carpentry course at my local college and then became a liaison officer on women's issues. I feel good putting an ordinary skirt on for work.'

Prostitution will always exist. Those who believe otherwise are blinding themselves to reality. As I hope this book shows, British legal attempts to subjugate the sex-for-sale trade have failed miserably. No one wins – prostitutes are arrested, punters are shamed and residents remain troubled. Privately, many police officers of all ranks admit that the laws do not work but they have jobs to do and must be seen to be doing them. The 'revolving door' policy of arrest, fine, re-arrest, continues to spin endlessly on.

The campaigning group aptly named Soliciting for Change (SFC) could lead the way forward. What started in 1988 as a Christian action group providing support and advice for prostitutes in Walsall has gradually mushroomed into a movement which has built up a broad range of support. It is made up of former and working prostitutes, clergy and health and social workers, and aims to combine the interests of working women and the community together in the fight to change the laws.

The SFC wants all laws relating to prostitution to be abolished and sex trade workers to be governed by exactly the same laws as every other member of society. The group believes there is no need for specific laws, as there is plenty of legislation available to deal with vice-related crime. Pimps, for example, could be charged with assault or demanding money with menaces (blackmail), street-walkers with disorderly behaviour or obstructing the highway. Indeed, there is a strong argument that separate vice laws are unnecessary.

SFC's spokeswoman Cheryl Overs explains: 'We don't want prostitutes to be made a special case. On the contrary, we want them to be treated like everyone else. We want to encourage them to work in the most satisfying circumstances, which by definition will be indoors. We are not into cleaning the streets of these women, but looking for a solution that will suit everyone.

'Residents need to look beyond the 20 yards past their front gate to a long-term solution. The reason why they have to put up with nuisance is because the laws prevent prostitutes having access to ordinary commercial activities such as discreet advertising or being allowed to deal with customers like other businesses can.'

Ms Overs believes if a woman or small group of women want to sell sex from a house, they should be allowed as it would alleviate many problems, so long as their work does not impinge on neighbours. 'If you get two secretaries or designers working from home, they would cause little upset and the same goes for two prostitutes. Any commercial activity – whether selling sex or pizzas – should operate under strict guidelines in residential areas.

'If a nuisance is caused by those who continue to work the streets and a complaint is lodged there and then by an impartial third party, a woman should be dealt with in the same manner as other people who cause affrays. Convictions should not be uncorroborated or rely on the word of a lone police officer.

'But if someone wants to open a 50-woman brothel, then it should be subjected to the same planning, health and safety regulations that a 50-person office or factory is. Many industries have the potential to offend and annoy. All have the capacity to exploit and abuse workers. The rules and regulations which govern other industries do not rely on criminalizing workers, so why should the laws which govern prostitution?

'We want to find a solution that will be politically palatable and workable for all people affected by the anti-prostitution laws.'

Campaigners are right when they say the lack of prostitutes' rights and status thwarts the rights and status of all women. With most females enjoying active sex lives in and out of marriage these days, the bridge between 'pure' and 'fallen' women has narrowed greatly, yet the prostitution laws continue to create such a gulf. 'You're a drag if you don't want to have sex with men and a bag if you sell it to them,' said one brothel madam.

The Government does not have the right to venture into the beds of consenting adults just because money changes hands. It argues that the criminal law concerns itself with the nuisance that may arise from prostitution rather than the activity itself. Others argue that the criminal law exacerbates the nuisance.

Given that the commercial sex trade will never cease, surely our society has the ability and courage to deal with it realistically for all concerned.

Perhaps the final comment should come from the architects of much of the law examined in this book – the Criminal Law Revision Committee – who noted in its 1985 report into off-street prostitution: 'Prostitution exists and no law, except perhaps a Draconian one which no democratic society could, or would, contemplate, can make it disappear. Prostitutes and clients have to meet.'

Home Office Statistics

F igures from the Home Office research and statistics departments showing the number of women found guilty of soliciting/loitering under the 1959 Street Offences Act in English and Welsh courts between 1989 and 1991, and the number of men convicted of kerb-crawling under Sections 1 and 2 of the 1985 Sexual Offences Act during the same period.

		PROSTITUTES	KERB-CRAWLERS			PROSTITUTES	KERB-CRAWLERS
Avon & Somerset	1989	149	6	Cleveland	1989	340	0
	1990	153	6		1990	389	4
	1991	131	15		1991	319	45
Bedfordshire	1989	106	62	Derbyshire	1989	26	9
	1990	89	45		1990	32	20
	1991	65	40		1991	40	21
Cambridgeshire	1989	2	0	Devon & Cornwall	1989	77	0
	1990	0	0		1990	52	1
	1991	1	0		1991	33	9
Cheshire	1989	4	0	Dorset	1989	10	5
	1990	0	0		1990	9	8
	1991	0	0		1991	16	41

	PROSTITUTES	**KERB-CRAWLERS**		**PROSTITUTES**	**KERB-CRAWLERS**
Essex	1989	27	16	Metropolitan Police Area	1989	4,501	54
	1990	14	8		1990	4,341	56
	1991	8	53		1991	4,459	120
Greater Manchester	1989	1,056	153	Norfolk	1989	238	9
	1990	1,125	175		1990	260	14
	1991	826	154		1991	224	25
Hampshire	1989	55	2	Northampton-shire	1989	88	18
	1990	45	0		1990	55	7
	1991	136	10		1991	66	9
Humberside	1989	8	0	Northumbria	1989	0	0
	1990	0	0		1990	1	0
	1991	8	0		1991	0	0
Kent	1989	9	2	North Yorkshire	1989	0	0
	1990	4	0		1990	0	0
	1991	1	0		1991	1	0
Lancashire	1989	67	0	Nottingham-shire	1989	294	41
	1990	80	3		1990	215	75
	1991	80	27		1991	177	101
Leicestershire	1989	117	20	South Yorkshire	1989	110	4
	1990	107	21		1990	138	69
	1991	81	20		1991	137	19
Merseyside	1989	351	2	Staffordshire	1989	137	72
	1990	297	28		1990	88	33
	1991	497	7		1991	88	46

APPENDIX

	PROSTITUTES	KERB-CRAWLERS		PROSTITUTES	KERB-CRAWLERS
Suffolk 1989	48	23	West Yorkshire 1989	671	196
1990	56	12	1990	561	343
1991	42	4	1991	464	232
Sussex 1989	0	0	Wiltshire 1989	134	24
1990	0	0	1990	125	14
1991	1	0	1991	40	7
Surrey 1989	0	0	South Wales 1989	127	17
1990	0	0	1990	152	21
1991	0	0	1991	116	1
West Midlands 1989	1,401	231			
1990	1,632	321			
1991	1,503	177			

TOTAL CONVICTIONS FOR EACH YEAR

PROSTITUTES

	1989	1990	1991
England	10,026	9,868	9,443
Wales	127	152	116
Total	10,153	10,020	9,559

KERB-CRAWLERS

	1989	1990	1991
England	950	1,264	1,182
Wales	17	21	1
Total	967	1,285	1,183

BIBLIOGRAPHY

Vern Bullough and Bonnie Bullough: *Women and Prostitution: A Social History*, Prometheus Books, 1987

Jack English and Richard Card: *Butterworth's Police Law*, 3rd edn, 1988

Helena Kennedy: *Eve Was Framed*, Chatto & Windus, 1992

Roger Matthews: 'Beyond Wolfenden? Prostitution, Politics and the Law', *Confronting Crime*, ed. Roger Matthews and Jock Young, Sage, 1986

Ken Pryce: *Endless Pressure, A Study of West Indian Lifestyles in Bristol*, Bristol Classical Press, 2nd edn, 1986

Nickie Roberts: *Whores in History*, Grafton, 1993

Gordon Wilson: *The Beat Officer's Companion*, 4th edn, Police Review Publishers, 1992

REPORTS AND PAPERS

The Wolfenden Committee: *Report of the Committee on Homosexual Offences and Prostitution*, HMSO, 1957

Criminal Law Revision Committee, 16th report: *Prostitution in the Street*, HMSO, 1984

Criminal Law Revision Committee, 17th report: *Prostitution: Off-street Activities*, HMSO, 1985

Hilary Kinnell: *Prostitutes' Perceptions of Risks and Factors Related to Risk Taking*, Birmingham Safe, April 1990

Hilary Kinnell: *Prostitutes and their Clients in Birmingham: Action Research to Measure and Reduce Risks of HIV*, Birmingham Safe, 1990

National Children's Bureau: *Young People Leaving Care*, June 1992

Neil McKeganey and Marina Barnard: 'Selling Sex: Female Street Prostitution and HIV Risk Behaviour in Glasgow', *Aids Care*, iv/4, 1992

INDEX